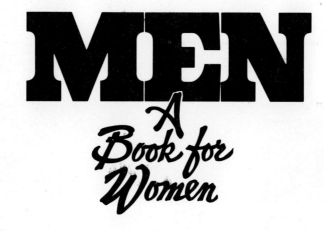

MEN

A Book for Women

MEN
A Book for Women

PRODUCED BY
JAMES WAGENVOORD
AND PEYTON BAILEY

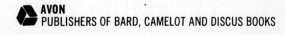 AVON
PUBLISHERS OF BARD, CAMELOT AND DISCUS BOOKS

MEN: A BOOK FOR WOMEN is an original publication of Avon Books.
This work has never before appeared in book form.

AVON BOOKS
A division of
The Hearst Corporation
959 Eighth Avenue
New York, New York 10019

Copyright © 1978 by Product Development International Holding, n.v.
Produced by Plenary Publications International, Inc.
10 East 49th Street
New York, New York 10017
Library of Congress Catalog Card Number: 78-66692
ISBN: 0-380-40212-2

First Avon Printing, October 1978

AVON TRADEMARK REG. U.S. PAT. OFF. AND IN
OTHER COUNTRIES, MARCA REGISTRADA, HECHO EN
U.S.A.

Printed in the U.S.A.

an oak alley book created by:

EDITOR
James Wagenvoord

WRITERS
Peyton Bailey   Douglas Gasner   Joel Homer
Dan Ross   Paul Siudzinksi   James Wagenvoord

DESIGN
Donald K. Wright

ILLUSTRATIONS
Sandra Forrest   Keith Right

SENIOR EDITORS
Peyton Bailey   Ellen Foley

ASSOCIATE EDITORS
Janet Goldstein   Ted Johnson   Dan Ross

LAYOUT
Kathleen Woloch

INDEX
Maro Riofrancos

PROOFREADER
Hilary Fried

EDITORIAL ASSISTANT
Tim Adams

We express our appreciation to the following people and organizations for their cooperation during the creation of this book.

American Blue Print; Cardinal Type Service: Andrea Fagin, Dean Franklin, Elizabeth Fabian, Joan Nasta, Michael Hayes, Michael Israel, Neil Gorman; Filmstat; Lockheed Information Systems; New York Academy of Medicine; New York Public Library; New York Society Library; New York Times Information Bank; System Development Corporation. William Budinger; Karen Brown; Shirley Homer; Frank Kendig; Peter Meyer; Susan Meyer; Fiona St. Aubyn; Freida Saltzberg; Ab van den Berg.

PEYTON BAILEY is an editor, writer, and columnist whose work has appeared in *Bride's, Glamour, Cosmopolitan, Co-Ed,* and other magazines. She was an editor for eight years with Condé Nast Publications.

DOUGLAS GASNER has been writing on medical subjects for a decade. He has been chief medical correspondent for *Time,* managing editor of *Nursing,* editor-in-chief of *Medical Dimensions,* and senior editor of *Saturday Review.* He is currently writing a book on the best hospitals in America.

JOEL HOMER is a freelance writer in New York City. He has been an editor and columnist for *Saturday Review, City, Family Health,* and *MBA* magazines.

DAN ROSS has been a writer and journalist in New Mexico, San Francisco, Jerusalem, and New York.

PAUL SIUDZINSKI has written extensively on men's issues. He also teaches painting, and is author of *Sumi-e: A Meditation in Ink* (Drake Publications, 1978).

JAMES WAGENVOORD, the author of nine books, including the widely acclaimed *Hangin' Out* and *City Lives,* is also a professional photographer and film-maker.

FOREWORD

This is a book about men. It is about the way men are, not as they should be or even want to be. It is about flaws, short-sightedness, power, and powerlessness. It is about the way men perceive who and what they should be. And it is about images—self-images, sexual images, images of friendship, of infinity, and images of love—the newest taboo. In recent years, many of the cultural elements that dictated a certain form to a social existence have crumbled or been transformed. Profanity—that's all right now, it indicates a certain freedom and relaxation; random sexuality—why not partake of more freedom and self-expression; death—it's all right to face up to it and watch it happen to others. But to care desperately and openly for someone or something—that just might be evidence of weakness, or at least a confession of need. And to acknowledge and state needs, well, that requires some thought. It can cause problems.

This is a book about men. It is about the uncertainties faced as cultural roles are redefined and the necessity to question comfortable assumptions is acknowledged. It is about men who as a result of willingly accepting historical prerogatives (termed rights) have discovered that there is no such thing as a status quo but as yet have no firm grip on how quickly or how dramatically they must themselves change. The uncertainties inherent in the roles are both the reason for and the thrust of this book. Definitions and understandings of roles are in an impacted period of change never before experienced. The Male Mystique has begotten the male quandary; and although the quandary grows, it is not necessarily self-propagating or self-inflicted.

This is a book about men. It is intended primarily for women. It concerns physical and emotional realities and the marked and subtle differences that set men apart from women. It is objective and subjective information offering not answers but form and context for more questions. And it has been developed as an extended statement concerning the physiological makeup of the male of the species and the general social attitudes that have been assumed as part of the genetically dictated role of being a man in an era dominated by "information."

A recent article in *The New York Times* pointed out that seventy-five percent of the world's available information has been compiled within the past two decades. Seventy-two billion new "pieces" of information are arriving yearly and the total amount is doubling every ten years. In a physical sense this is probably all to the good. More is now understood about the care and feeding of the human body. Some diseases and physical limitations are being dealt with. The planet as a finite reality is being considered. But these "pieces" of information have their limits. We have not become more literate, more contemplative, more willing to seek out intimacy, more vulnerable, more aware of being alive. But there *are* all those "pieces" of information around. Seventy-two billion new "pieces" a year? If the information were divided equally among people currently living in the United States it would mean an allocation of 360 items for each citizen. Terrific "pieces"—the effective stress of a titanium-laminated heat shield moving at supersonic speeds; the life expectancy of "red wigglers" in alkaline-charged soil in Samson County, North Carolina; the rate of male facial hair growth during pre-orgasmic intercourse; a new batting average every day for every active baseball player. Answers are increasingly available to questions requiring, or amenable to, statistics. But the realities of living that resist quantifying—the attitudes, the yearnings, the loneliness, the surges of joy—remain within each of us. The technology of information may succeed in rapidly adding to a seemingly endless computer tape, but the simple fact remains that when one is born, or faces death, or seeks physical and emotional warmth, the feelings, the sensations, are seldom related in one's mind to statistics. Twenty-one days to a movie star's face, seven ways to a smaller waistline, ten steps to improve your vocabulary, three ways to acquire power—few if any would consider these reasonable contributions to an epitaph.

This is a book about men. Here they are. This era's models—all sizes and shapes—more styling in common than they would willingly acknowledge—more design differences than can be handled statistically. They seldom come in tidy little packages, but they're available for questions.

There is an important bit of information you can discover for yourself. And a question is submitted for the asking. Try it out on a man you care about. And you might also address it to yourself. Ask, "Who do you love, what do you love?" If it's asked honestly it will probably be addressed honestly. The answers won't translate into bar graphs or mathematical formulas. But you'll begin to get a glimpse of someone.

CONTENTS

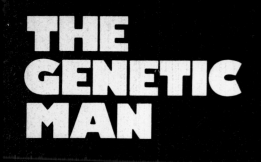

THE GENETIC MAN

THE GENETIC MAN

**aleness—what determines it?**

They are aggressive, physically active, independent, inquisitive. They tend to cry less, eat more, go off on their own earlier.

Obviously we are talking about male babies. But are these characteristics inborn, or merely the result of conditioning—of the way boys are raised? Is the male genetic nature myth or reality?

At the root of this question, and at the root of the myriad differences between men and women, lies a mismatched pair of chromosomes that have puzzled geneticists ever since they were discovered. These are the sex chromosomes, part of the set of 46 chromosomes that carry all the genetic material required to turn a single cell into a human being. Yet no one knew of their existence for thousands of years, much less that they could determine the sex of a baby. During a large part of the Middle Ages a mixture of equal parts of wine and lion's blood administered under the prayerful gaze of an abbot during the influence of the full moon was the appropriate nostrum for begetting a male child. When lion's blood was in short supply, there were other rituals; for example, both

How To Make A Boy

Folk tales about how to produce sons have always been popular:

In Sweden small boys were brought into the wedding bed to insure male offspring.

Husbands in one part of Germany brought axes into the wedding bed and chanted, "Ruck, ruck, roy; you shall have a boy."

Hippocrates, the father of medicine, recommended tying off the left testicle with a string.

In some Slavic countries, a wife pinched her husband's right testicle during intercourse.

Elsewhere, hearty red meat was eaten, brides wore men's clothing, or intercourse took place under a full moon.

The Modern Method

Modern science has produced its own method to boost your chances for a son. As outlined by David Rorvick in *Your Baby's Sex—Now You Can Choose*, it includes:

Abstaining from sex from the beginning of the monthly cycle until the day of ovulation.

Preceding intercourse with a baking-soda douche.

Vaginal penetration from the rear, and deep penetration at the moment of ejaculation.

Delaying ejaculation at least until the woman reaches orgasm.

partners were advised to lie on their right sides during intercourse. Vestiges of this thinking lingered until the early part of the 20th century, when a popular pseudoscientific theory held that eggs arising from a woman's right ovary produced male children, and those from the left produced female children.

Now it is known that a minuscule amount of genetic material locked inside the sperm of a prospective father determines at the moment of fertilization what sex the child will be. If the sperm that penetrates the egg carries an X chromosome, it will align with the X chromosome in the mother's egg and produce a female. Under normal circumstances, 50 percent of a man's sperm carry X chromosomes. The rest carry Y chromosomes and produce males. Though there are techniques to shift the balance in favor of either X- or Y-bearing sperm, once the sperm and egg unite, the genetic message has been transmitted; wearing loose clothing or getting out of bed on the right side every day for nine months will have no effect on the sex of the child.

The larger of the two chromosomes is the X. It carries a full cargo of genes, lined up like so many beads on a string, and every human cell has at least one of them.

The other is the furtive Y chromosome. It is mysterious because, like mouthwash or insect spray, the bulk of it is inert. It contains relatively few genes, and this distinction sets it apart from the X and all the other 44 chromosomes that mingle and combine to produce everyone's individuality.

The function of the Y chromosome

The Y chromosome has a single purpose in life. It causes a fertilized egg to develop into a male. That much scientists have known for 70 years from studies done on the lowly mealworm. The question they have been asking lately is: Does the Y chromosome make men behave any differently than women?

The answer is that it probably doesn't, at least not in the sense with which we're most familiar. The Y chromosome doesn't make men dominant, superior, or even more aggressive than women in any direct way. Nor does it account for their curiosity, independence, or temperament.

It is no longer genetic heresy to separate male characteristics from biological imperatives. In fact, the very theory

Are Genes Irrelevant?

While there is reason to believe that not every Tchambuli [a primitive tribe in New Guinea] woman is born with a dominating, organizing, administrative temperament, actively sexed and willing to initiate sex-relations, possessive, definite, robust, practical and impersonal in outlook, still most Tchambuli girls grow up to display these traits. And while there is definite evidence to show that all Tchambuli men are not, by native endowment, the delicate responsive actors of a play staged for the woman's benefit, still most Tchambuli boys manifest this coquettish play-acting personality most of the time.

—MARGARET MEAD
*Sex and Temperament in Three
Primitive Societies*

that there is such a thing as a male genetic nature has fallen on hard times. Anthropologists such as Margaret Mead have been sounding the death knell for the theory since they began observing other cultures in which men are not aggressive and women are not emotionally dependent. And now biogeneticists have joined the requiem. They have amassed evidence that neither the Y chromosome nor male hormones lead to specific behavior patterns, echoing the conclusions of anthropologists. And they've shown the remarkable degree to which parental influence can override anatomical destiny.

Where does that leave the Y chromosome? Well, for the first six weeks following fertilization, this bit of sex-determining genetic material has no apparent effect at all. During this time, the sexes are indistinguishable except by a laboratory analysis of the chromosomes (which is done in cases where couples suspect sex-linked genetic disorders, such as Tay-Sachs disease). The embryo looks the same whether it is male or female. The head, arms, legs, and torso have begun to take shape. The eyes and ears are recognizable. Within its body cavity, the embryo has a cluster of cells—the primordial gonad—that will become either testes or ovaries, depending

on a genetic instruction that has been communicated but not yet acted on. It also has an internal ridge that will form into a penis and scrotum or a clitoris and labia, and two sets of hollow channels or ducts.

If no other sex-determining message arises in the embryo when it is six weeks old, it will continue to develop as a female. One set of ducts will nearly vanish, while the other will develop into the Fallopian (uterine) tubes, uterus, and vagina. This led to some speculation that we all start out female—indeed, that we all are inherently female. But actually the embryo, from the moment that it's formed in conception, carries the sex chromosomes (either XX or XY) that will direct its eventual sex, male or female, barring any hormonal miscues.

During the six-week "sexually neutral" period the embryo has other things to do before it gets around to developing the organs appropriate to its sex. It is forming its basic human shape, securing its attachment to the womb, and growing at a phenomenal pace.

Sometime around the sixth week, if the embryo is genetically male, the Y chromosome turns the unisex gonads

—How do you tell a Y chromosome from an X chromosome?

—Pull down its genes.

—DOUG GASNER

into testes. This is the singular event that distinguishes the sexes, and no one knows how it happens in detail. However, it does seem that to make a male, nature has to add some extra ingredient.

Geneticists doing research on laboratory animals have found to their considerable amazement that if they remove the developing testes from a genetically male embryo, the sex-determination mechanism goes awry, and the animal develops not as a neuter but as a female. Removing the ovaries from a genetically female embryo, on the other hand, has no apparent ill effects on the development of sexual anatomy, though the animal is, as could be expected, infertile. From this and similar experiments, they have arrived at the conclusion that males, anatomically speaking, are more difficult to make than females. The reason, they thought, was the extra ingredient.

On closer inspection of human embryos, researchers subsequently discovered supporting evidence to bolster this conclusion. The genetic female, they found, lags behind the male in initial sexual development. In other words, while the testes are taking shape and beginning to produce the male hormone testosterone by the sixth week of development, the gonadal cells of a six-week-old female embryo remain quiet and do not produce either of the ovarian hormones, estrogen and progesterone. It is not until about six weeks after the male system has begun hormone production that the female system begins.

estosterone—the extra ingredient

This may seem a small point, but the implication is that the elusive extra ingredient that confers the stamp of male-ness on an embryo is testosterone, the male hormone that is more associated with male puberty and sexual potency than with a developing baby boy. Yet the embryonic testes, though they cannot produce sperm until puberty, start manufacturing testosterone as soon as they're formed. Without it, the embryo develops into a female, with a vagina instead of a penis.

Now researchers had something tangible—a discrete hormone—which they could chemically trace throughout the embryo, looking for sites where it might exert its masculinizing

Abe Lincoln's gangly appearance was caused by a hereditary condition called the Marfan Syndrome. People with this syndrome are usually thin, nearsighted, have heart murmurs, long legs, and an arm span greater than their height. It is a dominant trait, which means that 50 percent of a sufferer's children will inherit it. Lincoln's great-great-grandchildren, then, have a 6¼ percent chance of being long-legged. Their chances of inheriting his beard are exactly one-half: It depends on whether they are men or women.

effects. This was certainly more concrete than looking for some elusive genetic influence of the Y chromosome.

Geneticists had known that at about the time testes form in the male embryo, a set of embryonic ducts begins developing into the glands and tubes that activate and carry sperm from the testes to the penis. As they had suspected, testosterone was responsible for this transformation.

Then came the news, again from research on laboratory animals, that testosterone influences certain pathways in the brain during a few critical days in the development of the central nervous system. The pathways that were affected by testosterone were the ones suspected of being the master controls for our sexual behavior. They are located in the hypothalamus, a section deep within the brain that was already known to affect our emotions.

Scientists now believe that one effect testosterone has during brain development is to influence how we eventually perceive our genital organs. Normal amounts of the hormone account for the way men normally think of themselves. The production of too little testosterone during the first three months of pregnancy may make a man uncomfortable with his maleness; in fact, it might make him feel more like a woman trapped inside a male's body. Too much testosterone may create the potential for sexual aggressiveness and violence.

Could it be that testosterone, released during embryo development, has other far-reaching effects, effects that could

account for the differences that have been noted between the way men and women think? This was the question that drew together seemingly unrelated research findings from psychologists and human development specialists around the world.

It was known from repeated and confirmed laboratory studies that newborn male rats, deprived of testosterone, grew up to display female behavior, and that female newborn rats, given injections of testosterone, later displayed male behavior. If the hormone was that potent in predetermining behavior in some animals, it stood to reason that it had to have some effect in humans.

The danger of extrapolating directly from animal research to humans was well known to the researchers who had been investigating the psychological differences between the sexes. Even so, the question of testosterone's effects came up again and again.

Does testosterone influence behavior?

The first person to show what is thought to be a direct link between testosterone and altered behavior in women was John Money, Director of the Psychohormonal Research Unit at Johns Hopkins Medical School. Because human behavior is a mixture of so many variables, including genes, hormones, and environment, no one, least of all Dr. Money, could say beyond a shadow of a doubt that testosterone was the single factor involved in his startling discovery, but the evidence certainly pointed in that direction.

What Dr. Money and his colleagues found out was that girls who had been accidentally, or through some quirk of nature, exposed to male hormones during a critical time of their fetal development not only had genitals that resembled those of a boy, they also behaved like boys, and many of them had unexpectedly high IQs. Earlier animal experiments done in other laboratories had made it quite clear that testosterone is responsible for the final shape—male or female—of the genitals. But few scientists were willing to buy lock, stock, and barrel Dr. Money's suggestion that exposure to the male hormone for a short time before birth has profound effects on intelligence and behavior for the rest of a woman's life. They questioned the size of his sample—one study included ten girls, the other 70—and the methods by which he assessed masculine, in contrast to feminine, behavior.

These questions were the quite normal "head-scratching" reaction that scientists often have to one another's work, particularly when the work tends to prove or disprove a widely held belief, and they were in no way intended to discredit Dr. Money, who had already distinguished himself as a leading researcher in his field. In this case Dr. Money's work, subsequently confirmed by similar studies in other countries, did seem proof enough that once the brain is exposed to testosterone during the so-called critical period, it is indelibly imprinted with certain masculine behavioral characteristics as well as the potential for a higher IQ.

The individual pieces of Dr. Money's findings eventually came under even more intensive scrutiny. His suggestion that testosterone-encoded brains generally produced higher IQ and more masculine behavior than testosterone-free brains has so far held up.

Dr. Money and his co-researcher, Dr. Anke Ehrhardt, described high activity levels and outright tomboy behavior—from preference for pants over dresses to keeping company with boys over girls in their peer groupings—as the behavioral measurements that indicated masculine over feminine behavior. They also found that many of the masculinized girls scored high in both verbal and spatial ability.

Meanwhile, across the country at Stanford University, two psychologists had begun cataloguing all the psychological differences between the sexes that had appeared in the scientific literature up until the early 1970s. Their idea was to separate the wheat from the chaff, so to speak, and lay to rest the myths about psychological differences while substantiating the facts.

When Eleanor Maccoby and Carol Jacklin had finished their search—conducted in over 2,000 books and articles—they had a picture of boys and girls that hardly conformed with the sugar-and-spice/snakes-and-snails image. They found that boys are equally as social as girls, that the sexes were equally likely to succumb to peer group pressure, and that girls have as much self-esteem and motivation to achieve as boys.

The lines of equality, though, diverged on aggressive behavior, verbal ability, and visual/spatial ability. These were distinctions that Drs. Money and Ehrhardt recognized in their earlier studies on masculinized girls. Boys were, by every criterion, the more aggressive. They fought more, they postured more, and they daydreamed about aggressiveness more. They also did consistently better than girls on problems that tested three-dimensional perception. Girls, on the other hand, excelled in grasping verbal concepts, in making analogies, and in all tasks that involved language comprehension.

Drs. Maccoby and Jacklin concluded their study with a list of inconclusives. There just wasn't enough objective data as yet to determine whether or not one sex is more passive, maternal, noncompetitive, timid, or submissive than the other.

That left researchers with a very narrow field from which to choose. They could try to find what it is about a man's brain that makes him more aggressive than a woman. Or they could delve into the verbal-spatial dichotomy between the sexes.

Dr. Sandra Witelson, of the department of psychiatry at McMaster University, Ontario, chose to delve into the latter. She studied 200 children, ages six to 13, and found that in boys the right hemisphere of the brain—which is dominant for processing spatial information in right-handed persons—matures as early as age six. The same hemisphere doesn't process spatial information as well in girls until they are 13 or older.

For verbal ability, according to Dr. Doreen Kimura, an experimental psychologist at the University of Southern Ontario, just the opposite is true. The speech center located in the left hemisphere (in right-handed persons, again) matures more rapidly in girls than boys. Could the male hormone be responsible for this cerebral divergence? Theoretically, yes.

This is only theory now, but it gives some inkling into the way hormones affect the brain from the earliest days of development. And, for the first time, these studies show that sex hormones, especially testosterone, account not only for differences in our sexual organs, but also for subtle differences in the way men and women perceive their own sexuality, as well as the world around them.

Testosterone definitely determines the shape of the external genitals. The presence of the hormone in an embryo causes a slight outcropping of cells to develop into a penis and scrotum (its absence means that these same cells will develop into a clitoris and labia). This sets into action the final biological event that assures that when the child is born, the parents will react in the same way parents have throughout

Everybody's Fancy

Some are fancy on the
    outside.
Some are fancy on the
    inside.
Everybody's fancy.
Everybody's fine.
Your body's fancy and so is
    mine.

Boys are boys from the
    beginning.
Girls are girls right from the
    start.
Everybody's fancy.
Everybody's fine.
Your body's fancy and so is
    mine.

Only girls can be the
    mommies.
Only boys can be the
    daddies.
Everybody's fancy.
Everybody's fine.
Your body's fancy and so is
    mine.

I think you're a special
    person.
And I like your ins and
    outsides.
Everybody's fancy.
Everybody's fine.
Your body's fancy and
    so—is—mine.

—MISTER ROGERS
©Fred M. Rogers, 1967

time and across cultures: It's a boy! And testosterone continues to make a male a male throughout his life, as we shall see in later sections of this book.

enetic accidents

Sometimes the embryonic hormonal signals are confused and a baby is born who is not clearly either a boy or a girl. The external genitals resemble a large clitoris or a minuscule penis. This condition, known as hermaphroditism, has given some medical researchers the opportunity to ask what happens when the internal chromosomal label—boy or girl—disagrees with the external anatomy.

In some instances, the external genitals resemble those of a boy rather than a girl, but the internal organs are ovaries, not testes. These individuals have two X chromosomes, so they're genetically female, but an imbalance of hormones at a critical time during development resulted in the conflicting anatomy. This imbalance can arise two ways. The adrenal glands can malfunction, manufacturing excess testosterone, which alters the shape of the external genitals. This is known as androgenital syndrome, and girls born with this confusing set of sexual instructions resemble boys. In fact, if nothing is done to reverse the situation—by suppressing the production of testosterone—the baby will go on to develop a male build.

The other way genetically female hermaphrodites form is if the mother is taking a hormone that has a masculinizing effect. This was a problem about 10 years ago, when doctors prescribed the hormone progestin to prospective mothers who had a history of miscarriage. The hormone allowed them to carry for nine months, but in some cases at a drastic price. It seems that the progestin, like excess testosterone, caused the external genitals to malform, leaving the newborn with a questionable sex.

Genetic male fetuses can also undergo hermaphroditic changes if a metabolic error renders their testes incapable of producing male hormone. In another seemingly malevolent twist of fate, a genetic male fetus may be insensitive to its own male hormone. At birth, he would appear to be a girl, and while an astute obstetrician or pediatrician might diagnose the problem, there wouldn't be any way of correcting it because the boy's cells remain insensitive to male hormone.

hromosomes vs. conditioning

What becomes of these children? That depends on what their parents and the consulting doctors decide. Some are raised as boys, some as girls. "To use the Pygmalion allegory," says Dr. Money, who has counseled dozens of parents with hermaphroditic children, "one may begin with the same clay and fashion a god or a goddess."

Two such cases involved genetically female hermaphrodites born with the androgenital syndrome. One underwent feminizing surgery—her clitoris was reduced in size, and the rest of her external organs were fashioned into unmistakable female genitalia—and was raised as a girl. The other underwent "penis repair," as this corrective surgery is euphemistically called, and was raised as a boy. According to Money, both grew up secure with their sexual identities. The girl was somewhat tomboyish, her mother reported, but she "appeared attractively feminine to those who knew her." The boy too had no trouble being accepted for what he was, a boy. He even expressed romantic interest in girls, Money said—despite the fact that every cell in his body carried the female chromosomal complement, XX.

If conclusions can be drawn from studies such as these, one might be that male genes and hormones don't automatically confer maleness. Parental and social influences have to be taken into account. To a large degree, boys behave like boys and girls behave like girls because of what they're taught, because of what they're permitted to do, and because of how they think of themselves.

Male genes and hormones don't keep boys from wearing dresses or playing with dolls—parents do. At least, that's how we assume things work. But Money, and researchers like him, don't deal in assumptions. They look for evidence—proof, so to speak—that environment can override heredity.

They found their best proof to date in the case of a normal boy who lost his penis in a circumcision accident. He was seven months old at the time, and until the accident, he had been raised as any normal child, along with his twin brother.

For the next ten months after the accident his parents continued to treat him and his brother the same, and both grew into active toddlers, with little interest in dolls or

What Are Little Boys Made Of?

Snakes and snails,
And puppy dogs' tails;
That's what little boys are
    made of.

What Are Little Girls Made Of?

Sugar and spice,
And everything nice;
That's what little girls are
    made of.

housecleaning or other sexually stereotyped female behavior. Then, on the advice of specialists trained in assigning gender to children with genital abnormalities, the parents authorized the transformation from boy to girl. An operation was performed to change the boy's external anatomy, and his parents began rearing him as a girl. Within months, their newly assigned daughter took on female behavior characteristics, with prodding from her parents. She developed an interest in grooming and clothing, unlike her brother, who was encouraged to protect his sister. By the time she was four and a half, she was much neater than her brother, and she interacted with her parents much differently than he did.

She's now in adolescence and, if the medical plans are being followed, she is now being treated with female hormones that will make her breasts develop and her hips enlarge and will generally complete the feminization process that was begun when she was seventeen months old. She'll never be fertile, nor will she be capable of menstruating. Yet, from all evidence, she thinks of herself as a woman.

All this goes to prove that sexual identity is not simply a matter of chromosomes. Masculine and feminine roles, and the behavior that goes with them, aren't etched in stone. They can be modified, and sometimes switched around entirely, in response to changing times, experience, and learning. Even the basic anatomical differences between men and women can be altered on the operating table and by hormone therapy. Nothing, though, can eradicate the telltale sex chromosomes in each of our cells.

When one of those chromosomes is a Y and nothing interferes with the production and effect of testosterone, the infant will be born with the potential to respond to parental cues that, from birth onward, will coax him, sometimes gently, sometimes not so gently, into the male role.

IMAGES

IMAGES

ot to worry

The secret has not been particularly well kept. Men are scared. Sometimes they are terrified. Fear, of course, is supposed to be a product of lack of knowledge, lack of control, lack of understanding, lack. And, as the culture moves through the final fifth of the century, shrouding the fear most men have is the development of a coolness—a public and even private reticence—that conceals what is felt most often to be an irrational reaction. The male children of the depressed '30s, the war-torn '40s, the complacent '50s, the turbulent '60s, the yet-to-be-categorized '70s were taught not to fear. They were taught to be brave, but to be so passively, coolly.

If a man lacks confidence, if he experiences fear, well, he should just get over it, for crissakes—get a grip on himself. Most men try hard to accomplish this feat, and they do this by dealing with fear as a distraction rather than as an emotional reality. Fear is simply something to handle, to ignore, or to squash like a nagging mosquito.

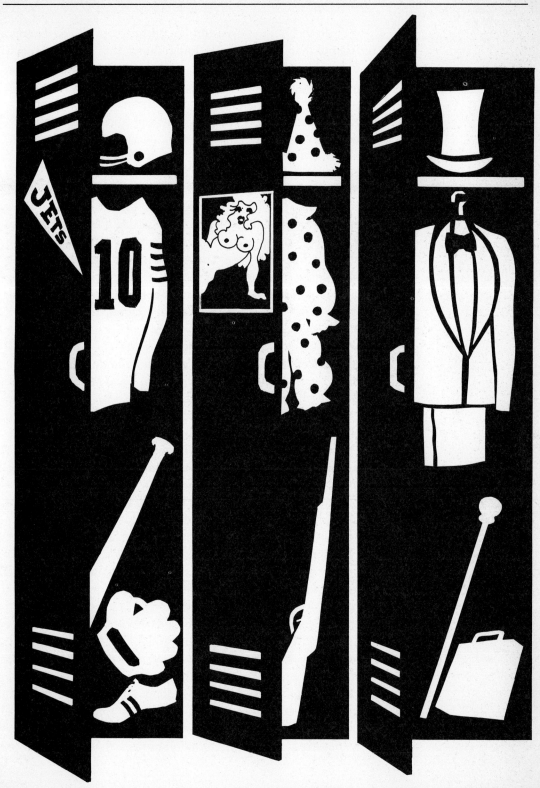

Anthropologist Weston La Barre wrote in *The Human Animal* that "the ability to know things that are not so is a unique peculiarity of humans among animals." One of these not-so things is *knowing* that a human baby, because of a particular combination of sex-determining chromosomes— XY instead of XX—has the potential and responsibility to develop as a better athlete, better leader, better profit-maker, better bricklayer, or better surgeon. X + Y = Braver and Emotionally Stronger. The cultural truth is in the broad stating of the formula to both men and women; if a man is told consistently that he is supposed to be brave and free of tears and responsible, then he will soon believe that that's the way things are supposed to be. He may not feel that way, but he will believe that other men do, hence he should. The uneasiness is an obstacle that is to be overcome. And the challenge is more often than not accepted, for the alternative is to be less than what one is told is acceptable—a failure. X + Y (failed) = X + X.

Accepting the challenge amounts to the deliberate repression of basic sensory signals, sometimes almost to the point of emotional freeze-drying. Men learn to do it very well. Repression begins with the earliest consciousness of a male child, and it ends with the death of a man. In this way the Male Mystique develops, and it becomes integral to the Male Outlook—and to the Male Inlook, which is really just a function of the Outlook. The condensed version of the expounded-to-the-point-of-distraction Male Mystique is simply this: "You're a man. Don't be *really* scared, but if you have to be, for God's sake, don't let anybody know it."

If you can't stand the heat, get out of the kitchen.

—HARRY S. TRUMAN

Handling the fear

The necessity of coping with personal uncertainties and fears affects the way a man views himself. What does he think he is? Most men think they are tough because they've been told for years that they're supposed to be tough. And that they are sensitive (in addition to being tough) because they seldom feel tough for long. He thinks he carries a heavy burden, in spite of whatever the Women's Movement has accomplished. He thinks what's required is working hard, showing imagination, earning money, passing knowledge on to his children, being fair, paying taxes. He believes all this and simultaneously that every day things are getting better, that this is the first day of the rest of his life, that he's blown it all, that he has power and can still make it, that he will someday understand what "making it" really is, that he is owed some favors, that he'll never collect, that he's in love—that it might not last. He thinks he's going to lose weight or at least not gain any more, keep a full head of hair or at least as much as he has, take the trouble to understand politics, bring back capital punishment, get a job that is worthy of him, be screwed by management—or if he's management, be screwed by labor—cheat a little on taxes and not get caught, cheat a little on his wife and not get caught, and pay more than his fair share for just about everything.

Sound contradictory? It is, and the contradictions make him uneasy. To complicate matters further, this self-defining takes into account not only his self-perceptions but his perceptions of others and his awareness of others' perceptions of him. A triple bind.

In the burgeoning pop psychology of our time, "defining" is frequently dealt with in strict clinical terms, leaving out the flesh-and-blood experiences. In reality it comes down to "Just who the hell does he think he is?" And the beginning of the answer is that he thinks he is a lot of different people at different times—not because he is schizophrenic but because he is a normal man in a complex world that makes many demands on him.

The first hero

A man's father is usually the most affecting model and, as a rule, the only hero directly challenged. He may cherish the relationship, merely accept it, or even reject it or receive rejection from the father, but there will never be a day in his life when he does not feel or sense or see or hear something in himself which is connected with his role as a son.

One of the critical points in most father-son relationships is reached sometime during the son's adolescent years. The young man feels that it's time to get back at his father. He doesn't want to kill his father—merely to return the emotional and physical whacks suffered in childhood and to enter adulthood. Relatively few express this desire violently. But most men, if asked, will confirm that the moment is reached and is memorable. That small boys want and need approval from fathers, or at least from older men, is obvious and has long been accepted. But the reaction to fathers by sons who are no longer boys is no less important.

Playing the roles

Being a son is a role that a man carries with him through a lifetime. It matters little how many children he may himself father—he still remains someone's son. And the acting out of a nearly lifelong role is often emotionally draining. This is not to diminish the importance of his mother. To most men she is, among other important things, an ally in a world dominated by the presence, or absence, of the father. But it is a father's victories, imagined or real, in a man's world that are first learned and used as self-measurement and then studied with increasing intensity. When the study of the father's achievements as a "man" begins to turn up less than truly heroic aspects, the son begins to reshape his views of his father, of his mother, and of himself. Often this results in a period of embarrassment over his father's limitations. Though these feelings do initially diminish, they frequently return as a son ages and feels more and more of his father within himself.

> *I must have been 30 the first time I noticed it. I was*
> *walking past a shop and saw a reflection in the*
> *window. It was me, but for a second I thought,*
> *dammit, it's him. I'm not even physically on my own.*

One of the many lessons received by many men from their fathers is the message "Be your own man, but don't embarrass your mother." An important part of the father's role is determining the mother's place and defining it to the son. More often than not the father heard much the same kind of information from his own father, and if the messsage was good enough for his father it is usually good enough for him. The passing on of rote statements that no one particularly believes happens with maddening predictability.

As for their own roles, fathers may have definitions that they find difficult to live up to. Most fathers believe that they should take the boy to a ball game, go camping and fishing, teach boxing, teach the lad about sex. Many do take the boy to a ball game, a few go camping and fishing, some teach boxing. But sex—that's something few fathers feel expert about anyway.

Certainly the instincts are there. Consider camping.

Like Father, Like Son

The old man thrived on work. He told the kid, "Always work as hard as, or harder than, anyone who works for you." The old man owned a shipping company.

The kid did even better than that. Now the kid is 47 years old, and he's chairman of the board of the American Ship Building Company, which is expected to do $180 million worth of sales in 1978. And he's principal owner of the New York Yankees.

From the father, the kid says he learned to be tough, to drive and succeed, to win; he doesn't believe in entering a contest just to compete. He believes in keeping score; he doesn't mess around with No. 2.

—TONY KORNHEISER

Nearly all fathers would like to take their sons camping, but only a few have any idea how to go about it. Camping is but one of the failed activities that can become representative of the gap between sons and fathers. It is potentially an idyllic and satisfying man-to-man scene, but for most fathers and sons that's not how it turns out. A week or two traveling on expressways from one fully outfitted trailer campsite to another is not what mythic camping is all about. So instead, there may be weekly scout or Indian-guide meetings that the father has little to do with.

Second thoughts

One of the earliest moments of truth, and a nearly traumatic acknowledgment of growing older, is when a son who wants to be thought of as a good son realizes that his father is less than a perfect son to his father. It is the first in what will be a lifelong series of challenges to the concept and the realities of a father and a man—as a son. That love between the two men is often present, or at least a possibility, does not make the appraisals and reappraisals less painful. As the child is father to the man, so the man believes that he is, indeed, emotionally and physically bound to the biological father. And if a total split ever develops between a son and a father, a void is invariably left that time, the great healer, seldom does more than cover with a temporary Band-Aid. If a split is avoided, as it is in most situations, still, an edginess is usually present in the relationship between the two men. A son may profess to want to be close to his father, but not to the point of limiting his own potential. After all, he's been right there and seen some of the cracks in the exterior, some of the flaws in the model. And the father? He feels he should maintain some distance. After all, the boy has to carry on by himself. The father, living with his own uncertainties and seeing traces of them in his son (as well as seeing more of the mother in the son than the son feels), is, not surprisingly, often wary of his son.

As son and father get older, the situation doesn't necessarily get better, though it gets different. A man feels a special confusion as he sees his father age—indisputable proof that he will age himself. He almost feels that his own mortality is his father's fault, like a fatal flaw passed in the genes. He is increasingly impatient with this first role model.

And you, my father, there on the sad height,
Curse, bless, me now with your fierce tears, I pray.
Do not go gentle into that good night.
Rage, rage against the dying of the light.

—DYLAN THOMAS

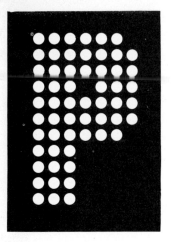

ublic Heroes

In the old days, before the '60s, an old saw had it that if you wanted to know what a man thought, what he admired, and who he admired you had only to study his bookshelves and then consider the magazines and newspapers he read. Today, however, things are different. Now it's television first, then movies (although most are shown on television), and the music he listens to a not-distant third. But television is the big one. This dominant communications medium, acting as a one-way convex cultural mirror, has been flashing images of strength, durability, and style to an audience which, in order to complete the far end of the communications contract, must remain both relatively silent and relatively still.

A television viewer survey compiled in early 1978 reported that the average viewer spent 1,500 hours a year in front of a television set. This figure takes on meaning when it is compared with the average student's 1,100 hours a year in the classroom.

Certainly the communicating has not been just to males. There is something for everyone within the electronic media, as there is in newspapers, books, and schools, within families, on billboards, in the churches, and on the back of cereal boxes, to name just a few of our cultural sources.

Anthropologist Edmund Carpenter in his book *Oh, What a Blow That Phantom Gave Me!* pointed out that "TV is the psychic leap of our time. It's a trip far more potent than LSD. It turns thoughts inward, revealing new, unsuspected realities. Those who prefer this inner reality live in a world apart.... Children west of the Rockies, from 11 to 12 on, are turning off TV, but their parents stick with it, becoming stoned in the process. Drugs, by comparison, are kids' stuff. It's really the silent majority over 30 that gets stoned nightly."

The involvement with the public images experienced by a man are different in texture if not in sense from those experienced by a woman. The heroes of men are usually, not surprisingly, other men. What is consistent is the coolness of the archetypical male hero. In the late '60s and through the '70s the good thing to be was "laid back." The work world calls it having "excellent control" or being "well-targeted." On television and in films the hero should be somewhat beleaguered, capable of excellence when the moment demands it, understanding of orange sunsets, tender, yet heroically resilient. Men's heroes are men who basically just sit there and do it with their mouths.

The field of media heroes is extremely wide. It includes entertainers, sturdy dramatic actors, talk-show iconoclasts, and, increasingly, "information." The newsmen have become heroes, and the news is heroic. Field reporters tend to be more significant male heroes than anchormen, not because they are more physically active but because they appear standing before varying backgrounds. The assumption is that they must have been somehow involved in the action, at least in getting to the changing backdrops, where they stand or sit and do it with their mouths, usually in less than 120 seconds.

Grown men imitate their heroes no less than they did when they were small boys. The difference is that they do it within a slightly larger personal context, so it's not always apparent. News heroes, sports heroes, TV and film heroes, all can and do become elements in most men's changing externalized makeup. Verbal phrasing, clichés, catch phrases, pregnant pauses—most can be traced to identifiable sources, and the great majority of the sources are public figures. Men show this through physical moves, cutting hand gestures, their pace leaving a basketball arena after a professional game with shoulders slightly loose.

The Problem With Young People

The young people of today get their ideas from postcards, cheap shows, serial love stories, and cheap novels.

One-third of the pictures exhibited at the cheap shows and plays at operas and theaters consists of every possible mode of spooning.

Nine times out of ten the sensual artist makes the young man to appear innocent and passive and the young woman is made the aggressor.

—THOMAS W. SHANNON,
Personal Help for Men, 1918

**eal life**

It is not the heroes as individuals that men so much identify with and emulate, rather it is the heroes as representatives of states of mind and states of nature. A new member of a telephone line crew will invariably recognize the dominant member of the crew and within a few days will have adopted certain of this man's moves and attitudes. If he likes what he sees—for instance, a shrug when a job appears to be acceptable—he will very probably "try it on" within his own world away from the job. If it appears to work it will become a fixture in his own repertoire and the source will soon be forgotten. It will be his. And it will very probably be borrowed again, taken further, by someone else who "likes his style."

The absorbing of actions and attitudes, the selecting of those that a man wants, begins early. The first acquisitions often serve to widen the gap between the sexes. One only wants a new attitude or attribute that will be beneficial or add to one's own stature. Mistakes happen to nearly everyone.

When I was eight I came out of a YMCA shower with my towel wrapped around my chest. The other boys laughed at me and said, "Hey, he's wearing his towel like a girl!" I had three older sisters at home and that's the way they wore bath towels. How the hell was I supposed to know? I thought everyone wore them that way. I didn't go back to the Y for weeks. But when I returned I wore the towel around my waist.

Attitudes and postures rejected, and roles left to be assumed by girls, who later become women, are legion. There is, however, an awareness that women have more options than men. It is a situation acknowledged, not envied. Small options. As a girl you could play with marbles or a yo-yo if you wanted to, but a boy who jumped rope could avoid teasing only if he established clearly that he was training to be a boxer. A girl could wear either a dress or a pair of pants.

Girls carry books in front, clutching them to the chest with arms bent. A boy carries his at his side, with his arm straight. Perhaps one of the most arbitrary gender distinctions is seen in leg-crossing. Men in America cross their legs with ankle or, at most, calf over the knee in a "figure 4" position. The knee-over-knee pose, although more comfortable, is consid-

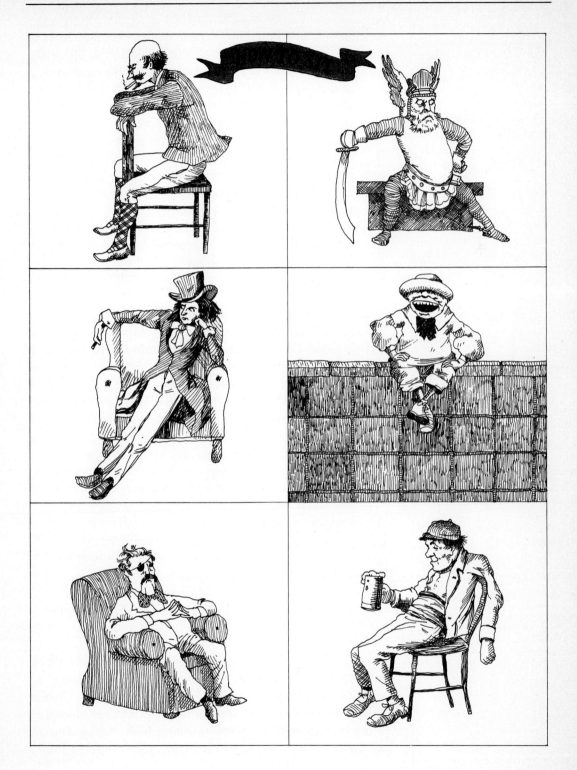

ered effeminate, primarily because women adopted it, or at least had it dictated to them because of the clothes they wear.

When I was a kid I was sitting on the sofa reading and my legs were crossed, right knee draped over left. My father said, "You're sitting like a girl!" and demonstrated the right way: He placed his left ankle on his right knee so that his thighs were separated at the immodest masculine angle. For a couple of years after that I thought men were supposed to cross legs left over right, while women cross them right over left. Or was it the other way? I could never remember which. So rather than make a mistake and do it like a girl, I preferred not to cross my legs at all.

The important point is not that one posture is masculine and the other feminine, but that if a man thinks there is a difference it makes a difference to him. He will attempt to get it right. And if a major male star appeared a few times on television talk shows with legs draped knee over knee, the new posture would begin to gain favor in a hurry.

A man's rational brain may tell him that the "man's way" is arbitrary and that he should be satisfied being his own model, that it's his own masculinity that he is stating, but...

I was out by the mailboxes talking with my next-door neighbor, a football coach, whom I respected enormously. We were standing there talking. I had my hands on my hips. He said jokingly that I was standing a woman's way, with my thumbs forward. I was 27 years old and I had never really thought about the best way to stand with my arms akimbo. But now, whenever I find myself standing with thumbs forward I feel an effeminate flash, even when I'm alone, and I quickly turn my hands around the other way.

The self-woven fabric in which men wrap themselves, and often tailor into straightjackets, is in many ways an example of accidental art: men as elements in a circular bucket brigade expressing attitudes and postures offered to them from diverse directions, retaining, rejecting, passing on, all the while attempting to settle into a comfortable stance which varies only slightly, if at all, from those of other men. Common in public schools in the South and the Midwest during the '50s and early '60s were Personality Books, little tablets in which classmates would have their names scrawled. Then the books would pass from hand to hand and unsigned comments about the individuals would be hurriedly scribbled onto the pages under the appropriate names. It could be ego-boosting or it could be devastating. But in either case it was taken to heart.

Focusing

Heightened awareness that the perceptions of others are important creates a situation in which one's self-perceptions are forced to do battle. Often this results in compromises that lead to the conclusion that the true goal is survival. Getting by. Not to be recognized as a failure becomes enough success for many. Above surviving come the varying degrees of accomplishment. It would be nice to be a leader, but being a sidekick beats being an also-ran. It would be good to be a star, but being a fan has more merit than being unaware. Being able to identify what others consider winners is critical, and implicit in this is the ability to spot losers—and avoid them. Since these judgments tend to be subjective, the individual has occasion to view the world as spinning on an orbit centered within an inch or two of his own breastbone.

The continuing teachings—be strong, be better, be polite, be honest, be kind, and true, and unassuming—become the expanded teachings—"Be fair, but you might as well get your share;" "Be honest, but you may get cheated so make your move first;" "You're equal, but if you discover that you have an edge don't be a jerk, use it;" "Be modest, but if you want to be appreciated make yourself heard."

And with the attitudes come the uniforms that are the mark of success. To wear a uniform, or at least a T-shirt with colors and words that match those worn by friends or hoped-for-friends, becomes of prime importance. "You look like a man" eventually becomes "You look like a banker, an auto-assembler, a fisherman." Nevermind the personal compromises a man makes along the way; the uniform remains paramount. What does deepen is the male quandary: Things are not always—or even often—the way they appear. And although appearances do become somewhat altered, they do not diminish in importance.

Most men sense that outside their immediate families few people wish them success. Perhaps even more important, a man becomes aware that he often resents another man's success if he feels the other person has enjoyed more than what he feels he himself has received. To be a better salesman than his father, a better football player than his classmate, a better scientist than his teacher, a more desirable lover than his roommate—this is the stuff that male competition is made of. But even here success is measured not so much in winning as in "not losing." Settling with "not losing" happens because most men admit to themselves that they don't really know what success actually means.

Sooner or later most men determine that relaxing may be as satisfactory as winning, or is, indeed, a form of victory. Most eventually realize that they exist in a finite world, both personally dictated and outer-imposed, and they either accept or resign themselves to the boundaries. But dreams themselves do not vanish. Usually it is only the direction of the dreams that change—from looking toward the future to reconsidering the past.

Dream world

Ask a man what he truly hopes for. As a rule, creature comforts are listed first: money, housing, the knowledge that he and the people he cares about are economically safe. But the dreams, the *real* dreams, generally center around the motivations he has been conditioned to consider his nature. This can be the "big, bigger, best" syndrome, coupled with keeping himself at a physical and emotional prime. And it often has to do with completion.

> *All of a sudden headlights came tearing down at us on our side of the parkway. We missed a head-on collision by less than 18 inches. I kept driving and all I could think was, "I could've been killed and I wouldn't have finished." And I don't even know what it is I haven't finished.*

It is the unfinished business of a man's life that can be the key to the question "Who the hell does he think he is?" It can be anything, but usually what it amounts to is simply "making a mark." The mark can be graffiti scrawled on the side of a bus or pediment, the creation of a modern building, or a stated insight. But it's a mark, a symbol.

renas

In your lifetime sports has become, for many, the male metaphor. The quality most admired by men in role models and heroes is competence. And it is within the realm of major league sports that individuals test and display their skills and attitudes in front of audiences that frequently number in the millions. Sports does serve as a valid illustration of judgments that are made concerning many men, and the individual compensations that men make in the face of outside judgments. It's easy to discern who's a winner and who's a loser, and it's also easy to make subtler and more profound judgments: who won well, who lost well.

Sports is the dominant media-dream focus—big heroes, big audiences, big business. For the spectators there is a sense of predictable gratification. Games and matches have definable boundaries, familiar beginnings, middles, and ends. As a rule, most occur within a time period that seldom exceeds three or four hours. One sports essayist has called it the male answer to the Gothic novel.

Thousands upon thousands of joggers, male and female, puff their ways down roads and sidewalks, tennis and racquetball players nick each other with their weapons as they wait to get time on local courts, parks teem with touch-football players, swimming pools choke with aerobic perfection-seekers. Yet the simple fact is that most of the active individuals—who are in any case greatly outnumbered by inactive individuals—are basically still spectators. They may be "participating"—but in their minds it isn't really their own two-handed backhand or perfect christie or deadly cool putt they're executing. They are playing out fantasies, running out dreams—seeing themselves in the roles of the big guys, the pros, the champions. And the pros? Most spend their entire careers still trying to show the style of their identifiable heroes, at least until the rarely reached point of attaining dominance in their particular field.

In a way it's a problem of simple arithmetic. In a relatively small public high school with 500 male students, at most 100 will be able to participate in organized sports. That means 80

Miguel Dominguin, Don Miguel, the Matador asked himself why men enter the arena and found his answer in women, in the presence of women. "If there were no women there, no man would face the bulls. At least I should not."

—JOHN CIARDI, "Their Eyes Watching"

percent do not participate other than to attend physical-education classes, in which any show of interest or enjoyment earns the ridicule of classmates. During the teenage years only the 20 percent will hear the scattered cheers and/or boos that are supposed to be the lifeblood of athletic heroes. Only about 2 percent of those that do participate in high school will ever move on to uniform-wearing play on the college or low professional level. And of these, only a similarly tiny percentage will go on to become the genuine article, the card-carrying, play-for-pay professional. For the rest it's occasional pickup games, or dedicated individual amateur efforts.

Sunday heroes

Those who will be actual athletes are usually spotted by coaches before they're 12 years old. Thus, most males—those the coaches pass over—are marked as also-rans at this early age. But the significance of sport as a life-force analogy is not lost on these unselected children. The language itself is peppered with sport analogies and insights. Study for a few days the sports pages of your local newspapers, or really pay attention to the smiling thick-chested sportscaster on the local television news.

It is at the early 12-year-old stage that many young men begin to learn that if they can't be number one themselves, at the very least they can identify with number one. They can be fans. They can share the emotional rewards of competiton with their selected surrogates.

I was ten, I think, when I decided to cheer for the Detroit Tigers. I didn't live there. I just picked them because my friends already had teams they followed. I collected everything about the team I could get my hands on—knew every statistic ever compiled, watched television every time they were on, learned to lope the way Al Kaline, their great centerfielder, did, and joined a Little League team. I only hit a little better than .180. Kaline's lifetime average was .297. I was benched when I was 13, but I still think I know how Kaline felt when he would drift under a flyball, glove it, and spin to nail a base runner who was fool enough to try to run on his arm.

Trot like an athlete, and smile like one—a bit reticent but warm and honest. Brush off distractions, know more than most coaches, be misunderstood, and feel that deep down there's a strength and ability that can complete a third-down-eight-to-go pass on a rain-swept field to keep a drive alive and win the Super Bowl. And, most important, insist on getting what's deserved. These are a few of the attributes the fan can add to his emotional arsenal. "Who does he think he is?" Well, not exactly an Olympic gold medal winner, but if the training had been available, a few breaks offered, maybe, just maybe, it could have happened. What the hell, the legs are still pretty good. Even now, if there were the luxury to get involved again, to work out every day, a few people might be surprised.

Big Sports becomes a meeting ground for Big Fans. And even those relatively few men who profess absolutely no interest in the sports world acknowledge its significance through their rejection. As men age, as they come closer to and then exceed the perennial youth of those on the actual playing fields, the conception of sports that began as childhood hopes and dreams turns to secondary fantasies and ultimately becomes a memory not of the way it was but of the way it was supposed to be. But on those Super Sundays, whether it's the big football game, the basketball or hockey playoffs, or a decent end-of-the-season backyard tennis match, shoulders tighten, blood pressure increases, pupils dilate, and the competition—someone else's competition—becomes extremely personal. Most modern men are blooded on spectator moments rather than actual sporting kills, but the blooding is no less permanently imprinted somewhere in the soul. There aren't too many opportunities in a man's life for flashing acts of personal heroism. For most men it has to be enough to share in the glory of the acts of "my team," or "my favorite player." The excitement is real, the emotional reward is definite. The disappointment can be staggering. The memory can be long.

Perhaps the pride and shame of the spectator are all the more intense because they exist in the mind only, like the triumph of the crafty Odysseus, the humiliation of the arrogant Oedipus. Win or lose, well or badly, the big guy does it for the little guy, and the little guy takes what he's been shown about how to play the game and tries to apply it in the boardroom and bedroom.

irror, mirror

Shortly after the onset of puberty a young man begins to spend a considerable amount of time facing a mirror. Shaving and washing the forehead and the lower part of the face begin to become a ritual. And what does he see beyond a mirror image of his face? Physically, he sees his upper body—face, shoulders, and chest. Only if he looks down will he see his stomach, genitals, and lower body (this from a distorted angle that diminishes the actual size). Most men have only limited visual perceptions of their bodies, and even, for that matter, of their facial profiles. Three-piece dressing-table mirrors are often granted to girls as toy promises of impending adulthood, but boys and young men don't get them. But by the time he reaches manhood the flat, one-piece mirror has become yet another place for full-face self-testing, for judging, for preparing for the rest of the world. It becomes a daily opportunity for conversation with his disembodied presence.

> I've heard a lot of people say they get their best ideas while they're shaving. I don't. But what I do get is a grip on myself, giving myself little pep talks and deciding that it's not bad, that everything's looking all right. It's as though there's a moment when I can pay attention to myself. Maybe I really do need the mirror to be able to convince myself that I'm actually around.

For many men the chest-high shaving mirror may become a best friend. It can also serve as a friend who is not above deception. Shoulders sagging? Push them back and admire that posture. Suck in that drooping stomach. Nod acceptance and move away, and for part of the day, until the blood sugar level begins its dip, that final reflection in the mirror becomes the way a man *feels* he looks. It is little wonder that most men, when asked where they perceive their physical center, wave their hands somewhere from shoulder to shoulder over their upper chest.

The point is not that men never see themselves full-body but that they seldom see themselves full-body in an undressed state. In the vast majority of team or club dressing rooms, there *is* a full-length mirror, but it's nearly always at a point near the door where one seldom ventures while nude. It's for confirming the fully-dressed back-to-the-world countenance, not for studying the unclothed body. Questions and answers reflected off a mirror are nearly always face-to-face conversations—not man-to-man.

Body image

What most concerns a man about his physical form is its effectiveness and how it feels. The important element is how well the body performs. If a man likes his legs it's because they work well, they move him with sufficient speed and agility. This is more significant than if they are symmetrically or photogenically formed. If he is comfortable with and aware of his hands, it's not because of their texture, curve, or smoothness, but because he is capable of doing what he wants to do with them. He can throw, catch, use them as physical tools. When he considers his penis (and he does) he is less concerned with how it looks or its size or texture than with how well it works. His body is an instrument. And if he feels that overall his body is effective in making his activities turn out successfully, he will enjoy a positive body image, feel confident, and be more at ease in situations that involve social contact.

Most men, even if personally satisfied with their bodies, rarely think of their bodies as beautiful or sexually appealing. The male difficulty in accepting a compliment on their physical appearance stems less from embarrassment than from pure lack of confidence. Few men consider their bodies visually appealing. This reaction results in part from pre-puberty training in rejecting things female, and later from an intensified reticence to identify with traits that are considered feminine, or at least less than masculine. Concern with one's body has been, until very recently, a mark of vanity, and vanity has never been an acceptable male value. It is not that most heterosexual men fear that they possess feminine qualities. What they fear and fear deeply is being *perceived* as feminine or less than 100 percent man. The opinion of the beholder is of extreme importance. In recent years, however, with the growing media stress on health and public conditioning, and the fashion focus on wearing garments designed initially for professional tennis players, runners, and skiers, men have begun to show more acceptance of and openness toward acknowledging their own bodies in relation to other bodies.

Looks, of course, do count. Few men are unaware of this. Yet it has only slightly altered their disdain of preening.

The way to a man's heart is through his stomach, especially if you tell him how flat it is.

—MIGNON McLAUGHLIN,
The Second Neurotic's Notebook

Most men simply go with what they have and pay only minimal attention to dramatically altering their physical presence. However, men react to another man's appearance as definitely as do women. And each man creates his self-concept and much of his social personality from the reactions he senses others have to him. Individuals who fit the cultural standards of attractiveness are treated more favorably than those who don't. Researchers have documented that these reactions appear in children as early as nursery-school age. It's not surprising that a naturally "attractive" boy has a head start in life and turns out to be self-confident, outgoing, friendly, and relatively more successful than the young "unattractives." Quite naturally, judgment by others leads him to feel these qualities in himself. The "unattractives," however, are forced from an early age to deal with less than favorable judgments, and the experience can either break an individual's spirit or it can result in a fierce anger that in the true "macho" sense is not going to be denied.

Attractiveness, however, is but one of several physical elements significant to a man's life. Overall size has also been shown to be of importance. If a man is both attractive and tall he will probably enjoy more than just the sum of the parts. Aside from the reactions it produces in others, a man's body affects his personality in a direct and personal way. This is because in the boyhood arenas where physical contests are the universal norm, in forms ranging from the earliest organized sports to friendly rough-housing and out-and-out brawls, a male's physical size can and usually will affect the experiences he's likely to have.

A young man who is smaller than his immediate circle of friends is likely to lose more confrontations than he wins, and repeated defeats can make a mark that can prove to be indelible. Similarly, a larger-than-average young man may initially have a noncompetitive nature, yet when he becomes involved in physical showdowns with others his age, chances are good that he will emerge the winner. Repeated experiences as a winner or loser can leave an imprint on a self-image, an image that is a critical part of a man's social and private personality.

A deeper biological process may be at work here, acting to turn experience into potential. Winning or losing may be followed by a change in the concentration of the male

Short Guys Finish First

New York Yankees manager Joe McCarthy, who won eight pennants in his 14 years at the helm, was only 5'8½" high in a clubful of tall athletes. He was so conscious of stature that he ordered all the Yankee uniforms a half-size too large—to make the players look bigger on the field.

hormones which alter the future chances of winning or losing. Researchers have determined that if a male rat is confronted with another male that has previously beaten him in a fight, his blood testosterone level drops sharply. But if the subject sees a male that he has previously beaten, his male hormones surge to a higher concentration than normal. It is conceivable that a man's experience may, in a similar way, affect body chemistry, which in turn affects future possibilities. Winning and losing can become habits—habits that are at the same time learned and biologically reinforced. Self-confidence perpetuates itself, and so does a lack of it.

A MAN'S BODY

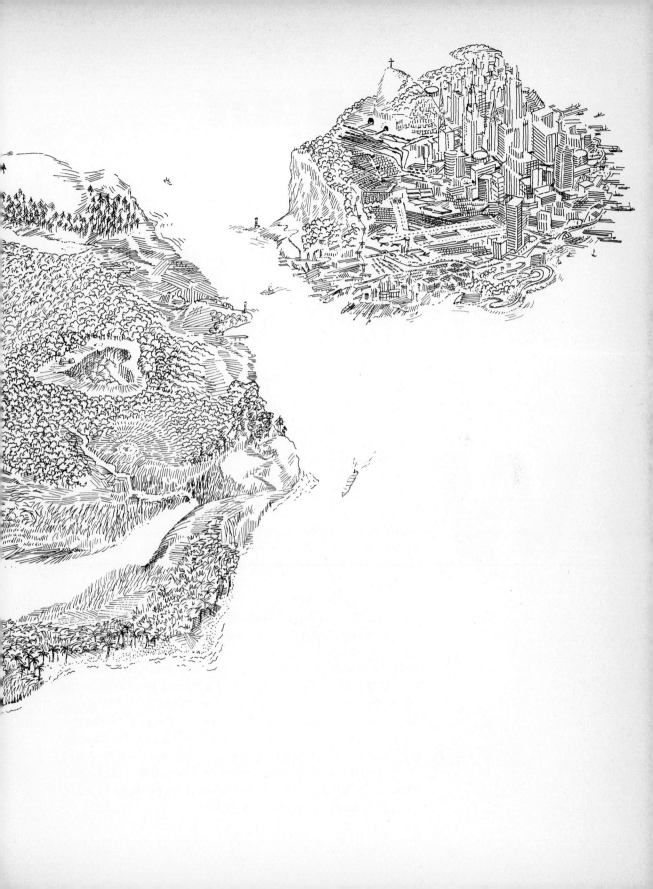

A MAN'S BODY

What is a male body?

You probably last heard this question in junior high, sitting through a biology class while a very embarrassed teacher tried to explain the difference between men and women, in all likelihood not doing a good job of it. Bodies are something most of us take for granted. As for the sexual differences, well, the major external ones can be hidden with a few fig leaves.

What most people know about their bodies they have learned from trial and error, and the instruction that came in crowded classrooms. But a man's body? That's best left to him, isn't it? Actually, no, it isn't. The more you know the better you will understand how men feel and react.

If you think that what makes a man a man is all in his mind, you are only partially right. The way he is built, the way his pubic hair grows toward his navel, the bulge of his biceps, and the shape of his jaw all help you perceive his masculinity. He may not be consciously aware of the subtle differences between his body and yours, but somewhere in the back of his mind he's tucked away dozens of little facts about himself, about his body and the way it works.

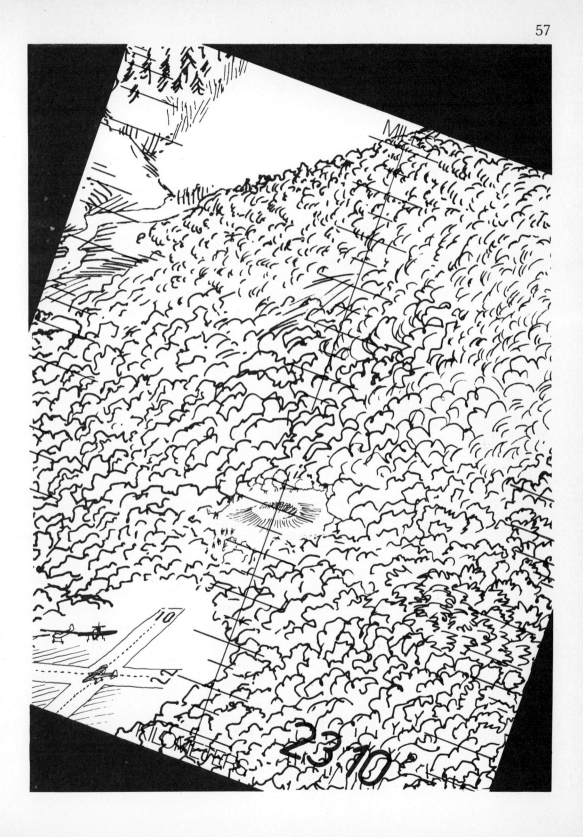

Is it normal that one of his testicles hangs lower than the other? Is he losing his virility along with his hair? Why does he get backaches and ulcers? Why does his anger seem to be unpredictable, or why is it so maddeningly predictable? Where on his body is he most sensitive? Why can't he keep an erection if he is in good enough shape to jog a couple of miles a day?

At one time or another every woman has questions about men's bodies—questions all too seldom asked. Such questions may embarrass a man or make him feel insecure. So the facts about why his body works, and why it works the way it does, often remain unphrased and unavailable.

And even if you have worked up the nerve to ask a man a question about his body, he probably won't know the answer. Or his suspicions will be aroused because he is afraid that you are comparing him to other men you have known. That's only normal. Most of the things you know about male bodies you've learned from experience.

uriosity

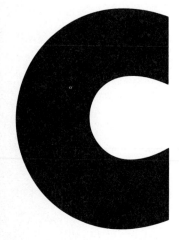

There's nothing unnatural about being interested in bodies. In fact, everyone starts out that way. A large part of your infancy was spent getting acquainted in general terms with your own body. No matter how many playthings were crammed into your crib, you were still more intrigued with your fingers and toes. X-rays of pregnant women show that fetuses occasionally suck their thumbs. And this interest doesn't diminish until the middle of childhood, when, through a combination of parental pressure and a stage of development to which Freud gave the term "latency," children suddenly become very private about their bodies and embarrassed about the obvious differences between the sexes.

This happens even in the most sexually "open" situations. Youngsters raised on communes in the late 1960s and early 1970s accepted nudity as if it were the natural condition. In fact, for many of them it was. But when they turned five or six, they invariably began asking their parents—or the adult authority figures, in any case—for underwear. Bathroom doors closed for the first time. They announced that they were old enough to take baths by themselves. And they sought secluded corners for dressing and undressing.

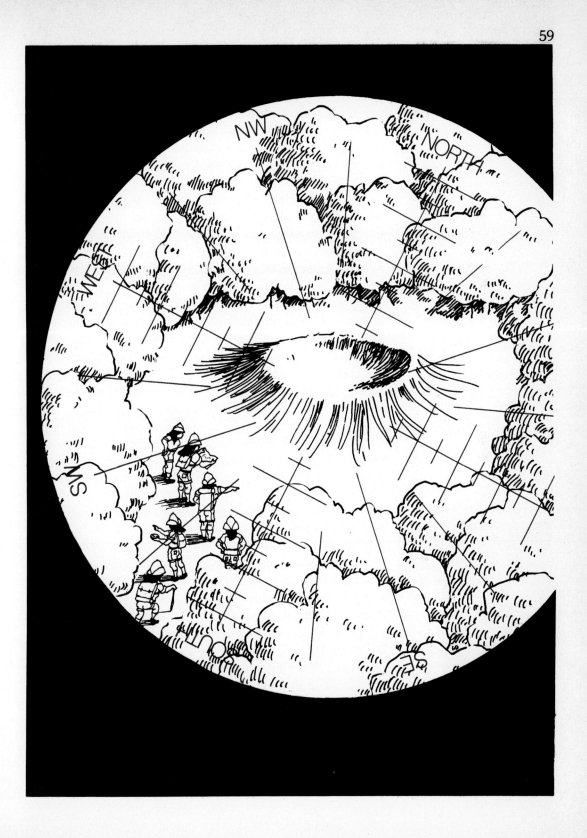

Until adolescence, most of what you knew about little boys you had learned by the the time you were five or six years old. The fact that a little boy has a penis and a little girl doesn't is one of the most startling discoveries of childhood. And if you were bold enough to touch it as well as look at it, you couldn't help being amazed by how funny and strange it felt, as if it were stuck on.

In all likelihood someone told you that the little boy's penis was for making babies when he grew up. But didn't he use it for urinating too? Whatever you knew about penises during childhood went into hiding somewhere in your memory, only to be summoned up again during puberty. Then penises were a whole different story.

So were their owners. They were changing into men, and their bodies took on a new significance along with noticeably different dimensions. Somewhere between the time of the first crush and the first sexual experience, mental images of the "ideal man" have formed. And usually he is big and strong, like all the men who ever marched across the silver screen to take a woman into their arms.

More often than not, the reality of seeing a man in the flesh was illusion-shattering, though most women weren't aware of it at the time because there were other things on their minds. What would he feel like—what would *it* feel like?

he rest of him

Images of a man's body are irrevocably intertwined with images of sex and images of watching men perform in sports or strut down a beach. That's unfortunate in many respects, because a man's body is, of course, more than an erect penis and rippling muscles.

Take a closer look. His ring finger is slightly longer than his index finger, a relationship that's curiously reversed on your hand. If it isn't, don't worry. Some women's ring fingers are longer than their index fingers, just as some women's shoulders are broader than some men's, and some women's hips are narrower than some men's. In fact, if hip and shoulder measurement alone are used to distinguish the sexes, 10 out of every 100 women would be classified as men, and 10 out of every 100 men would be classified as women.

On the average, though, a man's shoulders are broader

Where The Pounds Are

More than half a man's weight is in his muscle and fat. In a 160-pound man (73 kg.) with an average build, his weight could be distributed as follows.

Muscles:	68 lbs.	(31 kg.)
Fat:	28 lbs.	(13 kg.)
Bones (without marrow):	15 lbs.	(6.8 kg.)
Blood:	12 lbs.	(5.4 kg.)
Connective tissue:	8 lbs.	(3.6 kg.)
Bone marrow:	6 lbs.	(2.7 kg.)
Skin:	5 lbs.	(2.3 kg.)
Stomach & intestines:	4½ lbs.	(2 kg.)
Liver:	4 lbs.	(1.8 kg.)
Brain:	3½ lbs.	(1.6 kg.)
Lungs:	2 lbs.	(910 g.)
Lymphoid tissue:	1½ lbs.	(680 g.)
Kidneys:	11 oz.	(310 g.)
Heart:	11 oz.	(310 g.)
Spleen:	5 oz.	(140 g.)
Bladder:	5 oz.	(140 g.)
Pancreas:	2½ oz.	(71 g.)
Salivary glands:	2 oz.	(57 g.)
Testes:	1½ oz.	(43 g.)
Eyes:	1 oz.	(28 g.)
Spinal cord:	1 oz.	(28 g.)
Teeth:	1 oz.	(28 g.)
Thyroid:	1 oz.	(28 g.)
Prostate:	½ oz.	(14 g.)
Adrenals:	½ oz.	(14 g.)
Thymus:	¼ oz.	(7 g.)

than yours and his hips are narrower. He has more muscle, larger hands, stronger thumbs, a thicker skull, heavier bones, a deeper voice, bigger lungs, and more blood cells than you do. But he has the same number of hairs over his body, though some of them are more densely colored and thicker than yours, and he has less insulating fat under his skin, so he's more sensitive to cold.

If he stands up and holds his downstretched arms against his body, you'll be able to investigate another difference. Have him move his lower arms, from the elbow down, as far away as he can from his body. Then you try it. You should be able to move yours farther away. If you think of your elbow as the top of a triangle, and your forearm and torso as two of the sides, the angle formed when you hold your forearm away from your body is about 6 degrees greater than his. This is called the carrying angle, and yours is larger than his. It's advantageous for carrying a child around perched on your hip. You can easily support the child with one arm, leaving the other free. Your larger carrying angle also evens things out a bit for lifting and helps compensate for the fact that your shoulders tend to be narrower and less muscular than a man's.

Even so, there's no way that your upper-body strength can match a man's, if both of you are physically fit. The average man is muscularly stronger than the average woman, and he can use that strength to hit a tennis ball harder. Before Renée Richards underwent sex-change treatments, she had the hormones and body musculature of a man. At that time, as Dr. Richard H. Raskind, she had played in the men's division at Forest Hills, and had reached the semifinals one year. Most, if not all, women athletes will concede that a man who is good enough to reach Forest Hills' semifinals is capable of winning a match against the best of the women tennis players. Renée Richards used to play tennis with this sort of power, but after years of hormonal adjustment, her muscles no longer respond like those of a man. Her serve no longer booms across the net. Age certainly has also diminished some of her skills, but it is the replacement of testosterone by estrogen that has fundamentally altered her muscular strength.

But muscle alone doesn't make a man's body what it is. Nor do skin and bone and blood. In an average 160-pound man, skin and bones weigh 34 pounds, and muscle and blood

weigh another 80 pounds. That accounts for two-thirds of his weight. The remaining 46 pounds is divided among fat and 20 organs and tissues. His body is 60 percent water, 18 percent carbon, 3 percent nitrogen, 1.5 percent calcium, and 1 percent phosphorus, with traces of various minerals and ash.

That's equivalent to 10 gallons of water, a 30-pound sack of charcoal, and enough phosphorus to light a 5-foot fuse. The net chemical worth of this average man is about six dollars on today's market, up from 98 cents during the Depression.

The value of these chemicals soars astronomically when they are combined into cells and then into organs. And if you've ever thought that a specific man was priceless, you'd be right on this count alone. Most of his organs are priceless, though there are a few bodily parts he could do without—the appendix, for instance, and the coccyx at the base of his spine. His earlobes don't serve much use, except for an occasional nibble, and the nail that grows from his small toe has no known function, unless he likes wearing holes through his socks. Of course, your own body has the same unnecessary parts. By and large, though, most of his parts are useful, and, with the exception of his reproductive system, he has the same parts that you have. His cells may be assembled somewhat differently than yours, but you both have about 60 trillion of them. Some last longer than others. Some are made to be worn away or worn out and replaced.

It may come as a surprise but, if nothing else, his body at least is constantly changing. He sheds about half a pound of skin cells a year. In fact, the dust that accumulates under the bed harbors a goodly number of sloughed cells. As if that weren't enough, he loses about 8 million blood cells every second. Fresh replacements are manufactured by his bone marrow and lymph glands. Nevertheless, contrary to popular misconception, a man's body doesn't renew itself every seven years, so there's no biological foundation for the "seven-year itch."

Fortunately, most of his other cells aren't exposed to abrasion or wear and tear, so they last longer. But, according to current theories of aging, all of his cells have a built-in genetic time clock that begins ticking from the moment they are formed. As the clock runs down, the cells wither and die. In the brain, this process dampens the memory and shortens attention span. In the kidney, poisons that should have been filtered out escape back into the bloodstream. Every one of his organs is on its own time schedule. When a vital one no longer functions, all the others suffer, run down, and stop.

Contrary to grisly myth, nothing continues to grow after the heart stops—not even fingernails, though they appear to grow because the skin around them shrinks.

Except for mature blood cells, which float loosely through his circulatory system, most of the cells in his body exist in compact arrangements called tissues. Groups of tissues form his organs, and collections of organs form his systems. If you're having flashbacks to those days in junior high biology class, try replacing them with this slightly more up-to-date version of how remarkable a man's body really is.

His face is capable of 250,000 expressions. Among them are ones that show when he's happy, sad, angry, depressed, scared, tired, annoyed, and satisfied. His eyes weigh only a little over an ounce, but it is said that you can read his character by looking into them.

His brain has the consistency of soft gelatin, yet he can be hard-tempered, hard at thought, hard to understand. The only thing his muscles can do is contract, but his touch can be gentle or rough. The seams in his skull don't entirely close until he's in his forties, but his thoughts rarely escape.

The largest blood vessel in his body, the aorta, is only an inch in diameter, yet it carries enough warm blood to keep

Anatomy of a Smile

What's behind his smile? Eight small muscles connecting his lips to the bony structure of his head. The expression of his face depends on which of these muscles he uses.

If he uses the *risorius* to pull down the corners of his mouth, it means he's scared. When he's sad, he also contracts the *triangularis* and the *mentalis* beneath the lower lip. At times of love and passion he relaxes all the muscles around the mouth, leaving a slight opening between the teeth.

In most smiles, the upper corners of the mouth are pulled up and outward by the *zygomaticus major* and the *buccinator*. If his canine teeth are also showing, he's using the *levator labii superioris* behind the upper lip. And when Jimmy Carter flashes all his teeth at a press conference, he's using all eight of his mouth muscles equally.

him from getting cold feet. All his endocrine glands have a combined weight of no more than 5 ounces, yet without the hormones they produce, he'd be hard pressed to get an erection, he couldn't eat candy, he'd get fat and lazy, his bones would start dissolving, and he'd be about as aggressive as a lily pad.

He uses more than 80 percent of the energy extracted from the food he eats just to keep his body at the standard operating temperature of 98.6 degrees. Even when he's

asleep, his lungs take in a pint of air with every breath—and this process may be noisier than when he's awake.

With no effort at all, he makes 30 billion sperm a month, compared to your one egg. How many of those sperm he releases is another question entirely. And that, for the most part, depends on his sexual activity.

If you think his body is one in a million, it's not. It is one in a zillion, or a number so large that it's followed by 3,000 zeros. That's the figure geneticists have calculated as the potential number of different human beings.

Body systems

Among all the bits and pieces of information that you assemble about a man's body, some are more memorable than others. His shape, the texture of his skin, the sound of his heart beating, the way his body and yours fit together, his smell, the feel of his flanks, the angle of his smile, and the hairs on his chest are some of the things you are likely to recall when you conjure up an image of the man you know best.

BONES

Behind this image—or better yet, beneath it—is an architectural framework that puts skyscrapers and suspension bridges to shame. If bones have one thing going for them, it's that they're hard, not soft and pliable like most organs. Bones have to be that way or else he'd collapse in a heap. They also have to connect up with one another, and for that we have joints and ligaments, which are actually thin, strong bands of fibrous tissue. If you've ever torn a ligament or known someone who has, you know how incapacitating it can be. Ligaments get torn when they are stretched beyond their capacity. Then the fibers pull apart from the bone, and the experience, to say the least, is painful. But the damage isn't permanent, for ligaments can heal in a process known as regeneration, with cells manufacturing new fibers.

Broken bones mend in the same way. Cells in the outer, covering layer activate and knit the rift together. The repaired section is as strong as the original. And bones are strong. The sturdiest one, the femur or thighbone, can withstand 20,000 pounds of pressure per square inch, about as much as a deep-diving submarine. In fact, nothing short of steel is as strong as bone. Yet bone has only a fourth or a fifth the weight of steel.

A stirrup-shaped bone in the middle ear, called the stapes, is 1,000 times smaller than the femur, making it the tiniest bone in a man's body. Still, it withstands almost constant vibration as it transmits sound waves from the eardrum to the inner ear.

In between these are some 204 named bones, and a few that don't have names. One, though, has a story attached to it. It's the upper arm bone, known as the humerus. It is notched in the inner part of the elbow, and one of the nerves that run down the arm lies in this notch just under the skin. When you strike your elbow the wrong way against something hard, this nerve knows it. It's called hitting the funny bone, and got its name because of the humerus. This is perhaps the standard joke in an osteologist's repertoire. Apparently they don't have time to dream up other whimsical names for bones, because they're too busy arguing over how many bones a body has.

Extra bones are more the rule than the exception. In fact, one in twenty men has an extra rib—not one less, as the Bible would have us believe. Lest you think men are being favored with spare parts, the same goes for you, too.

But that's nothing compared to newborns. They have about 100 more bones than adults. Most of these are soft, flexible cartilage that will fuse and then lengthen into hard bones as the baby matures. When this fusing process is not completed, there is a solid residue in the form of an extra bone, and this is what anatomists find so disconcerting.

The junctures between all the movable bones in the body are lined with cartilage, a tissue that's smoother than silk and lubricated with a slippery fluid. The most common malady—if it can be called such—that afflicts a man's joints is creaking. It's the noise joints make when air that has become trapped in the joint socket is suddenly squeezed out.

Creaking can be annoying, especially if a man creaks on purpose. Then it's known as cracking the knuckles. Why some men do this and others shun the behavior can only be attributed to manners. Accidental creaking is forgivable, unless it wakes you up in the morning.

BLOOD
and circulatory system

If bones only kept us from collapsing, they'd be useful enough. But they have another function as well. They contain the marrow, which manufactures blood, keeping a man's body supplied with over 20 trillion blood cells. Some are white cells, the body's scavengers, which are capable of squeezing through the walls of blood vessels to hunt down and destroy invading germs and other organisms. The majority of blood cells are red and doughnut-shaped, and they carry oxygen to every cell in the body.

That average man mentioned a while ago has some 1 million more red blood cells in every 20 drops of blood than a woman does. And, on top of that, he has more blood: a gallon and a half compared to your four-fifths of a gallon. This enables his blood to carry more oxygen to his larger muscles, and, in concert with his heart, which weighs 2 ounces more than a woman's, and his larger lungs, which can hold 2 quarts more air than a woman's, it gives him a sizable edge in energy.

The average red blood cell makes a round trip through the circulatory system—from the heart to the toes and back again—every 60 seconds, traveling at speeds of up to 10 miles per hour in the largest blood vessels. By the end of four months, it's worn out and begins to disintegrate.

The spleen, which is part of the circulatory system, filters out the spent red cells and has a hand in restocking the blood with white cells, called lymphocytes. These cells manufacture

antibodies that are capable of neutralizing bacteria and viruses and producing immunity. The spleen is aided in this filtering and restocking process by lymph nodes, such as the tonsils, and those under the arms and in the groin that have a tendency to swell when we're sick.

Keeping the whole system running smoothly is the responsibility of a simple hollow muscle, no larger than a clenched fist—the heart. It works like a pump, only no pump devised by technology can duplicate its awesome performance. It pumps a quarter of a pint of blood a beat, 72 times a minute. That's 6,000 quarts a day, or some 50 million gallons in a normal lifetime. It can increase its pumping rate to 180 times or more a minute in the bat of an eyelash, pushing out 20 gallons a minute when it's called on to do so in strenuous exertion or during orgasm.

Under normal circumstances, the heart beats a minimum of 40 million times a year. It has its own built-in electronic system to keep beats coordinated. With each *lub*, the valves separating the heart's chambers close; with each *dub*, they open again, and other valves leading to major vessels close.

The blood it pumps flows through 60,000 miles of vessels that reach everywhere in the body. But men are most concerned with a short section of blood vessels that feed the heart muscle itself. These are the coronary arteries, and in some men they are apt to clog up with stiff, fatty deposits in a disease known as atherosclerosis or arteriosclerosis. If not enough blood is able to get through one or another of these vessels, the region of heart muscle that the vessel feeds will starve, go into spasm, and die. That's a heart attack, and it's the number one killer of men, even when they are in their prime. More than 500,000 men will die from heart attacks this year alone. That makes it seven or eight times as frequent a cause of death for men as for women. An estimated 4 million men have suffered at least one heart attack and are still living with the psychological burden of knowing that their hearts have been damaged.

If the region of heart muscle that dies is small and doesn't impede the electronic circuitry that keeps the heart beating rhythmically, the heart attack won't be fatal. But the heart will remain damaged, and scar tissue will form over the injury. Heart muscle, like other muscle throughout the body, is incapable of regenerating itself.

#

No one can voluntarily—by willpower alone—make heart muscle contract. But the majority of a man's muscles—400 of them—do contract at his command. Called skeletal muscles, these bulky bands, consisting of millions of elongated cells wrapped into bundles, are responsible for all human movement.

The skeletal muscles have connections with the circulatory system, which carries in oxygen-rich blood, and the nervous system, which coordinates the muscular contractions. Most skeletal muscles move in tandem; when one contracts, the other relaxes. When the biceps muscle contracts, bending the forearm toward the upper arm, the triceps, on the underside of the arm, relaxes.

All the skeletal muscles are attached to bone by cords of fibrous tissue called tendons. If you want to get some idea of what a tendon feels like, there's a handy one just above the heel, called the Achilles tendon. It's the attachment that the calf muscle has to the heel bone, and it's used primarily to point the foot downward.

There is another type of muscle, smooth muscle, that functions automatically, under control of the involuntary (or autonomic) nervous system. These muscles are found in the eye, where they constrict and expand the pupil; in blood vessels, where they help keep the blood flowing; and in the digestive tract, where they help move food through the stomach and intestines.

At least one skeletal muscle can contract both voluntarily and involuntarily. That's the diaphragm muscle, which separates the chest from the abdomen. When it contracts, it helps expand the chest, along with the ribs and their muscles, and air is sucked into the lungs. When it relaxes, the air is forced back out again. As such, the diaphragm is one of the most important muscles of respiration. Spasms of the diaphragm cause hiccups.

RESPIRATORY
system and vocal cords

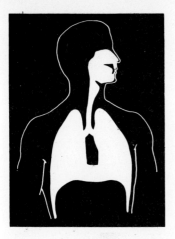

The lungs themselves are a series of branching tubes, much like an upside-down tree, ending in bubblelike air sacs that transfer oxygen to the blood and pick up carbon dioxide. The entire respiratory system includes the tubes leading to the lungs, beginning with the trachea or windpipe, which branches into two bronchi, one for each lung. The vocal cords are located in the larynx (visible as the Adam's apple) at the entrance of the trachea. Air that moves out of the lungs passes up through the larynx, where it's molded and shaped into sounds.

A man's voice is deeper than a woman's because his larynx is larger and his vocal cords thicker. The voice change begins during puberty, and though it might not be noticeable until he wakes up one morning and finds himself singing baritone rather than soprano in the shower, the events that cause the change don't occur overnight. They begin when cartilage in a boy's larynx responds to fresh supplies of testosterone, the male hormone, which are produced in abundance by the testes during puberty. The laryngeal cartilage grows thicker and outward, forming the characteristic bulge, known as the Adam's apple, that distinguishes a man's neck from a woman's. (One of the surgical procedures that can accompany the reshaping of external reproductive organs in sex-change operations from male to female is a reduction in the prominence of the laryngeal cartilage. Not all surgically transformed women request this adjustment; those who do always bear a telltale scar on the neck.)

The vocal cords, which are two folds of tissue with a V-shaped opening between them when no sound is being made, also thicken and lengthen in response to testosterone.

Later on in life, sometime in the forties, a man's voice undergoes another, though more subtle, change as the effects of aging decrease the flexibility of the vocal cords. His voice can no longer hit high notes—think of Frank Sinatra's voice now compared to 20 years ago. And the quality of his voice becomes more nasal, less sharp, less clear. But his voice is recognizable, because his mouth, soft palate, and tongue all transform the sounds that arise from his larynx and thus contribute to his own individual style of speech.

SKIN

Probably nothing in or on a man's body imparts as much individuality as his skin, particularly in the way it clings to the underlying bony structure of the face. The skin is a man's largest organ. It houses the richest supply of nerve endings of any organ. It's the domain of hair roots, pigment cells, and three types of glands—sweat, oil, and musk—that keep him cool, lubricate the skin, and impart an odor to the skin.

The skin on unexposed surfaces of a man's body may feel smoother than that on his hands or face, but nonetheless its outer layer is as dead as the rough, scaly skin of chapped hands. The sweat glands on his hands secrete a clear fluid, mostly water, that ordinarily keeps the thick layer of dead cells pliable. The drier his hands are, the more easily they'll chap and crack. Also, dry fingers don't grip or sense the feel of objects as well as damp fingers.

Although sweat glands are most abundant on the palms of the hands and soles of the feet, they are distributed over the entire surface of the skin, including the scalp. A man (or a woman) has 2 to 5 million sweat glands, depending on how large he is, and they all empty onto the skin's surface through pores.

The sweat fluid, which is generally called perspiration, is excreted all the time, not just when it is visible during exertion. In fact, the average man excretes about half a pint of sweat a day. Sweat glands are the main temperature-regulating system of the body. If a man couldn't lose some of the heat produced by the activity of his cells, he'd cook his own tissues in a matter of hours. Instead, sweat constantly evaporates from the surface of his skin, cooling down the blood that circulates in the superficial blood vessels. The hotter his body gets, the more sweat his glands pour out to moderate the internal temperature. When he's cold, the glands restrict their activity, and muscles throughout the body start contracting to cause shivering, thereby producing more heat from increased cellular activity.

During puberty, other skin glands—apocrine sweat glands, located primarily under the arm and around the nipples and genitals—enlarge and secrete an odorless, fatty, milky liquid in response to emotional stress and sexual excitement. This excreted fluid, which empties out through hair follicles, has a gluelike consistency that's ideal for

A teacher is reported to have sent a boy home because of his smell. The boy's mother sent her this note: "Dear Miss, our Johnny smells the same as his dad and his dad smells lovely. I should know; I've slept with him for 25 years. The trouble with you, Miss, is that you're an old maid and don't know what a proper man smells like."

—Biologist

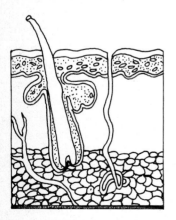

trapping bacteria. The bacteria decompose the fluid, causing the typical underarm odor. A man's body odor may be stronger than a woman's, but that probably has more to do with the fact that he doesn't shave under his arms. Hair tends to harbor bacteria as well as provide a convenient attachment for sticky apocrine sweat. Any spicy foods, coffee, and alcohol can alter the odor for the worse.

A third type of skin gland, the sebaceous glands, are attached to hair shafts just under the skin everywhere in the body except on the palms and soles. They produce sebum, an oily, waxy substance that keeps the skin and hair from becoming too dry. Sebum is also largely responsible for waterproofing the skin.

Indeed, skin can be thought of as a waterproof container that envelops the entire body, even the eyes, where it's modified into a transparent windshield known as the cornea. Over the fingertips, it dips into an individually unique pattern of ridges and whorls, not for the convenience of the FBI, but simply to provide a better grip, like treads on a tire.

Fingerprints aren't the only skin pattern that distinguishes people from one another. They are just the easiest to reproduce on a three-by-five card. Look closely at the back of your hand or your knee, or anywhere else on your body for that matter, and you'll notice that your skin is lined in geometrical patterns that are as individual as fingerprints. An elbow or nose print would work for identification, though fingerprints produce a deep relief that's easier to classify.

Men who blush easily have skin with blood vessels nearer the surface. Talk about a man with thick skin and you're referring—anatomically—to skin over the palms and soles, which may reach 1/16 inch in thickness. Mention that a man has thin skin, and you're referring to skin on the eyelids or behind his ears, which is only two thousandths (.002) of an inch thick. The average man has about 20 square feet of skin, some 3 square feet more than the average woman, because it has to encase his larger body. Men and women the same size have the same amount of skin.

HAIR

If all our hairs grew thicker in diameter and lengthened, we'd be as hairy as apes. Some hairs remain fine rather than thick, some short rather than long. Even the forehead, which appears to be hairless, has hair. So does a bald head. Most hair on a man's body, except for that which grows on his head, cheeks, and chin, grows only to a specific, genetically determined length at the rate of 1/3 millimeter a day during the growth phase. Then the hair root, which is the only living part of a strand of hair, enters a rest phase. When it reactivates, it forms a new hair bulb, which proceeds to push the old hair out. The growth-rest phases differ for hairs in different parts of the body. Scalp hair, for instance, has a three-year growth phase and a three-month resting phase.

Men lose about 100 scalp hairs a day. And, according to an inherited sequence and the activity of testosterone, some of these hairs don't grow back. The follicles, responsible for producing the new hair, shrink and eventually shrivel up, leaving more or less of the scalp bald. For men who are destined to become bald, nothing can stop the process. Nothing, that is, short of castration. A clue to how and when a man will lose his hair can come from his maternal grandfather, since the genes for baldness seem to be carried by the X chromosome, which he inherits from his mother.

One possible explanation for hair turning white overnight comes from William Montagna, professor of experimental biology at the University of Oregon Medical School. He suggests that coarse hairs are the first to turn gray or lose their pigment. These hairs are usually masked by the more numerous, thinner, normally pigmented hairs, which are less resistant to stress. After a traumatic or particularly stressful experience, the thinner hairs fall out, leaving the coarse white ones.

Of course, this is only an educated guess, because Dr. Montagna has never actually witnessed hair turning white overnight. But it is plausible, because hormones that are released during stress cause the smooth muscles that are attached to every hair follicle to contract, pulling the hair up and causing the skin around it to pucker in a characteristic goosebump. Older scalp hairs could be loosened by this activity and thus fall out easily.

HORMONES

The hormone that is released during stress, and the one Montagna blames for loosening hairs, is adrenalin, the "fight or flight" hormone. It works like a panic button, raising blood pressure, tensing muscles, dilating pupils, speeding the heart rate, and slowing down digestion. All this would be fine, if it was released only when a man needed it, but adrenalin knows no such selectivity. It gushes out of the adrenal glands, which sit on top of the kidneys like three-cornered hats, at the slightest hint of trouble. So a man may be calmly sitting in a restaurant waiting for his rare steak, and in the second or two that it takes him to realize that he's forgotten his wallet, adrenalin has prepared his body to take on anything up to a saber-toothed tiger.

Unfortunately, saber-toothed tigers haven't been around for him to do battle with for some time, so all the pent-up energy, all the muscular readiness, goes into crumpling his napkin. As the amount of adrenalin in his blood subsides, his grip on the napkin becomes less forceful. All this can occur in less than a minute, from panic to calm. Or it can last longer, depending on emotional factors. Some men are hot-tempered, and don't cool down quickly; others aren't as easily excited, perhaps because they've been in the situation before and know how to handle it without it being stressful.

But whenever anything is perceived as stressful, be it a near-miss collision, a blind date, or even an approaching birthday, adrenalin is the mischief maker that causes the heart to pound, the palms to sweat, the tongue to dry out, and butterflies to emerge in the stomach. Too much stress—in other words, too much adrenalin—chips away at an otherwise healthy body. In fact, stress has been implicated in an appalling array of diseases: peptic ulcers, rheumatoid arthritis, hyperthyroidism, ulcerative colitis, heart attacks, and cancer.

Despite this dreadful image, adrenalin isn't all bad. Under nonstressful circumstances it is one of the hormones that regulate the body's internal environment, helping to keep all the tissues and organs running smoothly. There are some two dozen hormones, produced by endocrine glands, and they flow through a man's blood all the time, controlling his metabolism, the growth of his bones, his ability to reproduce, and the development of all his secondary sex characteristics from the hair on his chest to the length of his penis. A fraction of an ounce too much or too little of a hormone can change a man's life drastically. Lack of growth hormone from the pituitary gland was responsible for the midget stature of Charles Stratton, who is better known as General Tom Thumb. A malfunctioning thyroid gland has the same effect, but it leaves its victims not only short, but misshapen as well. Too much growth hormone, and giants grow; too much thyroid hormone, and the eyes bulge from a body that is thin as a rail.

The effects that glands have on the body were known long before hormones were discovered. Aristotle kept pages of notes on the effects of castration on birds and men. Little did he know that he was paving the way for a new science called endocrinology (the study of endocrine glands) when he wrote that removal of the testes in a young rooster causes the bird to grow larger, with more tender meat, than an unaltered male. What's more, the comb and wattles that ordinarily adorn a rooster's head don't form on the head of a capon.

Aristotle also recorded that boys castrated before puberty never develop the secondary sex characteristics of men; their beards fail to grow, their pubes remain hairless, and their voices don't change. This fact was taken advantage of—in a perverse sort of way—during the late Renaissance when it was considered immoral for a woman to appear on stage. Yet someone had to carry the soprano parts. Boys chosen for this honor—and it was an honor in those days—sacrificed their manhood for the stage, and became members of an elite group known as the *castrati*. Their voices remained high-pitched, and they grew uncommonly tall, with long limbs, narrow shoulders, and a wide pelvis.

The Thyroid—100 Years Ago

The thyroid gland is situated in front of the trachea, and upon the side of the larynx. The use of this organ anatomists have never determined. It is larger in the female than in the male, and tends to give fullness and beauty to the female neck, if it serves no other purpose. As an offset to the projection on the neck of the male, known as Adam's Apple, may we not suppose the thyroid gland to be of special use in lubricating the larynx and throat of the female— she having much greater need of such a fluid to prevent serious difficulty in the use of the tongue and vocal organs?

—HARMON KNOX ROOT,
*The People's Medical
Lighthouse, 1854*

Castration before puberty also leaves a man infertile and, usually, impotent (unable to achieve an erection). These facts, too, were taken advantage of. Such castrates, or eunuchs, as they were commonly called, were the favored harem guards of desert sheiks.

The explanation for all these changes is another hormone—or rather the loss of it. Testosterone, manufactured by the testes along with sperm, is responsible for the development of secondary sex characteristics and fertility, as we have already noted in our discussion of genetic man. It is the principal male hormone. Removal of the testes is equivalent to removing the body's major source of testosterone (though small amounts continue to be manufactured by the versatile adrenal glands, which manufacture small amounts of the female hormone estrogen as well as the principal male hormone in both sexes).

Until puberty, testosterone is not produced in abundance. "Abundance" in this context doesn't mean quarts or pints. This substance, like most other hormones, is extremely potent in minute quantities. Only one ten-thousandth (.0001) of a gram or less is sufficient to cause sensitive cells to undergo changes.

Testosterone, and each of the other hormones for that matter, can be pictured as a chemical messenger. It's secreted by a gland—in this case the testes—into the bloodstream, in which it travels throughout the body, affecting other cells and tissues. Testosterone promotes the growth and maturation of a boy's reproductive system, and it also stimulates his muscular development. During puberty, it works in coordination with hormones from other endocrine glands, including the pituitary, the thyroid, and the adrenals.

After puberty, testosterone continues to be secreted by the testes, but the amount produced dwindles steadily from the time a man is about 20 years old. A 60-year-old man produces about as much testosterone as a nine-year-old boy. Most men produce measurable quantities of the hormone throughout their lives—certainly enough to maintain their ability to produce sperm and to keep their reproductive system functioning. But more on that later.

Dwindling male hormone has also been unfairly blamed for a common male concern, the receding hairline or bald spot. Neither worry nor the burden of too much responsibility causes this problem. Baldness is simply genetic destiny, and it's triggered by testosterone, not the lack of it. What about the 50-year-old man with a full head of hair? Well, his genes may not have been programmed for baldness in the first place.

A prevalent myth is that treatment with extra testosterone will improve waning sexual vigor. In fact, except for a brief benefit, the reverse is true. Extra hormone will diminish, not enhance, sexuality because it has a depressing rather than a stimulating effect on the testes. Certain testosterone-sensitive cells in the region of the brain called the hypothalamus record the level of testosterone circulating in the blood. Too much hormone, and these cells, through a system of intermediary chemical messengers, tell the testes to shut down testosterone production for a while. When the blood level of the hormone drops, the brain's testosterone-sensing cells remove their restriction, and the testes begin producing their hormone again.

These regulatory controls in the brain work the same way for each hormone and each gland in the endocrine system. The amount of hormone secreted by each endocrine gland is kept in balance with the need for that hormone by the hypothalamus. Think of the hypothalamus as a thermostat, the testes as an oil burner, and the hormone as the heat. Too much heat and the thermostat shuts off the burner. The brain's thermostat is a good deal more sensitive than the wall model in a house, so it's able to regulate hormones without too many surges and lapses.

Nonetheless, there is an ebb and flow to hormone production, and there is increasing scientific evidence that a man's sex hormones fluctuate in cycles somewhat akin to a woman's monthly cycle. But a man's hormone peaks are probably related to his sexual activity rather than to any internal mechanism as in a woman. The evidence for this variation in his hormone level comes from observations that after a period of sexual abstinence a man's beard grows faster the day before anticipated intercourse than the day afterward. One note of explanation: These were carefully controlled laboratory observations, not casual, on-the-street spot checks. In any case, there may be more to that five-o'clock shadow than meets the eye.

ize and shape of the body

At birth the average male has less than 2 square feet of wrinkled skin wrapped around a collection of incompletely formed bones, tiny muscles, and immature organs. He weighs about 7½ pounds and measures about 15 inches from crown to rump. The head forms a quarter of the body length, the legs only an eighth.

He's 5 ounces heavier and less than a ½ inch longer than the average female newborn. His forearms are slightly more muscular (a difference that persists, accounting for his stronger handgrip). Otherwise, there's no substantial difference in height, weight, body shape, or muscular strength between males and females until puberty.

Puberty and growth

How tall a man grows and the eventual shape of his body are determined by a mixture of genetic, hormonal, and environmental factors that by and large await a biological alarm clock set to go off when he's about 12 years old. Records of Bach's boys choir in Leipzig, Germany, show that in the 18th century puberty probably started four or five years later. The boys lost their soprano voices to the changes of puberty when they were around 18 years old. A comparable study done on London schoolboys in 1959 showed that their voices changed at an average age of 13.3 years.

Today, the start of puberty may be a year or two earlier or even three years later than the average of 12, but the bodily events that it triggers follow a preordained sequence that was the same in the Middle Ages as it is now.

Puberty begins when the hypothalamus, a cluster of specialized nerve cells deep within the brain, releases droplets of a certain chemical messenger that flow down axon paths, like beads of rain down a window, to the pituitary gland. The pituitary responds by releasing into the bloodstream two of its eight hormones, the gonadotropins FSH and LH. Together these hormones stimulate the testes to begin enlarging and to begin forming sperm and the principal male hormone, testosterone. The enlargement of the testes occurs very slowly, and, at first, goes easily unnoticed. However, it is the primary event of male puberty and it proceeds to set the stage for all subsequent changes.

Testosterone production during puberty

Before a boy's body can begin taking on male dimensions, it must wait about a year until the testes, under constant prodding of LH, produce sufficient levels of testosterone. The sprouting of the first pubic hairs is the signal that testosterone is flooding into the bloodstream in quantity for the first time since the boy was an embryo, when this same male hormone induced his anatomical development as a male. From then on, growth and masculinization progress rapidly and dramatically.

As the testosterone level increases in the bloodstream, it causes the penis to begin enlarging and the growth spurt to begin. Under stimulation of this hormone, nearly every cell in the body starts making adjustments in accordance to its genetic blueprint. Bone cells multiply, adding length and thickness. Bone growth starts in the feet and hands, progressing to the arms and legs, giving the adolescent a gangling string-bean appearance. Eventually the other bones catch up. The shoulder girdle, which supports the rib cage and arms, widens proportionally more than the pelvic girdle, just the opposite of what happens in girls. The wide shoulders and relatively narrow pelvis give the framework a shape that produces man's characteristic gait. Cartilage in the nose pushes out, and the rings of cartilage that support the larynx enlarge. The vocal cords lengthen and thicken, and a boy's high-pitched voice squeaks and breaks into a man's.

Oil glands lying quiescent in the deep stratum of the skin begin filling and exuding their secretions. Hair emerges under the arms, in the nose, and on the chin. Sideburns lengthen. Then one night, under the potent stimulation of male hormones and the wondrous fantasies and apparitions of dreams, the first ejaculation occurs. This is the culmination of biological puberty, and it is the first and only entirely new event of puberty. All other changes are simple growth and enlargement—nothing, biologically speaking, as novel as the development of reproductive fertility.

Secondary sex characteristics

The elapsed time thus far: about two years since the appearance of the first pubic hair. The anatomical changes, though, are hardly over. During the next two to three years many of the secondary sex characteristics emerge. The pubic

hair darkens and grows upward toward the navel instead of terminating in a horizontal line as it does in the mature female. The beard fills in (fast or slow depending on genetic signals), and the number of hairs increases on the eyebrows and chest and in the ears and nose.

His veins and muscles enlarge and bulge beneath the skin. Women are endowed with an extra-thick layer of subcutaneous fat that can serve as a supply of nutrients in case of hardship during pregnancy. This fat hides much of their muscular development, even among women athletes. By the time a boy is 16, he has 14 times as many muscle cells as he did when he was five. The size of the individual cell has the potential to increase, depending on use, until he's 40. A woman's muscle cells increase to their maximum size by the time she's 10 or 11. Thus some of the disparity in muscle strength between adolescent boys and girls is unquestionably a consequence of their sex, though some is due to the way they are brought up.

By the time a boy is 17 his heart has assumed adult proportions, increasing in weight to about 10 ounces and in size to 5 inches long by 3½ inches wide, slightly larger than a woman's. The number of times it beats per minute slows from 80 or more to an average of 72. The blood pressure, number of red corpuscles, total blood volume, and the lung's capacity for air and ability to exchange oxygen all increase.

After puberty

Sometime during the 17th year, or a year earlier or later depending on genetic individuality, the raging flow of hormones subsides. The high level of testosterone signals the pituitary to diminish the supply of LH, and, in turn, the hormones all over the body begin to taper off to adult levels.

At the end of puberty, the boy's body is 98 percent grown. The sex hormones that initiate and maintain puberty cause the growth plates at the ends of long bones to begin closing. For a few more years, these plates will remain sensitive to the same hormone, somatotropin, that was responsible for growth before puberty. (At the turn of the century, when puberty started later, men stopped growing at about 26.) They'll extend another inch or two before closing for good at age 18 or 20.

Average height has increased by 1½ inches in each of the

last two generations, but the trend toward taller males seems to be leveling off in Western society as we extract the maximum benefit from our diet. On the whole, men are about 10 percent taller than women.

In general, a man's profile is straighter than when he began puberty, his nose more projecting and his jaw more prominent. These features supposedly contribute manliness to his appearance, but drawing behavioral conclusions from anatomical details has always been dangerous. Aristotle, for instance, in one of the earliest objective studies of the face, concluded that men with small foreheads are fickle, and those with rounded or bulging foreheads are quick-tempered. Straight eyebrows indicated to him softness of disposition. Bulbous noses meant insensitivity, while irascibility was a characteristic of those whose noses ended in sharp tips. But then Aristotle thought that men were entirely superior to women, and even that they had more teeth.

Proportions of the face

The face has defied most attempts to define its perfect proportions, but no less a man than Leonardo da Vinci took a stab at it. His geometrical descriptions offer some insight into the complexity of facial anatomy.

From the eyebrow to the junction of the lip with the chin, and from there to the posterior angle of the jaw, and from there to the upper edge of the ear near the temple, there is a perfect square, the side of which measures half a head, and the hollow of the cheekbone is halfway between the tip of the nose and the back portion of the jaw.

From the edge of the orbit to the ear, there is the same distance as the length of the ear—in other words, one-third of the head. The distance from the hairline to the chin is three ears long and also three noses long. The distance from the chin to the nose and the distance from the hairline to the eyebrows are both equal to the height of an ear.

The distance between the eyes is equal to one eye. The face from the chin to the hairline is the same length as the hand, and the nose is the same length as the thumb. The eyes are situated between the top of the skull and the chin.

Bigger Kids

Men are growing taller earlier than they used to. These are the average heights of American and European children today, compared to 60 years ago:

Age	Height 60 Years Ago	Height Today
5 years old	4'1"	4'3"
9 years old	5'0"	5'3"
11 years old	5'3"	5'7"

By comparison, adults are only 2½–3½ inches taller today than they were a century ago.

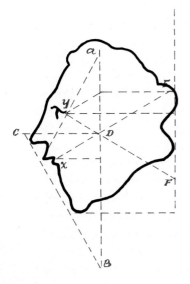

Somatotypes

The rest of the body, though, has proved much simpler to categorize. The idea of classifying body shapes is nothing new. Hippocrates, the father of medicine, devised such a scheme. But the classification system was reinvented for what appears to have been the final time in the 1940s when William H. Sheldon, an American psychologist, sorted bodies into three basic shapes, which he called "somatotypes."

He had examined thousands of men and found that some were fat, others lean, and others muscular. Those with rounded stocky bodies, short thick necks, and heavy arms and thighs he called "endomorphic," because their bodies took on the characteristics of the digestive system. They were supposed to be easygoing and jovial, and of course they liked to eat. Men with slender, tall bodies, thin arms and legs, and elongated muscles were classified as "ectomorphs," intellectual, sensitive, and restrained. In between were the powerfully built, muscular, broad-shouldered "mesomorphs," who kick sand in the faces of the ectomorphs. They were typically aggressive and competitive.

Leaving off the correlation with personality types, Sheldon's system, called somatotyping, seems to be a fairly accurate way of sorting out men. Not only that, it seems to hold true for prepubertal males as well. Ectomorphic boys grow into ectomorphic men, and so on. Some researchers who have studied body shape before and after puberty believe that it is linked genetically with rate of growth. Thus they find that ectomorphs tend to mature late, mesomorphs right on schedule, and endomorphs a little early.

Body size, though, doesn't seem to be linked with growth rate or any other single factor. How tall a boy grows seems related to genes he inherits from his father, as well as freedom from childhood diseases and an ample diet.

Individual variations

The normal mature male body ranges in length from 4 feet 3 inches to 6 feet 7 inches and in weight from 112 to 204 pounds. On the average he comes wrapped in 20 square feet of skin. The head makes up only a seventh of the body length, the legs half.

Extreme variations occur once in a while. The tallest man on record was Robert Wadlow of Alton, Illinois, who died in

Not Too Big, Not Too Small

The body size of humans is just about right. An ant-sized human might be able to put on clothes, but surface tension would prevent their being taken off. On the other hand, for humans to be twice as tall as they are would be disastrous. In a human who was, say, eleven feet tall, a spill would have some thirty times the impact it has for one between five and six feet.

—PETER FARB,
Humankind

1940 at age 20. He stood 8 feet 11 inches and weighed 500 pounds. An overproduction of the pituitary's growth hormone, somatotropin, is responsible for this condition, known as gigantism. Although pituitary giants are large in most dimensions (Wadlow's feet measured 20 inches long), their bodily proportions are different from those of normally tall individuals.

Height also varies among people living in regions of extreme temperatures. Eskimos are stocky and compact, rarely exceeding 5 feet 6 inches, a shape and size suited for the conservation of bodily heat. The Tutsis of central Africa and some of the Nilotic tribes of the Sudan attain an average height of 6 feet, with thin bodies suited to the hot, dry climate where a capacity to dissipate heat is genetically advantageous.

Yet, despite what looks like a reasonable explanation for the differences in size—genes collaborating with the environment over eons to foster a particular characteristic—nature seems to defy her own rulebook. Not far on the African plains from the towering Tutsis are the diminutive pygmy tribes, where a height of 4 feet 6 inches is considered tall. For some baffling reason, the cells of a pygmy's body respond only slightly to growth hormone issued by their pituitary glands.

Pituitary dwarfs, on the other hand, don't produce sufficient quantities of growth hormone, and, although the dimensions of their bodies are properly proportioned, they can be less than 2 feet tall as adults.

Muscular hypertrophy

No matter how bones are stretched, pulled, or tugged, they retain their basic size; only doses of growth hormones can make them sprout during puberty. But that's not true for muscle. Men can—and do—alter the size and shape of their muscles, in work, play, and sport.

Body building takes maximum advantage of muscular hypertrophy, as this type of enlargement is called. Unlike true growth, in which new cells are formed, hypertrophy is simply an enlargement of existing cells. All muscles, including the heart, can hypertrophy through overuse.

Ordinarily, without hypertrophy, muscle tissue accounts for some 40 to 45 percent of a man's body weight, a proportion that's at least 10 percent higher than for women. A man's upper body is particularly stronger than a woman's, because his broader shoulder girdle provides better leverage for his larger muscles. How much of this muscular strength difference is innate and how much developed, no one will know exactly until women and men train on the same ground. But it's a sure bet that men will retain a muscular edge. That doesn't mean that every man is stronger—or even potentially stronger—than every woman. But on average he's 10 percent taller, has 10 percent more musculature, and by some accounts is 50 percent stronger by the end of puberty than a woman of the same age.

Men who have always considered themselves superior because they're bigger and stronger are in for a rude awakening. Just the opposite is true, at least from a biological perspective. Through the ranks of all living things runs one constant that connotes superiority: survival. At every stage of life, from conception through birth, infancy, adolescence, and beyond, males are more likely to die than females. It's a plain fact that females are better at survival than males. And in the biological contest for superiority, women win hands down.

THOUGHT, STRESS, & SLEEP

THOUGHT, STRESS, & SLEEP

an's brain

Deep inside a man's brain, nerve cells are bursting with energy, firing off impulses along a tangled web of nerve fibers that float in the jellylike organ. Minute bundles of electrical energy—it would take some 60,000 brains, all juiced up at once, to energize a flashlight bulb—zip from nerve to nerve, relaying a man's thoughts, his feelings, his sensations, his memories first to one region, then another and another, until the energy is dissipated and the message, whatever it was, is absorbed and acted upon.

Researchers have probed into the brain's substance, measured the electrical activity of pain and pleasure, and analyzed the neurochemicals that transform light and air waves into the sights and sounds of memory. They have pinpointed the regions of the brain that control muscles and initiate dreams, measured intelligence and creativity, and located the seat of foresight and the center from which sex urges bubble up to levels of consciousness. They've unpeeled layer upon layer, and still the nugget they've been hunting for has eluded them. What is a man's mind, and what makes it different from yours?

Is his brain different from yours?

Men dream different dreams than women. They think different thoughts; they have different perceptions. Let's face it, they behave differently, and the differences cannot all be attributed to social conditioning or parental expectations. After all, men come from the same planet as women do, sometimes from under the same roof. So how come they act like they're from Mars every now and then? Why can they be so different—and so difficult?

If you've ever gritted your teeth about this, you're not alone. That's about all anyone could do until a few years ago when research findings began pointing in a startling new direction. It had been assumed that all newborns start out with basically the same biological equipment, and that the brain is a reservoir of potential. All that had to be done was to fill in the blanks provided by the genes in order to become a ballet dancer, a second baseman, a surgeon, a pirate, a poet, a pauper, a millionaire. Men were different from women because they grew up differently. They had different codes of honor, different games, different friends, different expectations.

One of the acknowledged masters of brain research, José M. R. Delgado, said that the mind as we know it does not exist at birth but develops from "a combination of genetic bias, the sensory information we receive, and our educational and cultural inheritance." In other words, the mind is not revealed as the child matures; it is constructed.

It turns out that even this sweeping view does not explain enough. While the brain is by no means fully assembled and ready for rational thought at birth, it is already distinctly male or female, and has been for months, ever since embryonic cells began producing sex hormones.

The fact that the presence or absence of testosterone affects the brain was first observed in laboratory experiments on rats and has since been generally confirmed in humans from studies of genetic hormonal imbalances. The differences are not visible in the way anatomical sex differences are, but they do show up in behavior.

Apart from a slight difference in weight (a man's brain is, on the average, 4 ounces heavier than a woman's), a man's brain and a woman's seem indistinguishable. They contain the same number of nerve cells—about 10 billion—and about ten times that number of supporting cells, which help guard against the transfer of certain substances out of capillaries and also insulate the nerve fibers, allowing them to carry impulses faster than they would if they were bare.

The number of nerve cells doesn't increase substantially after birth (although in some small regions of the brain as many as 90 percent of the nerve cells don't form until afterward), yet the brain quadruples in weight and size to attain full adult proportions. The additional bulk is made up of new supporting cells (called neuroglia), more capillaries, and a richer supply of interconnections between nerve cells. The more connections there are, the more each nerve cell can communicate with others.

Differences in development

At birth, the brain weighs between 324 and 350 grams. No matter if it belongs to a boy or a girl, it achieves about 50 percent of its adult weight in the following six months, and the remainder over the next six years, even though an estimated 10,000 nerve cells die each day, never to be replaced. Despite these similarities, researchers have noticed subtle differences between the sexes in the way the newborn's brain expresses itself through behavior.

As soon as a month or two after birth, boys tend to be attracted to visual patterns, while girls seem to be more attracted to sounds. Also at this age, the cells that are maturing fastest within a boy's brain reflect themselves in jerking, twitching body and limb movements, while those in a girl's brain produce almost rhythmic mouthing motions. That's not to say newborn girls don't twitch or that newborn boys don't move their mouths—simply that there are differences in frequency that can be observed by long hours of watching many newborns, which researchers patiently did to come up with this first set of behavioral differences.

They also noticed, after hundreds of studies on older children, that girls learn to speak earlier than boys, but that girls and boys then have an equal command of language until about age 11, when the girls surpass the boys. Then a year or two later, boys' mathematical skills increase faster than girls'. These differences seem to persist, though not as consistently as two other psychological differences: aggressiveness and superior visual-spatial ability.

No one has yet found out which brain pathways are primed by testosterone during embryogenesis to produce aggressiveness, but researchers have found clues to how this hormone influences visual-spatial ability in the brain. The perception of three-dimensional objects and the relationships of their surfaces seems to be the province of the brain's right hemisphere. At least one study has shown that the right hemisphere of boys six years old or older is more specialized than that of girls the same age. Evidence for this was gathered by testing the ability of children to identify the shape of various objects by feeling them first with one hand, then the other. When the final scores were in, researchers found to their surprise that boys were able to detect shape more accurately with their left hand than their right, and boys were significantly better at left-hand detection than were the girls.

By the same token, girls' superiority with language seems to stem from earlier maturation of the speech center, which is located in the brain's left hemisphere. Such presumptive evidence as this, added to the right-hemisphere specialization in boys, bolsters the argument that the brain is not as asexual as was once thought.

Sex hormones and the adult brain

If sex hormones play a role in the early organization of the brain during embryo growth, as researchers say, then one would expect these potent substances to influence the nervous system later on as well. So it turns out.

Women, after they've passed through puberty, have a measurably greater sensitivity to odors than do men. But if male hormones are administered, or if women are deprived of estrogen, this sensitivity disappears. Testosterone, it turns out, not only influences the sense of smell, it also stirs up sexual desire in women as well as men through its effects on a pea-sized cluster of cells, called the hypothalamus, deep inside the brain.

Small as the hypothalamus is, its size belies its importance, for this section of the brain contains the body's temperature-regulatory center, its thirst and water metabolism centers, and its hunger and satiety centers, as well as its sexual urge center. In men, testosterone, produced by the testes, is carried by the bloodstream to every part of the body, including the hypothalamus, where in concert with sensory *limbic system:* two central rings of brain structures which control your primitive emotions; also called "the visceral brain."

reticular activating system: a web of cells and fibers spreading up from the brain-stem, regulating the brain's activities and keeping you awake.

information transmitted to the brain by the eyes, the skin, and the nose, it turns up the sexual thermostat.

This hormone plays a similar role in women. Of course, it isn't manufactured anywhere in your reproductive system, but it is made in the assembly of various other steroids (testosterone is a steroid) by the adrenal glands, which also produce adrenalin. Women whose adrenals have been damaged by disease and subsequently removed notice a sharp decline in sexual desire. (By the way, no such decline occurs after surgical removal of the ovaries, which produce the female sex hormones estrogen and progesterone.)

By virtue of the normal tide of sex hormones that bathe the hypothalamus, most men and women have a recurrent need for sex, just as they have similar needs for food, water, and sleep. These "needs," as well as primitive emotions such as rage and fear, arise in a number of densely packed nerve-cell clusters, located in the center of the brain, that include the hypothalamus, the limbic system, and the reticular activating system.

ray matter

If it weren't for higher control centers, people would be forced to have sex, seek food, or fall asleep, as are many animals that have no choice but to obey these brain messages that result in instinctual behavior. Fortunately, the human brain has an intermediary filtering incoming messages. This intermediary is the cerebral cortex or gray matter. It's what's traditionally meant when we refer to the brain.

The cerebral cortex, 3 to 4 millimeters deep, forms the outer covering of the cerebral hemispheres. Beneath it is the white matter, containing the fibers that connect nerve cells in the cortex directly to every muscle and indirectly to every gland, every hair, every part of the body. Together, the gray and white matter of the cerebral hemispheres makes up about 80 percent of the brain's total mass.

The cells within the cortex process incoming data from the senses into what we call consciousness. Some of the cells conceive thoughts, others initiate muscular action, still others store and retrieve memories. Working together, they are responsible for intelligence, judgment, reasoning, creativity, feelings, will power, charity, appreciation of beauty, sense of awe, anxiety, morals, tastes, outlook, and inlook.

Anatomy of the cortex

The cortex looks very much like the surface of a walnut, which just goes to prove how deceiving looks can be. The wrinkles of the brain's cortex are not as individually unique as fingerprints—they form nearly the same pattern in every human brain that has ever been closely examined. The gullies are called sulci and the ridges or elevations are called convolutions. These dips and rises give the cortex a greater surface area so that more brain cells can be packed into a smaller space. This gave Aristotle the idea that the brain was no more than a radiator for the blood, cooling it near the surface of the skull when it became overheated. The heart, he wrongly guessed, was where thoughts arise.

If the cortex weren't convoluted, a man's skull would have to be seven or eight times its size to contain all his brain cells. As it is, some of the convolutions provide anatomical landmarks that identify for neurologists specific regions that control various activities. One convolution about 1½ inches wide that runs down the center of the cortex on both sides of the brain contains all the nerve cells that govern the voluntary muscles. The more complicated a muscular activity is, the more nerve cells are devoted to manipulating it. Thus more gray matter is involved in controlling the thumb than in the total control of the torso.

The body is represented on these two muscle-controlling convolutions in an upside-down and reversed fashion. The nerve cells that control muscles in a man's legs lie at the top, followed in descending succession by those that control his genitals, his torso, his upper limbs, and his face. The muscles on the right side of his body are controlled by the left side of his brain, and vice versa. This reversal arrangement is true for sight and sound as well. The right eye and right ear communicate to the left hemisphere, while the right hemisphere receives messages from the left eye and ear.

The surface of the brain is further divided by deeper fissures into eight lobes, four on each hemisphere. Most of the nerve cells in the lobes of the cortex are not devoted to specific tasks, unlike those that control muscular activity. The uncommitted nerve cells are involved in associating all of a man's past experience with the new incoming data that is absorbed by his brain every day.

1. The convolution of the corpus callosum.
2. The fissure of Rolando.
3. The parieto-occipital fissure.
4. The calcarine fissure is just above the number.
5. The corpus callosum.
6. The septum lucidum.
7. The fornix.
8. The anterior crus of the fornix.
9. The optic thalamus.
10. The velum interpositum.
11. The pineal gland.
12. The corpora quadringemina.
13. The crus cerebri.
14. The valve of Vieussens is to the right of the number.
15. The pons.
16. The third nerve.
17. The pituitary body.
18. The optic nerve.
19. The anterior commissure.

Cross section of the brain

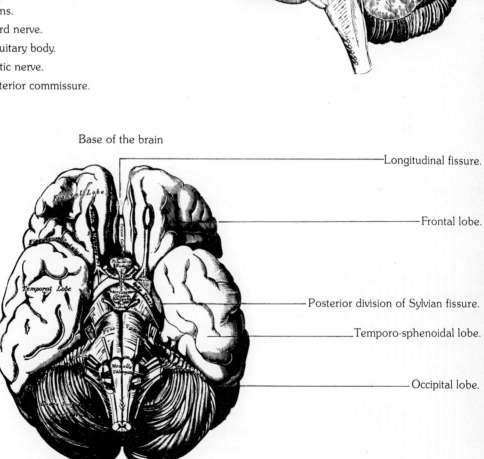

Base of the brain

Longitudinal fissure.

Frontal lobe.

Posterior division of Sylvian fissure.

Temporo-sphenoidal lobe.

Occipital lobe.

The frontal lobes

Some of this associative cortex is distributed among the four lobes of each hemisphere. The frontal lobes, in the forehead of the skull, are the repository of a man's foresight, and, among other things, they seem to exercise caution and restraint over his feelings and desires. But this wasn't known in the mid-1940s and 1950s when the tips of these lobes became the object of the neurosurgeon's knife in lobotomy operations (which have been abandoned). The operation was a popular, though dramatic and irreversible, treatment for a variety of psychotic disorders ranging from depression to severe anxiety. More than 30,000 such operations were done. Some people did indeed appear to be better after lobotomy. Their intelligence didn't noticeably suffer, and they claimed to feel better. Yet, there were a number of tragedies following the operation, and it is from these failures that psychologists developed the theory of what the frontal lobes actually do.

lobe: a rounded projection from any body part, such as an ear lobe. The brain has 4 pairs of lobes, located in the forehead (frontal lobes), in the back of the skull (occipital lobes), and above the ears (temporal and parietal lobes).

After a decade of studying lobotomy patients, researchers determined that the operation led to dehumanization. The emotions were blunted, moral standards were lowered, and moods swung from anger to laughter at inappropriate times. But the most striking change was that lobotomy patients were left with an inability to anticipate the future. Tomorrow did not exist for them. They lost the ability to plan, and with it the concomitant ability to delay gratification. They could no longer imagine working toward a goal.

The operation showed once and for all that the brain cannot be attacked lobe by lobe. Each specific area is integrated with other areas, and while one or another function may be primarily confined to a particular region of the brain, the organ works best intact, with nerve cells in different lobes communicating back and forth to provide the texture and flavor of full human consciousness.

No other lobe of the brain is as well studied as the frontal lobe, simply because the results of lobotomy put a damper on psychiatric surgery. Yet certain facts are known about the remaining lobes in a man's brain.

he nervous system in action

The occipital lobes in the back of the brain contain the visual interpreting areas where the impulses that begin in the eye finally wind up. On the first part of its journey, the message that conveys vision—let's say that it's the sight of someone a man recognizes across a crowded room—strikes the retina of his eye, where vision sense cells translate the image's light pattern into electrical impulses. These jolts of energy travel along the optic nerve to the end of nerve fibers, where they trigger small packets of chemicals to explode forth across minuscule gaps, propelling the impulse along to still other nerve cells. The image is carried in this manner of alternating electricity and chemicals along thousands of linked nerve cells to the visual center in the occipital lobe.

From there, fresh impulses, still carrying the electro-chemical counterpart of the visual image, dart to other regions of the brain, where the message is recognized as a familiar face. Memories are called up and judgments are made. Lower levels of the brain, connected to the autonomic nervous system, which links consciousness to a number of internal organs, signal the heart to begin pounding, perhaps even the palms to sweat. Thoughts arise, and the silent voice that talks to the brain when it is thinking—yes, apparently all of us talk silently to ourselves—offers choices. "Should I wave hello?" "Should I walk over?"

The man's brain is really humming with activity now. Nerve cells in the parietal region, which contains the muscle-controlling convolutions and the nearby reception area for the sense of touch, direct muscles in the face to form a smile. Pleasurable emotions that are evoked in the cortex continue to stimulate the autonomic nervous system, which responds in part by dilating the pupils of the man's eyes. Finally other nerve cells in the parietal lobe, bolstered by courage and the formation of a decision, begin firing off impulses that are relayed down the spinal cord to appropriate nerves that control muscles in the leg.

The man's leg rises to begin a step forward. Sense receptors in the joints of the ankle, knee, and hip shoot impulses along nerves that connect with the spinal cord. These impulses travel upward until they reach the cerebellum, which coordinates the complex muscular activity involved in walking. Tiny, stonelike chips, called otoliths, in the inner ear bounce off other sense cells in the semicircular canals, causing them to send information to the brain about the orientation of the body.

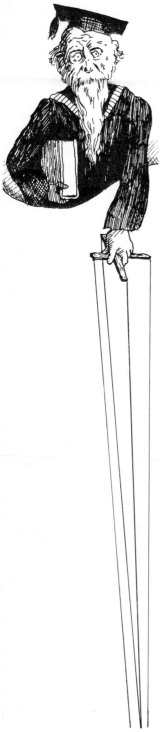

Aristotle not only erred in his description of what the brain does, he was also mistaken in his count of the senses. He enumerated five: vision, hearing, smell, taste, and touch. He did not include the kinesthetic sense, which is transmitted by joints and conveys an awareness of the position of the arms and legs, or the vestibular sense in the inner ear, which is the sense that gets upset in amusement park rides.

In the time it takes a man to recognize a face and initiate the first step that will move his body toward it, the temporal lobes of his brain, located just forward of the parietal lobes, have sorted through his memory banks and sifted through the sensory messages that are holding his attention, eliminating all the other intervening faces in the crowded room. In this process, the temporal lobes, in association with all the other lobes, have formed a perception which represents the kindling of an idea or the blooming of a thought. The temporal lobes, which house, among other things, a man's speech and auditory centers, are a vital link in his brain's ability to organize simple sights and sounds and weave them into an accurate picture of the external world, complete with references to past experience. Thus, he's able to interpret all the evidence gathered by his senses and then figure out what to do.

A perception can take place in a thousandth of a second, as it sometimes does when a man feels the touch of a wasp as it lands on his skin and forms the perception that he is about to be stung. Or it can take minutes, even days or years, depending on the complexity of the problem that he's confronted with and the resources drawn from his experience that he can bring to bear in solving the problem. The formation of perceptions is just one aspect of thinking, which is the main feature of a man's brain. When he swats at a wasp, it's not instinct that guides his hand, it's thinking. His brain has identified the insect from past experience, interpreted the danger, and instructed the muscles of his arm to contract.

The interpretation stage can be modified by learning. In the case of the wasp, some men learn that it's best to remain perfectly still until the danger has flown away. Others, though, can't resist trying to beat the bug at its own game.

Thinking

Thinking is, by far, the most complex activity that a man's brain engages in, and all its parts have yet to be identified. No one knows, for instance, where ideas come from or how thoughts about the future emerge. But it is known that when a man is thinking, other parts of his body are engaged in the process. That's not to say that thoughts don't originate in his brain—they do. However, researchers have found that specific muscles participate during thinking.

If a man is asked to solve a mathematical problem, the muscles that control the size of his pupils will relax, causing the pupils to steadily dilate. When he has figured out the answer, his pupils contract. His heart rate also increases while he is thinking about the problem and subsequently drops back to normal after he has figured out the solution. In experiments done in psychological testing laboratories, researchers used sensitive electrodes to measure the changes in muscular activity that went along with thinking specific thoughts. Sure enough, when a man was asked to merely think about walking, the muscles in his legs showed activity. Similarly, when he was asked to think about the words to the national anthem, the electrodes recorded muscular activity from his tongue and lips that was nearly identical to the activity recorded when he recited the words.

Memory

It's a poor sort of memory that only works backwards.

—LEWIS CARROLL,
Alice in Wonderland

The ability to recall the words of the national anthem or, for that matter, to recall any information housed inside the brain, is called memory, and every man has two types, a short-term memory and a long-term memory. A region of the brain called the hippocampus, within the limbic system beneath the cortex, is the way station in the transfer of information from short-term to long-term memory. Facts first enter the short-term memory in the cortex, where they last for about 30 seconds. If the fact is a phone number that won't be used again, it will be eliminated before permanent storage. But if it is something a man wants to remember, then brain cells associate the incoming message with information that is already present in the long-term memory and enter it for storage.

The process of associating a new fact with an old one is crucial for long-term memory, and some men are naturally better at this than others. Association mostly takes place automatically, but it can be consciously influenced. A man who has trouble remembering simple facts, such as names of people or addresses, can actually improve his memory by making a conscious effort to link the new fact to something that he's familiar with. There's a famous case of a man whose association process was so overdeveloped, through what is believed to have been a genetic error, that he could remember everything he ever experienced. The shape of the clouds, the taste of his lunch, the length of his fingernails all came flooding back to him when he was asked to remember a minor detail about an event that occurred a decade earlier.

His memory, though, was nothing to envy, because he had no way of keeping useless information out of his head. Along with his all-encompassing memory, he lacked the ability to forget anything, and he could remember all of his painful experiences, all of his problems, all of his failures as if he were reliving them. Most men have just the opposite problem. Minor details about events, even some of the events themselves, fade away after weeks or months or years.

Other times, the memory of something a man wants to recall finds its way to the tip of his tongue and stops flat. He knows it's there, but it keeps flitting away. Wrong memories come to mind in place of the one he wants to capture, and then, when he's least conscious of trying to remember what it is he forgot, the memory suddenly surfaces. His brain has been unconsciously working on the problem all along and when the correct association has been made, the memory reinserts itself into his consciousness.

Hypnosis can also be used to get at memories that cannot be retrieved at will, which has led psychologists to theorize that forgetfulness is comparable to selective memory blocking rather than complete erasure.

The place in the brain where memories are stored remains a mystery, but the case of one man who accidentally lost his long-term memory ability during brain surgery indicates that the temporal lobes are involved. The man, referred to as H.M. in written accounts of his case, suffered from severe epilepsy and underwent a brain operation in 1953, during which the surgeon removed parts of his temporal lobes to relieve the seizures. H.M. recovered and, at first, he seemed entirely normal. He remembered everything up to the time of his operation, and the surgeon was ready to claim his handiwork a success, when the nurses and the patient's family noticed that H.M. could remember new experiences for only a few minutes at a time. He couldn't remember who visited in the morning, whether or not he had taken his medication, or any other recently learned information.

While his short-term memory was left intact, his ability to store facts in his long-term memory was gone along with the brain tissue removed from his temporal lobes. To this day, H.M. lives in a minute-to-minute world. Needless to say, this type of surgery for epilepsy was quickly discarded.

re there two brains?

In the 1960s another neurosurgeon performed another dramatic operation in an attempt to relieve epileptic seizures in other patients. He severed the corpus callosum, a thick band of some 200 million white fibers in the middle of the brain, which allows the two hemispheres to communicate with each other.

Again the results looked successful. The patients appeared, for all intents and purposes, normal. But after extensive psychological testing a curious discrepancy in their apparent normalcy arose. Using their left hands to feel an object that was kept hidden behind a screen, and therefore undetectable by sight, they could not identify what in the world it was. When they switched hands, using the right hand this time, they had no problem.

The psychologists who tested these patients knew that previous research had shown that sensory information from the right hand travels to the left hemisphere of the brain, and similarly, the left hand communicates with the right hemisphere. If the two hemispheres were identical, they wondered, why didn't the right side of the brain know what was in the left hand? The only answer, they reasoned, is that the hemispheres are not identical. They were correct. The right side of the brain is different from the left; in fact, much more different than they guessed at the time.

Clues to the difference between the hemispheres had been discovered a century earlier, when neurologists in France found, by examining accident and stroke victims, that written language and spoken language were controlled by two adjacent regions in the left hemisphere. No comparable centers were found in the right hemisphere.

This century-old information proved the key to understanding why a patient who has had the bridge between his hemispheres surgically severed is not able to identify unseen objects with his left hand, but is able to identify them with his right hand. Information from the right hand crosses over to the left hemisphere and hence to the language center, which "identifies" the object that is touched as round or square or firm or soft or whatever it may be. This information ordinarily is relayed to the right hemisphere via the corpus callosum, so that it, too, is kept informed, so to speak, about what is going on next door. But with the corpus callosum cut, the information can't be relayed into the neighboring hemisphere. In the case of right-handed identification of objects, the severing of the communication between both hemispheres is no loss because the language center in the left hemisphere receives the information directly.

But the information that travels from the left hand to the right hemisphere can no longer be relayed to the language center. Once psychologists realized this, it opened up a whole new arena for testing the brain.

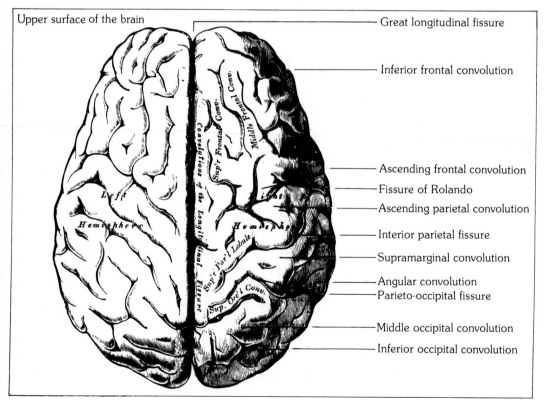

Upper surface of the brain — Great longitudinal fissure — Inferior frontal convolution — Ascending frontal convolution — Fissure of Rolando — Ascending parietal convolution — Interior parietal fissure — Supramarginal convolution — Angular convolution — Parieto-occipital fissure — Middle occipital convolution — Inferior occipital convolution

Split-brain psychology

The "split-brain psychologists," as they came to be called, began pasting electrodes onto the scalps of volunteers, who were for the most part normal right-handed men and women. (All right-handed people have left-hemisphere language centers, as do more than 50 percent of the people who are left-handed; but the other 40 percent or so of left-handed people use either the right hemisphere or both hemispheres to process language.) The plan was to test for brain waves emanating from either the left or right hemisphere when the brain was engaged in different kinds of activity.

They found that the left hemisphere is active when a person writes a letter, forms words to finish a sentence, or executes a task that takes manual dexterity. The right hemisphere is active when a person draws a picture, hums a tune, or recognizes a face.

A Man's View

Women would rather be right than reasonable.

—OGDEN NASH

In other words, the left hemisphere seems to be the rational, verbal side of the brain, where logic and analytical thinking rule; the right hemisphere seems to be the emotional, intuitive side, concerned with forms and feelings. This difference suggested a handy explanation for some—if not all—of the psychological differences between the sexes that have traditionally been assumed to exist, at least until recently. Those who embraced split-brain psychology believed men are more prone to listen to their left hemispheres and women are more prone to listen to their right hemispheres.

Robert Ornstein of the Langley Porter Neuropsychiatric Clinic incorporated this idea and expanded on it for *Psychology Today:* "Reason versus passion is one of its guises; mind versus intuition is another. The feminine, the sacred, the mysterious, historically have lined up against the masculine, the profane, and the logical. Medicine argues with art, yin complements yang. In fable and folklore, religion and science, this dualism has recurred with stunning regularity."

That was in 1973. Since then, the idea that the behavior of men and women is swayed by different sides of the brain hasn't had the impact on the psychology of masculinity and femininity that some of its early proponents thought it would. The novelty has worn thin, and on closer inspection of the split-brain theories, they seem no more revealing than other brain research that has localized certain functions in specific regions of the brain.

onnections

In fact, the whole idea of viewing a man's brain in tidy little sections is misleading. Neurologists and neurosurgeons, who have probed inside the brain and even isolated individual cells that, when stimulated, cause hunger or thirst or pain or pleasure, know that these cells would not produce such reactions if they were not connected by means of nerve fibers to a myriad number of other cells in the forest of the nervous system. A man's thoughts, his dreams, his ideals, and his emotions are not inhabitants of one region of the brain any more than they are inhabitants of a single cell.

If brain researchers have made anything clear about how a man's brain works, it's that all the regions of his brain collaborate with one another to impart the qualities, the attributes, the moods, and the reactions that make him a unique individual. The brain jealously guards its position as the body's premier organ by consuming about 20 percent of the body's total oxygen supply, even though the organ itself accounts for only about 2 percent of the total body weight. To carry this much oxygen to the brain, a quantity of blood that equals the weight of the brain travels to it every minute. If this flow is interrupted for as short a time as 15 seconds, consciousness will begin flickering.

The brainstem

The state of consciousness is normally maintained by a stalk of brain tissue, no larger than a man's small finger, that connects the brain with the spinal cord. A diffuse network of cells within this stalk—called the brainstem—forms the brain's activation system. These cells are extremely sensitive to oxygen in the blood, and it's their electrical signals that begin fading when oxygen is in short supply.

All of the messages that go to and from the brain pass through the brainstem, which also contains the control centers for the heart, lungs, and alimentary canal. These centers form an important link between the limbic system, where emotions arise, and the body's internal organs.

No matter what the emotion is—anger, fear, love, sadness—the message is recorded in the limbic system as stress. Higher centers in the brain's cortex interpret the stress depending on the nature of the stimulation which provoked it. Intense conflict registers as anger; threats of potential harm register as fear; warmth and comfort from hugging and kissing can register as love. These stress messages are also relayed via the limbic system to the brainstem, and then to the autonomic nervous system, which carries them to the internal organs.

The autonomic system

In any stressful situation, the autonomic nervous system disrupts the normal rhythm of the intestines, heart, and lungs, preparing a man's body for whatever change it has encountered. This is best seen in his body's nearly instantaneous reaction to an emergency, but it also happens when he's angry, or frustrated, or even when he realizes that he's in love. Signals from his autonomic nervous system increase his breathing rate, boost his blood pressure, dilate his pupils (and his nostrils), constrict some blood vessels and expand others, raise the concentration of sugar and fats in his blood, and quicken his pulse.

Some of these changes are produced directly by the impulses that fire from autonomic nerves, and others indirectly by hormones that are released by the pituitary and adrenal glands. The main feature of the autonomic nervous system is its ability to trigger nearly all of a man's internal organs at once, as if the brain's "panic button" suddenly began flashing.

This readiness reaction is a throwback to earlier evolutionary times when men were constantly exposed to life-threatening attacks. In those days, a man didn't have time to decide if he was angry or scared—he either had to run or fight, and his body had to be ready in a flash for either action. This system has not changed much since then, but men and their environment have. Now stress can be provoked by an overdue elevator, an unanticipated telephone call, a crowded street, a noisy office—the list is endless.

ffects of stress

The bodily reaction produced by any one of these events need not cause an all-out stress response, as happens, let's say, when a man is on the front lines of a battlefield and the bullets are zipping by. Even less heart-pounding situations, everyday frustrations, disrupt internal equanimity.

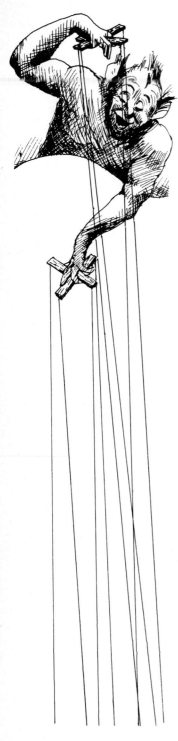

A Swedish team investigating stress and the commuter reported several years ago that men who take long rides to work appear, curiously, to suffer less stress than their fellow commuters who get on closer to the destination. The researchers measured urinary levels of stress hormones released in the two groups of commuters as a correlate to their stress levels. The longer the ride, the less hormone they found. Their explanation: The middle-of-the-run riders, with less control over where they sat and who they sat with, had less control over their environment and were therefore subjected to more stress.

When the economy takes a downswing and men fear losing their jobs, stress increases and so does illness. The physiological consequences of stress include tension headaches, migraine attacks, hives, depression, high blood pressure, bladder infection, irritable colon, and heart palpitations. The loss of a job ranks eighth on the Social Readjustment Rating Scale (SRRS), a checklist of 43 life events that produce stress-related changes in the body, devised by Thomas Holmes, professor of behavioral sciences at the University of Washington, and Richard Rahe, head of the Naval Health Research Center's stress medicine division.

The life events on the SRRS have values of 100 (for the death of a spouse, ranked first) to 19 (for a change in recreation, the bottom-ranked item). Dr. Holmes found that 80 percent of those who scored 300 or more points in any one year subsequently developed a major medical or psychological illness, including cardiac arrest, tuberculosis, leukemia, multiple sclerosis, diabetes, and phlebitis, which Richard Nixon suffered from in his final weeks in office.

A man doesn't have to be aware that he's nervous or tense for the impulses and hormones of the autonomic nervous system to be released and begin taking their physical toll. All he has to do is something as seemingly inconsequential as make up an excuse for being late for a meeting or a dinner engagement, and his autonomic nervous system steps up his pulse and respiratory rates and wrings out his sweat glands. In fact, these bodily changes form the basis for lie detector measurements. Chronic nervous tension repeatedly discharges fats into the bloodstream, and these can be converted into cholesterol deposits, which, in turn, can eventually plug up vital blood vessels that feed the heart.

Coping with stress

Not every man, though, risks physical or psychological damage from combating stressful situations. Some are better at coping with disappointment, frustration, and deadlines than others. The classic study of coping ability among men was done 19 years ago by Meyer Friedman and Ray Roseman, two research cardiologists who decided to test their theory about escalating stress on a group of tax accountants.

Their premise was simple: Find a group of men who had to get a job done under the pressure of an impending deadline and watch what happens to them. The researchers refined their objectives to measuring cholesterol content of the blood and clotting time of their subjects from January to June. If their theory was right, the two cardiologists reasoned, the tensions of filing tax returns ought to be reflected in elevated cholesterol levels and reduced clotting times—bodily changes that set the stage for heart attacks.

As the April 15 deadline approached, the group's cholesterol rose on the average 100 milligrams, peaking at a dangerously high 323-milligram level. Blood-clotting time dropped from an average 8.1 minutes in February to 5 minutes flat on April 15. In the course of the study, one 48-year-old volunteer died of a heart attack.

From this and subsequent studies, Friedman and Roseman devised their celebrated but controversial hypothesis of the Type A and Type B personalities. Type A men are frantic; there's a sense of urgency about everything they do, from dressing to eating. They are intense, driven, competitive, worrisome, and far likelier to suffer a heart attack than Type B men, who are more content and have a more relaxed lifestyle even though they are active and involved in all sorts of things. Obviously, Type B men cope with stress more successfully than Type A men.

There are shadings between these two personality types, and, as with most behavioral groupings, the division down the middle is not always clear-cut. What about, for instance, the man who is tense while he's at work, but relaxed at home? Or the man who appears relaxed, but who is seething under the surface?

In every case, the man who can get rid of his tensions—which is another way of saying that he can discharge the stressful feelings that build up in him—is better off than the man who keeps everything locked up inside him. The man who does a slow burn when the bank teller shuts the cash window for lunch break is coming closer to burning himself out than he's probably aware of. Fuming over situations that are beyond personal control leads to internal self-destruction. The key to releasing tension used to be "fight or flight," but neither one does much good in a bank, or in an office, or at home.

One of the best ways for a man to release the grip that tension has on his internal organs is to do relaxation exercises that quiet down the nervous system. Most of these are variations on the old practice of "counting to ten." They include transcendental and Zen meditation, but less extreme measures of conscious relaxation work as well. By focusing his attention on some neutral work or sequence, a man can, by sheer will power alone, decrease his heart rate, lower his oxygen intake, reduce his skin resistance (which means that his perspiration rate has tapered off), and slow down his brain wave activity.

The idea that a man can consciously influence his metabolism as well as other seemingly automatic processes was akin to witchcraft not all that long ago. Now the balance has swung the other way, and a few daring researchers are probing the fringes of mind control to find out what—if anything—is beyond the grasp of consciousness. No man's thoughts have yet been shown to penetrate even the flimsiest of external barriers, let alone move objects or bend keys. Yet when specific thoughts about relaxation are directed inward, they do produce measurable changes.

The steps a man can take to learn how to relax begin with actually slowing down—eating slower, talking slower, walking slower. His brain, in other words, can get its first relaxation cue from his body. These cues can be reinforced if he listens to soothing music; or, if that doesn't suit him, he can try alternately tensing and relaxing the muscles in his arms, face, shoulders, and legs. One of the easiest meditation techniques calls for the repetition of the word "one" with each exhalation during 5 to 10 minutes of concentration on breathing and letting the mind drift.

Simply getting a good night's sleep can bolster a man's ability to cope with day-to-day stress. For some men, this can be as little as five or six hours; others need eight or more hours to feel well-rested. It's strictly an individual matter. During sleep, a man's body recuperates from the stresses and strains of the day. The body's chemical building blocks are assembled within the appropriate cellular machinery for general tissue repair, growth hormone is released, and worn-out cells are replaced. Everything about a sleeping man may appear to be shut down for the night, but that's far from so. Even his brain is active.

leep and dreaming

When a man climbs into bed, pulls the blankets over him, and shuts his eyes, his body makes simultaneous adjustments in anticipation of sleep. Its internal temperature starts drifting down a degree or two below its normal daytime high. The brain waves, which had been fluctuating at 16 to 30 cycles per second, fall to about half that pace, into an alpha wave pattern, characteristic of rest with the eyes closed.

The transition period between being awake and asleep takes, on the average, 7 to 15 minutes. But no matter how long this transition period is, all men fall asleep in an instant. One second they're awake, the next they're asleep. Their muscles relax, their breathing falls into a regular pattern, and their brain waves slow. This is the first of the four stages of sleep that cycle throughout the night, but the singular event in the brain that triggers it has eluded scientists who have been studying why men spend one-third of their lives in a state of suspended consciousness.

One theory for why men fall asleep is that the oxygen flow to the brain diminishes, signaling the sleep center in the brainstem to cut off its arousal impulses to the cortex. This first stage lasts a few minutes, and then the deeper stage II sleep begins with erratic brain waves, slower breathing, and more muscular relaxation. After another several minutes, stage III begins, identified by sleep researchers as the first time the slow delta brain waves show up on the electroencephalogram (EEG). All the bodily processes continue to slow down throughout the next 10 minutes of this stage, leading to stage IV, which is the deepest sleep.

Although a man sleeps the soundest during stage IV—and it's the most difficult stage for him to be waked from—it is also the time when sleepwalking occurs (as well as

alpha wave pattern: a slow, regular wave pattern produced by your brain during reverie, the onset of sleep, meditation, and other relaxed situations.

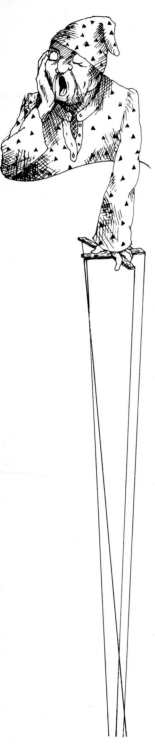

night terror and bed-wetting in children). Even though this curious phenomenon looks like the brain's way of acting out dreams, that's not the case, because dreaming doesn't take place during this stage of sleep. Sleepwalking happens when parts of the brain that control leg movements awaken for some unexplained reason. If the entire brain is aroused, by waking up a man who has been up and around in his sleep, he won't know where he's been, because the activities that his brain has engaged in don't enter the associative areas that were "asleep."

Stage IV sleep, which begins about half an hour after the onset of sleep, doesn't last all night. After about 40 minutes, the brain waves pick up speed, and the sleeping man ascends through stages III, II, and I. When he has recycled back to stage I, he doesn't awaken, but his body and brain undergo equally dramatic changes. His eyes begin darting back and forth under the lids, his breathing and heart rate fluctuate irregularly, his penis engorges with blood in an erection, his brain waves resemble those when he's awake, his muscles go limp, and last but not least, he begins to dream. (Presumably a man's limp musculature during this stage of sleep is an evolutionary adaptation that prevents him from acting out his dreams.)

This is known as REM sleep, for the rapid eye movements that were first noted in 1952 at the University of Chicago in volunteers who were carefully observed throughout the night. The first REM period ends after 10 minutes with the beginning of another stage II cycle. This is followed by stages III and IV, and then another REM period. In an average night's sleep, a man will have four or five REM periods, each one getting longer and longer, so in seven and a half hours of sleep, he'll spend one to two hours REMing.

The cause and function of dreams

Men who are awakened out of REM sleep usually recall a dream, but it will fade very quickly if they don't make a conscious effort to grasp at its receding images. Dreams occur, according to the latest theory, as the brain tries to make sense of electrical impulses from the changing position of the eyes during REM sleep.

Unlike Freud's theory, which holds that dreams are the guardians of sleep and represent the expression of unconscious fears and wishes, the new dream theorists say that dreams arise spontaneously out of random nerve-cell activity. Drs. J. Allan Hobson and Robert McCarley of Harvard Medical School dismiss Freud's idea that stimuli instigate dreams. Instead, they believe that dreams originate in certain giant nerve cells in the brainstem, called "on" cells, which send impulses to the cortical areas that control vision, memory, and even emotions. These regions explode into activity under stimulation from the "on" cells, and pictures—visual dreams—are constructed from the aroused nerve cells.

The two dream researchers reported experiments they conducted with cats in the *American Journal of Psychiatry* in December 1977, and they hypothesized that in man the cortex plucks out images from the long-term memory storage areas that correspond to the electrical signals that it receives from the eyes and brainstem. When the memory matches up with the signal—which doesn't happen all that often—the dream images are familiar people, places, and activities. But when the circuits cross, as they're bound to do, nothing in a man's memory relates to the signal, and the dream fills with bizarre images and distorted sequences.

Most dreams are a mixture of the two: reality images retrieved from memory and nonsensical visions. Men, it turns out, dream more often about other men than about women, while women probably dream about both sexes equally. Why this should be hasn't been figured out yet, but if a man calls out a name in his sleep, it's not because he's been dreaming about that person. Sleeptalking, like sleepwalking, occurs during the non-REM sleep phase when dreams usually don't occur.

Sleeplessness

The longest case of sleeplessness on record is that of a high school boy who volunteered to stay up for 11 days and suffered no serious physical or emotional changes. He was watched for those 264 hours by researchers from Stanford University's Sleep Laboratory, among them the lab's director, Dr. William C. Dement, who was beaten at pinball by the youngster well into the last stages of the experiment.

While the loss of a single night's sleep has little or no effect on physical or mental efficiency, after the loss of any more than that the average man is unable to perform at his

The conscious mind allows itself to be trained like a parrot, but the unconscious does not—which is why St. Augustine thanked God for not making him responsible for his dreams.

—CARL JUNG,
Psychology and Alchemy

usual level on physical tests, and he becomes irritable. Longer sleep deprivation leads to hallucinations, irrationality, and, eventually, death. Researchers found that REM sleep is most important for emotional stability. They studied two groups of sleepers, one waked during non-REM periods on consecutive nights, the other waked during REM periods. Those who missed non-REM sleep were virtually unaffected. But those who missed REM sleep were, to a man, more moody and irritable. They also did poorly in concentration and learning tests. From experiments such as these, it has been learned that a man needs REM sleep in order to prevent dreamlike brain activity, in the form of hallucinations, from impinging on his consciousness during the time he's awake, and also to process recently acquired facts into his long-term memory. Thus, a man who stays awake into the early-morning hours may not get sufficient REM sleep to incorporate the new material into his memory.

The men who were deprived of non-REM sleep, on the other hand, complained of feeling lethargic, though they were no more moody than before the experiment. None of the men in either group had any trouble getting a good night's sleep after the experiment, which meant that their sleep rhythm wasn't disturbed by their lack of sleep. But that's not the case for some men who suffer from an occasional night of insomnia. They drag themselves out of bed in the morning, and collapse back into bed at the first opportunity.

Chances are that a man who misses a night's sleep will fall asleep naturally the next night. But the fear of not being able to sleep, which is the leading cause of insomnia, can keep him tossing and turning. Sleeping pills may work once in a while, but a steady nightly diet of them is counterproductive. Not only do they become ineffective after three to four weeks of use, but the man who takes them this often risks aggravating his insomnia, not curing it.

Though there are other, more serious, causes of insomnia than the fear of sleeplessness itself—including breathing problems that occur when lying down and excessive nocturnal twitching—the man who lies awake worrying over the day's ordeals or the problems he has to face the next day will eventually succumb to the natural rhythm that induces sleep. He may have to struggle through a couple of nights of restlessness, of not getting a "proper" amount of sleep, but if he makes himself as comfortable as possible, gets enough exercise during the day, and stays away from the evening cup of coffee, he'll probably find himself dozing off.

A glass of milk, warmed or not, helps because it is one of the foods, along with meat, that is rich in tryptophane, a component of protein that is used by the brain in the assembly of what is sometimes referred to as "sleep juice" but is more properly known as serotonin. In some way, this brain chemical is probably necessary for sleep. A man who gets drowsy after a heavy meal has most likely just dosed himself with tryptophane. The effects are temporary, and he'll revive after half an hour or so.

Waking up

Like falling asleep, waking up in the morning is a natural process related to a man's internal alarm clock. When a sufficient concentration of "awakening" chemicals accumulates in the brainstem's arousal center, he begins stirring. In some men, the whole process can be over in a matter of minutes, but in others, full awakening takes an hour or longer. His pulse and respiratory rates climb back to daytime levels, as do his temperature and oxygen levels.

There are over 100 bodily functions in a man that oscillate from minimum to maximum over a 24-hour period. Known as circadian rhythms, these biological cycles affect his body's temperature (which peaks at midday and plummets during the early-morning hours), his blood sugar, his adrenal gland activity, and even his mental activity. The precise timing of these rhythms varies from man to man, and the individual differences account for why some men are energized in the morning while others don't get geared up until nightfall.

By and large, though, a man is tuckered out and ready for sleep during the depressed phase of his daily rhythm. By the time he awakes in the morning, these rhythmic cycles are back on the upswing. As his brain re-emerges into consciousness, the electrical impulses that flood into his cortex, upon opening his eyes and stretching his muscles, disperse the last remnants of the dream world he has occupied, like so many cobwebs, and his nervous system braces for the onrush of stimulation that will be sorted into the feelings and memories and thoughts that give him his sense of identity, that let him know he is a man.

REPRODUCING & AGING

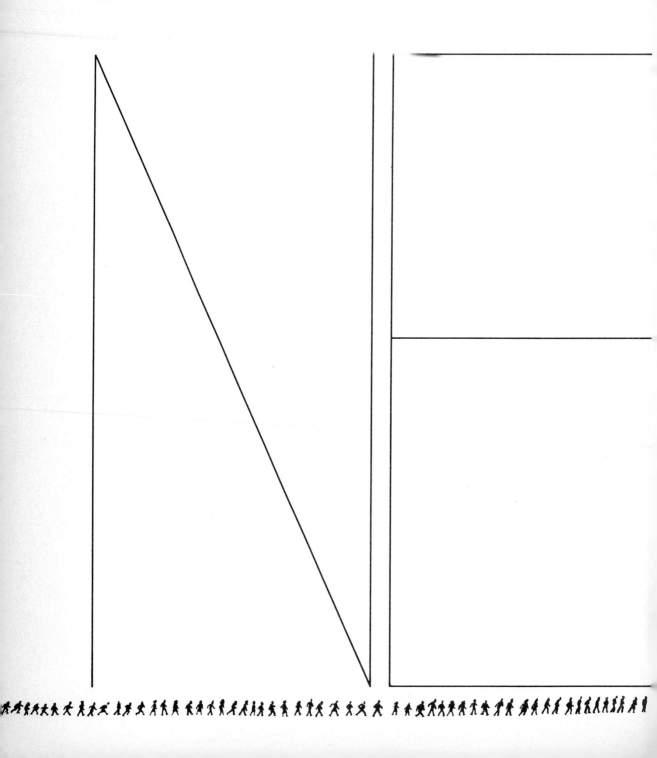

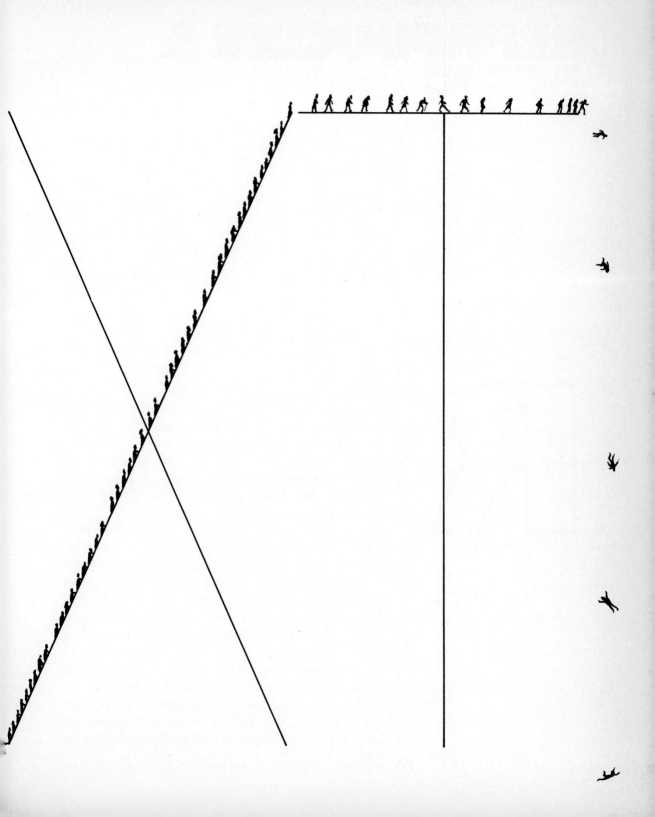

REPRODUCING & AGING

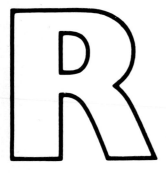

eproducing

There used to be a controversy over female orgasm. One side took the argument that a clitoral orgasm was the real thing. The other side claimed that exalted status for a vaginal orgasm. The finer points of each type were detailed in sex manuals, and psychologists decided one kind was better than the other—more mature, they said. And so the myth grew, and with it, efforts to achieve the ultimate orgasm.

Like most fables, this one has a moral. Along came Masters and Johnson, the first people to put science and the orgasm in one room without defeating the purpose of each. They found only one type of orgasm, which begins in the clitoris and spreads upward. They divided it into three stages and documented the physical events and subjective feelings at each stage. Lo and behold, a woman's body knew only a single way to say orgasm. To be sure, the intensity and duration of orgasm does indeed vary; but, biologically, a woman's body responds in the same way each time.

Why talk about a woman's orgasm in a book about men? Well, rumor has it that men can have two types of orgasm: one type that occurs with ejaculation, and another without it. In

other words, orgasm and ejaculation needn't be synonymous. According to the latest research studies, there may be a fine line between male orgasm and ejaculation, a line that, once crossed, leads to the inevitable. But once men learn to sense that "line"—and this takes a conscious effort—they'll not only be able to achieve an invisible orgasm, they'll also be able to have more than one.

Masters and Johnson notwithstanding, the last word on orgasm has yet to be written. But that's not for lack of effort. Man's sexual response would have been considered fully understood long ago if it weren't for the fact that he derives pleasure from an act that Nature intended for reproduction. There would be no such thing as premature ejaculation or striving for multiple orgasms if having babies were his sole objective in sexual encounters. Sex as a sensual experience, not just a biological process, has been around quite a while, despite *Time* magazine's proclamation a few years back that we're entering the dawn of sexuality. But as long as it has been around, men of each generation have had to learn about sex from scratch. That goes for women too, of course. Doing what comes naturally, it turns out, is anything but natural, in the sense that we're born with all the instruction we need to be sexually learned. The trial and error of all those who have come before us haven't added one iota of sexual experience to our genes. We don't start off as any better lovers than our Victorian ancestors. The social climate may be more or less permissive, but each of us has to take the same first steps.

It's true that the sex drive—the urge for copulation—is deep-rooted, and given no instruction, a man could succeed in impregnating a woman. But that's not enough to turn him into a lover, much less a half-decent lover. Some men, admittedly, are more adept at sex than others. This is a matter of attitude, experience, and a desire to give as well as receive pleasure. It's also a matter of self-control.

Among the many myths of male sexuality, there's one that says that men have little or no control over their own orgasms. Once they're aroused, nothing short of a knock on the door or ice water will thwart the process. Belief in the inevitability of ejaculation is, in many respects, a trap that both men and women fall into.

Men can and do enjoy sex without coming. It's not a sign that something's wrong with either party. Men can't have an ejaculation (under ordinary circumstances) without an erection, but they can have erections without ejaculation and they can have sex without ejaculation. This seemingly contrary situation most often happens after a man has already had an ejaculation. He might be able to regain an erection, but he doesn't necessarily need the release of sexual tension that ejaculation affords. In fact, although he may have an erection again, he certainly won't have the same degree of sexual tension in his body as he did during the earlier orgasm.

The capacity for orgasm and the ability to achieve an erection have more to do with automatic processes within a man's body than with anything that goes on consciously in his head. No man can will an erection or an orgasm. His sex organs don't work like his arms or legs. He can use his mind to raise his leg, yet the same mental effort redirected to the part of his anatomy between his legs won't have any noticeable effect. What his body is capable of and what his mind wants to do may not happen together as often as he likes.

A man's sexual prowess and limitations reside for all intents and purposes in what anatomists refer to as a pendulous appendage suspended from the pubic arch: the penis. What does it mean to a man? How does it work when it does, and what goes wrong with it when it doesn't?

enis size

Despite the mystique that's grown up around it, there is nothing mysterious, titillating, or awesome about a penis, certainly nothing to be envious about. Yet there's not a man who hasn't been concerned about the size of his penis sometime during his life, nor are there many women around who know what makes an erection harder some days (or nights) than others.

The size and shape of a man's penis has nothing to do with his ability to have orgasm, his physique, or his virility. Penises vary in size, like any organ, and personal preferences aside, men seem to be more concerned about this than women. Penises don't attain adult proportions until puberty, and since boys of the same age don't start puberty at the same time, concern about penis size can arise during this emotionally charged stage of life. The range of ages for the start of penis growth is from 10½ to 14½ years old, and the range of age for completion of penis growth is from 12½ to 16½ years old. So some 13-year-olds have finished their penis growth stage while others haven't even begun.

Then, too, a prepubertal boy who compares his penis to his father's is bound to feel inadequate. Usually this comparison does no lasting harm, but some men harbor feelings of penis inadequacy despite ample evidence to the contrary.

Reassurance from the opposite sex does a lot to help them. But the fact of the matter is that a man who has a comparatively small flaccid penis may have a larger-than-average erection, while the man with a large flaccid penis may not gain as much during erection. There is simply no correlation between before-and-after sizes.

How size changes

Penises don't enlarge through frequent use, nor do they shrink or atrophy from disuse. They aren't made of muscle, and they contain no bones, though gorilla and chimpanzee penises do have a bone called the os penis. By way of comparison, a gorilla for all his size has a penis that measures less than an inch long.

Among the anatomical records kept by medical researchers who have measured penis length, there are men whose erections extend as far as 12 inches. The average is 6 inches in length and 1½ inches in diameter. And there are men

Bigger Than Average

—How tall are you, son?

—Ma'am, I'm six feet seven inches.

—Let's forget about the six feet and talk about the seven inches.

—MAE WEST

who have fathered children and, from all accounts, have had satisfying sex lives with penises that measured under 1 inch erect.

Where most researchers on penis size recorded erect length, Masters and Johnson did a study to correlate flaccid penis length with height of the man. Of the 312 men they measured, the longest flaccid penis measured 5½ inches, which is 1½ inches longer than average, and belonged to a man 5 feet 7 inches tall. The smallest in the study measured 2½ inches and belonged to a man just shy of 6 feet tall. Again, the tale of the tape measure seems to puncture the myth.

The erectile capacity of the penis may have done much to secure its status as the repository of manhood, but, as most men know, the penis can temporarily shrink smaller than its average flaccid length. In fact, the flaccid penis tends to shrivel when it's chilled and constrict after an unsuccessful attempt at intercourse, to the chagrin of many men who, at one time or another, find themselves impotent. Shrinking is a function of the loose skin that enwraps the organ itself, not any intrinsic mechanism within the penis. This skin is supplied with some smooth muscle that automatically responds to temperature and emotion by contracting or relaxing.

Temperature regulation of sperm

The same arrangement of skin and smooth muscle accounts for the varying tightness or looseness of the

The Un-Punctured Myth

The normal length of a penis when erect is about one-twelfth of the height of the body, that is, there should be one inch of length for every foot of height so that a man who is five feet six inches tall would normally have a male organ 5½ inches in length when in the erect state.

—CHARLES A. CLINTON,
Sex Behavior in Marriage, 1935

testes (plural of *testis*): the two oval-shaped glands, about 1½-2 inches long, which hang next to the penis and produce the sperm.

scrotal sacs: the two loose bags of skin which contain the testes, and together make up the *scrotum,* or "balls."

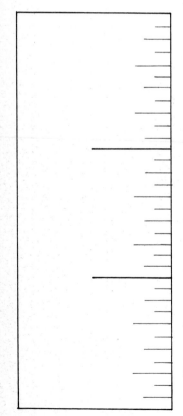

scrotum, only here there is a sound biological purpose for the adjustment. Sperm, which are manufactured in the testes, can be formed and mature only in an environment that's some 5 degrees below the normal body temperature of 98.6 F. It's not known why, but higher temperature can injure sperm, and even prolonged fever can cause temporary or, in some instances, permanent sterility. Men who wear jockey shorts in preference to the looser boxer shorts may unwittingly be lowering their fertility. Hot tub baths also suppress sperm production. But neither tight underwear nor hot water is effective for male birth control.

Under ordinary circumstances, the scrotal smooth muscle regulates the temperature of the testes for optimum sperm production by contracting when the external temperature is cold and relaxing when the temperature is hot. On relaxation, the scrotal sac drops away from the body and the testes cool. On contraction, the sac is raised with its contents, and the body's own heat warms the testes. These same smooth muscles also rhythmically contract during ejaculation, and for those of you who are wondering, that's why the testes seem to get tighter during orgasm.

The testes, like much of a man's genital system, have a dual function. They not only produce sperm, but they also supply most of a man's testosterone. A small amount of this hormone is also manufactured by his adrenal glands, which also manufacture a small amount of the female hormones. Men aren't alone in this hormonal transposition. You also produce a bit of male hormone in your adrenal glands. It's the balance of the two types of hormone, male and female, that keeps our respective sexual anatomy functioning. Without testosterone, a man would be infertile and impotent.

But with normal amounts of this hormone he is able to produce 200 million sperm a day and get an erection. How long it takes a man to get an erection depends on his mood, the amount of time since his last erection or orgasm, and the situation he's in. It can happen in three seconds flat if he happens to be in the right mood. And he can lose it just as quickly—or fail to get one at all.

rection

Surprisingly enough, a man can have two different kinds of erection. One starts in the erotic center of his brain and is called a psychogenic erection. The other results from stimulation of the penis itself and is called the reflexogenic erection. They are equally pleasant, but the psychogenic erection can be a mite distracting.

There's no telling when a psychogenic erection will occur, but the younger a man is, the more likely he is to experience this kind of erection at seemingly the oddest times. It can happen riding a bus, eating a hot dog, playing Monopoly. All it takes is some passing thought, some mental association that nudges against his erotic center, and an impulse is flashed down his nervous system to the lowest section of his spine, where the *nervi erigentes* or nerves of erection lie waiting.

From there, the erection message travels along nerves

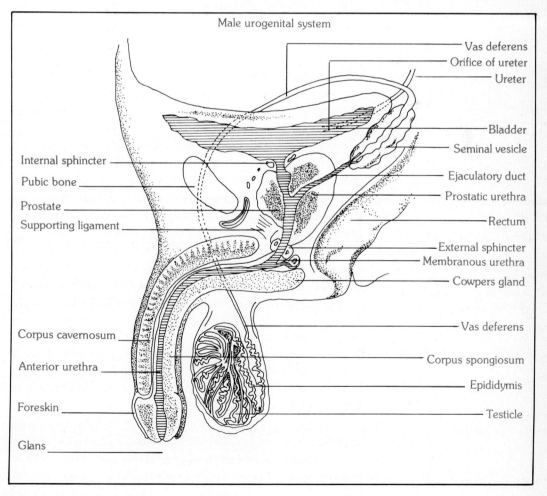

Male urogenital system

Vas deferens
Orifice of ureter
Ureter

Bladder
Seminal vesicle

Internal sphincter
Pubic bone

Ejaculatory duct
Prostatic urethra

Prostate
Supporting ligament

Rectum

External sphincter
Membranous urethra
Cowpers gland

Corpus cavernosum

Vas deferens

Anterior urethra

Corpus spongiosum

Epididymis

Foreskin

Testicle

Glans

that end in the arteries that bring blood into the substance of the penis. Like most nerve messages, one word is sufficient; in this case the word is "dilate." The arteries expand, as the smooth muscle (yes, here's that smooth muscle again) that encircles their walls relaxes. Extra blood begins flooding into the open spaces in the spongelike tissue that makes up most of the penis except for the hollow tube, the urethra, that is the channel for urine and semen.

As the tissue expands with blood, it squeezes the penile veins so blood can't escape back into the body. At some point a balance is reached, and the blood pressure in the spongy tissue reduces the inward flow of blood. This is the point of maximum erection. It can be maintained by some men for hours or it can begin to subside in a matter of seconds. The ability to maintain an erection gradually declines with age, as do all a man's sexual abilities, but circumstances and his mood also affect his erection.

The sphincter muscle

sphincter: any circular muscle which can open and close openings and channels in the body. Besides the mouth of the prostate, a man has sphincter muscles on his bladder, anus, and elsewhere. You have an additional one in your vagina.

How hard the penis becomes when it's erect depends in large part on a sphincter or circular muscle band in the prostate gland, which is one of the internal accessory glands that contribute fluid to the semen. The veins that carry blood out of the penis travel through this sphincter, so the tighter it clamps down, the less blood flows out and the harder the erection. Sphincter tightness isn't voluntarily controllable, which means that penis hardness is not a direct measure of sexual desire, even though it's rumored to be.

prostate gland: a pale, firm organ, partly muscle and partly gland, which produces much of the fluid in the semen and controls whether urine or semen will enter the penis.

The same sequence of vascular events takes place within a man's body during a reflexogenic erection. The difference is that the nervous impulses bypass the brain. The signal for erection arises, in this situation, from sensory nerves in the skin of the penis and travels to the erection nerves in the spinal cord, and then, via other nerves, the impulse tells the penile arteries to dilate. A man, peculiar creature that he is, can become aroused, or at least attain erection, from fondling his own penis while he is thinking about something as mundane as income tax. But the usual erection is more a mixture of physical and psychological stimulation, with the brain having the upper hand in the matter. If it were otherwise, then every time a man urinated he'd have to contend with an erection.

Additional physical responses

Sexual stimulation that triggers an erection has other effects on a man's body besides penis engorgement. Masters and Johnson call this the excitement phase of the male sexual response cycle, which is a clinical way of saying that he's getting hot and bothered. His pulse begins to race, his muscles tense, and his respiratory rate increases. In other words, he really does get hotter as muscular activity raises his body temperature.

spermatic cord: the cord that suspends the testes within their scrotal sacs, and contains the vessels and nerves connecting the testes to the rest of the body.

Getting bothered is another matter entirely. It's part mind and part body. His penis gets stiffer, his scrotal skin thickens as more blood is pumped into it, and a flat band of muscle around the testes and spermatic cord tighten and raise the testicles. These changes don't go unnoticed by his brain. Now is the time he'd like to be touched and fondled. All the physical adjustments his body has made up to this point have been geared to make his skin sensitive to touch. That's *all* his skin, not just around his genitals. If you're at the same excitement phase, the changes in your body have begun to prepare your vagina for intercourse. But your body also becomes more sensitive to touch, your nipples—and his too if you care to notice—become erect, and the shaft of your clitoris swells. The same kind of spongy erectile tissue that's responsible for a man's erection is, believe it or not, making your nipples protrude and getting your clitoris into position, so that it's more accessible to stimulation.

rgasm

The excitement phase can progress right into orgasm or it can be delayed. This is where individual preferences, sexual technique, and attitudes about satisfying one another have been compressed into one eight-letter word, "foreplay," that is the pivotal concept which makes going to bed with somebody either a pleasurable or troubling experience.

First the pleasurable. If sex is going to be good for both of you—heterosexual sex, that is—your lover has to have learned a thing or two. He has to know what feels good to you, and you have to teach him this through a combination of responses and words. He also has to be able to bide his time, which means that he has to delay the urge to come. Make no bones about it, this urge is powerful, and the desire to succumb can be overwhelming.

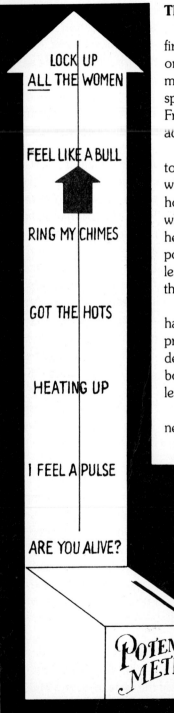

LOCK UP
ALL THE WOMEN

FEEL LIKE A BULL

RING MY CHIMES

GOT THE HOTS

HEATING UP

I FEEL A PULSE

ARE YOU ALIVE?

POTENCY
METER

The urge to orgasm

Both biology and, very often, the conditioning of a man's first sexual experiences put a premium on coming—reaching orgasm—as quickly as possible. Biology has equipped the male animal with a hair trigger, all the better to assure that sperm are sent on their final destination to fertilize an egg. From a purely reproductive point of view, the faster this is accomplished, the better.

So here we have him, all set with an erection—primed, so to speak, for orgasm. He can stay in this excitement phase, with his erection waning, but not flagging altogether, for hours. Or he can come within a matter of seconds, which is what his body is telling him to do. The important point is that he can override his body's commands through sheer will power alone. This takes training, like throwing a ball, or learning how to write the alphabet, and the more he does it, the better he'll become at delaying orgasm.

His body isn't amused by this cerebral trickery, but it isn't harmed by it either. Although an erect penis is physiologically prepared for insertion into a vagina, it can be coaxed into delaying ejaculation with no adverse effects. This gives your body a chance to catch up sexually with his, so you won't be left unsatisfied, and it prolongs his pleasure.

All this effort at seeking mutual pleasure wouldn't be necessary had our bodies been designed to operate at the same sexual pace. Alas, this wasn't taken into consideration. Nobody's to blame, but the fact of the matter is that Nature made only the male orgasm necessary for reproduction, not the female orgasm. That's not to diminish the value of your orgasms. They make sex all the more pleasurable, not to mention satisfying.

The excitement phase which prepares a man's body—and a woman's—for intercourse doesn't end with orgasm. In fact, there's an intervening phase just before orgasm. Masters and Johnson call this the plateau phase. This is when the penis increases to its maximum size. The tip, or glans, may darken to a reddish-purple hue, and a small internal gland (Cowper's gland) located near the base of the penis secretes a few droplets of a clear, mucuslike substance that lubricates the urethra before sperm pass through.

The mechanics of ejaculation

Men can get erections by just thinking about sex, but few if any can reach orgasm without some sort of tactile stimulation or physical pressure on the penis itself. A man's orgasm begins with a feeling that he can't hold back any longer. The phrase that biologists use to describe this is "sensation of inevitability." The sensation lasts only a second or two, but there's not a man who's not keenly aware of what is to follow.

During these two seconds of inevitability, nerves in the skin of the penis transmit impulses to the spinal cord, where they are quickly rerouted back to the testes, to the tubes that will carry the sperm, and to the glands that will add various secretions to the sperm, changing the consistency and composition of the fluid into a mixture that is known as semen. Contractions of smooth muscle, initiated by the nerve impulses of orgasm, propel the sperm from each tightly coiled epididymis, or storage tubule, in the testes into the vas deferens, a pair of 16-inch-long tubes that wind up from the scrotum, into the pelvic cavity, around the bladder, and into the seminal vesicles.

Here a fluid, rich in the sugar fructose, which serves as the chief source of energy for the sperm, is added. A single tube, called the ejaculatory duct, carries sperm out of the seminal vesicles and into the prostate gland at the bottom of the bladder. The prostate adds a fluid (accounting for more

epididymis: a tight mass of tiny coiled tubes in the back of each testis, where the sperm is stored until it can be used. If unwound, these tubes would stretch 20 feet long.

vas deferens: a continuation of the epididymis, which takes the sperm from each testis to the main body of the reproductive tract.

seminal vesicles: two pouches on the sides of the bladder, which keep the sperm alive and motile by adding their sugar-rich fluid.

than half of the volume of semen) which is composed of citric acid, calcium, and enzymes, among other things, and which activates the sperm.

The ejaculatory duct merges with the urethra within the prostate gland, and, as semen fills the urethra, the feeling of inevitability gives way to ejaculation. Most men can sense the fullness of the urethra an instant before the first orgasmic contractions start.

Up to this point, the semen has been moved along by contractions of smooth muscle, which produce very little in the way of sensations. The second stage of ejaculation begins when powerful striated muscles take over and expel the semen out of the penis. The main muscle of ejaculation is the bulbocavernous muscle, which stretches from the base of the penis backward along the floor of the pelvis. In your body, the same muscle begins at the clitoris, then divides and passes along either side of the vagina (it acts slightly as a sphincter around the opening of the vagina). This, and all the muscles that get swept along in orgasm, contract at rhythmic intervals of eight tenths (0.8) of a second, the same in men and women.

Men usually have between three and eight contractions per orgasm. The first waves of muscular contractions are the strongest, and most of the semen bursts out—with enough force in some instances to carry it 30 inches—during the first three or four contractions. If any contractions follow, they're weaker and not as regular, and the entire orgasm is over in a matter of seconds.

Male vs. female orgasm

This is where your body has a distinct edge. Contractions begin in the lower third of the vagina and spread to the uterus and many other parts of your body. The first contractions may last as long as four seconds, but then the 0.8 second rhythm begins. The orgasm can continue through 15 or more contractions, with the later ones getting spaced further and further apart, and it can last more than a minute. Then the waves can begin again and again in succession, without much loss of intensity. Between the waves of multiple orgasms, your body doesn't need to recover as a man's does. It stays at the plateau phase. Not all women experience multiple orgasm. Some are multi-orgasmic once in a while, others all the time, at least every time they reach orgasm.

The male multiple orgasm

The very fact that a woman can have multiple orgasms and a man supposedly can't has been a constant source of disappointment. Even if a man can manage self-control long enough for mutual orgasm, there's simply no way he's going to match you orgasm for orgasm. Or is there?

The question of male multiple orgasm—does it exist?—has two answers. Yes and yes. The first kind of multiple orgasm men can have is multiple ejaculation. The younger a man is, the better his body is at doing this. These aren't waves of increasing intensity, but separate, distinct orgasms, with more or less loss of tumescence (erectile rigidity) between each ejaculation.

Most men have to be aroused again to come a second or third or fourth time. No less a sex researcher than the towering Dr. Kinsey himself found that some men were able to have five or six orgasms a session, but the average was one and sometimes two. How much time must elapse between orgasms depends on the man's mood, the condition his body is in, and his age. The capacity for having orgasms declines, sadly, after a man passes that benchmark age, 20. As youthful as this age sounds, it's a man's physical sexual peak. His desires may not fall off—in fact, they might increase the older he gets—but his body's sexual ability starts the downslide. The decline is slow, and a man's sexual prowess may diminish, but it never entirely fades away.

The second yes to the question of the male multiple orgasm is a reserved yes, not a wholehearted yes. Some men, it seems, are able to come to the brink of ejaculation, and experience an orgasm by all physical and emotional signs, yet not come. Aside from the actual ejaculation of semen, the physical signs of male orgasm include a heart and respiratory rate twice (sometimes three times) normal, blood pressure elevated one-third to one-half above normal, and increased muscular tension with urethral and anal contractions.

Researchers, following in Masters and Johnson's path, have monitored all these physical signs in men who were plugged into laboratory equipment during their multiple orgasms. They found that some men were indeed capable of having orgasms without ejaculation, and these orgasms built up in successive waves to a final ejaculatory climax. Men's multiple orgasms, when physiologically measured in the

Better Red Than Dead

Russians are the world's greatest lovers, says the Soviet Union's first sex manual. Soviet sexologist A. M. Syvadosch, author of *Female Sexual Problems*, claims that 85 percent of Russian women have experienced orgasm, compared to 60 percent of French women and 59 percent of British women. And not a single Russian man in his tests ever failed to ejaculate.

laboratory, turn out to be biologically the same as women's multiple orgasms.

In all probability, anyone can have multiple orgasms, both men and women. The technique has to be learned, not forced, and, of course, the body has to be willing. There's no step-by-step instruction manual for multiples, but there is some good advice around from those who've already been there.

Men have to learn to hold back just long enough to impede ejaculation, but not lose the other sensations and contractions that go along with orgasm. This means being able to tense up at the instant the body is saying to let go. It's not something every man wants to accomplish. Nor is it possible to do every time. The more time—measured in days—between orgasms, the harder it gets for a man to hold back. So the ideal time for a man to try is when he's been having sex regularly, when he's not feeling forced to perform, and when he's comfortable about himself.

A man might like to experiment with different positions for sex, but he usually doesn't think about experimenting with his sexual drive. In fact, most men think that they are at the beck and call of their sexual feelings; once they start coming, the process is automatic and nothing can stop it. So he'll need encouragement, he'll need to know that it's perfectly normal, not harmful, and he'll need to know that it takes practice.

If it doesn't work, don't force the issue. There's no proof yet that the capacity for multiple orgasm is universal, though from all the evidence thus far it seems that men well into their sixties can experience the phenomenon.

Down to size

Once ejaculation has occurred, a man's erection hasn't long to last. It becomes flaccid in two stages, and no act of will can deter the deflation. The first stage happens within seconds after ejaculation when the penis begins to soften as the prostatic sphincter relaxes. Within a short time—30 seconds to a minute—only about half of the erection remains. The second stage lasts longer and can be delayed by keeping the penis in the vagina. In fact, the penis needn't lose all its hardness before it can be aroused to full erection again. Without stimulation, though—and sometimes despite it—the penis will return to its normal flaccid state within minutes.

This post-orgasmic stage is what Masters and Johnson call the resolution phase, and during it a man not only loses his erection but also his desire to stay awake. Men come down from ejaculation faster than women come down from orgasm, and it takes a bit of will power for them to do anything but curl up. Again, the intensity of the orgasm has something to do with the energy reserves a man is left with afterward. His heart rate, blood pressure, and pulse also begin falling back to normal within seconds after orgasm, even though the sound of the heart pumping doesn't seem to diminish as quickly as his erection. The entire resolution phase which brings his body back to its pre-excitement condition can take an hour or longer, as the body makes its subtle adjustments.

What does orgasm feel like?

From all accounts, men experience nearly the same sensations during orgasm as you do. At least their descriptions of orgasm bear similarity to descriptions women have written. That's what researchers found when they asked a group of men and women to type out a paragraph or two on their personal sensations during orgasm. The participants in the experiments were told not to identify their sex in their accounting. Other than that they were given a free hand to describe their most intimate feelings.

The researchers—men and women—read the descriptions and guessed the sexual identity of the writer. They were wrong half the time. Why, then, all the fuss about who's getting more enjoyment out of sex, if the sensations are much the same? Well, the trouble seems to lie in the timing of the sensations themselves.

Before, during, and after orgasm, the same nerves and muscles in a man's body as in yours perceive sexual tension and transmit these sensations to the brain. But that's where the biological similarity ends. The timing of arousal and orgasm differs considerably between men and women. Men can generally be aroused more quickly and reach orgasm much sooner than women. This is largely an unspoken difference between the sexes, but nonetheless a very real one.

No one knows precisely why a man's orgasm is set to go off as quickly as it does, but part of the answer seems to lie in evolution. Nature apparently put speed before pleasure, and men are heirs of this male evolutionary pattern. There would

What Orgasm Feels Like

Screaming physical pleasure where everything becomes blanked out in those nerve-shattering waves of orgiastic abandonment that leave the body spasm-wracked and helpless.

—MICKEY SPILLANE.
The Last Cop

be nothing troublesome about this if men didn't gauge a large portion of their masculinity on being able to sexually satisfy a woman and if women could time their orgasmic response to a man's.

hen he can't perform

Despite all that's been written and spoken about men's sexual prowess, about their ability to perform, about their instantaneous readiness, there isn't a man who has never been too tired, depressed, or anxious to perform in bed.

He may not get an erection at all, or he may lose it at any time before he ejaculates. Even though he may have no trouble getting an erection, he may ejaculate too soon, in some cases before intromission (insertion of the penis into the vagina) or just afterward. He may be able to delay ejaculation longer than he thinks humanly possible, but still not long enough to satisfy you. With as much emphasis as there is on sex nowadays, it's no wonder that the fear of not maintaining an erection has left many men feeling inadequate.

Too quick

The most common sexual problem men have is premature ejaculation. In its broadest definition, this means ejaculating before a woman reaches orgasm. Sometimes—especially after periods of sexual abstinence—premature ejaculation can't be helped. Occasionally, men do get carried away by the rushing tide of sexual stimulation, and no exercise of mind over matter can intrude.

Premature ejaculation becomes a problem when it occurs all the time and leaves a man feeling inadequate and a woman feeling frustrated. When it comes to ejaculation, men seem to be creatures of habit: If they are used to ejaculating quickly from their initial sexual experiences, the pattern will set or jell in much the same way as any habitual pattern, just as the way he holds his leg when he's putting on socks is conditioned from the time he first learned how to do it. Sometimes a man breaks the habit of ejaculating too quickly on his own. The desire to please a woman, for whatever reason—from proving his masculinity to securing a satisfying relationship—is strong enough that he may learn self-control.

Whenever his feelings are getting too intense and he realizes that he is about to ejaculate, he does something to ward it off, such as thinking distracting thoughts or even physically withdrawing his penis.

There's nothing wrong or abnormal with a man who has to stop thrusting and relax for a moment to desensitize. You shouldn't think he's losing his interest or loves you less. In fact, you should encourage him to slow down or speed up to keep pace with your progress toward orgasm. It might take some of the spontaneity out of sex, but communicating what is going on is about the only way to overcome the difference in sexual timing.

Sustaining an erection

The desire for sex and the ability to reach orgasm vary from day to day. Both desire and ability depend chiefly on mood and physical condition. Is he tired? Is he very aroused? These variables influence how long it takes him to reach orgasm. But if he wants to delay or speed up the process he can. Developing ejaculatory control is something he has to want to do. It doesn't happen if he doesn't learn how to do it, and he won't learn how to do it if he has no consideration for the woman he's with.

You can help or hinder him in learning ejaculatory control by how you act, what you say to him, and what you do. With some men, just mentioning your frustration may be sufficient; he'll get the message. But with others, blunt talk can compound the problem. If he thinks that you're questioning his masculinity or deriding his ability, he'll become more anxious about premature ejaculation, and the more anxiety he has, the less control he'll have.

Reducing his anxiety by taking the emphasis off his ability to perform can work wonders. Men have fears about sex—about being able to satisfy a woman—and it doesn't take much to make them feel threatened. If a man is overly worried about premature ejaculation, his fears can lead to impotence, the inability to get an erection or sustain it long enough for intercourse to take place.

There are several things you can do to help a man develop ejaculatory control without making him feel inadequate and without risking that he'll become impotent. The first is to tell him that it's okay for him to slow down and wait for you to catch up. After all, your satisfaction isn't just his responsibility—you have to take an active part in sex also. This may mean that he withdraws his penis while manually stimulating you, or it may mean that he just stops thrusting while you manually stimulate yourself. The main point is that the responsibility isn't all his.

The squeeze technique

If you expect him to bring you to orgasm by constant thrusting, you may be asking too much. When Kinsey did his pioneering study on sex he found that 75 percent of men ejaculate within two minutes after intromission. That amount of time has climbed steadily since then, according to surveys taken in the 1960s and early 1970s, and now hovers somewhere around ten minutes. Apparently men are getting the message. But in cases where they're not, Masters and Johnson have developed a solution that anyone can try. It's called the squeeze technique and it relies on both partners wanting to do something about premature ejaculation. The basic position calls for the woman to sit up with her legs apart and the man to lie down on his back, facing her with his legs astride her thighs. She then fondles him until he's on the verge of ejaculating, and, at his warning, she presses the tip of his penis where the glans meets the shaft between her thumb and first two fingers for three or four seconds. A fairly healthy squeeze (the erect penis can withstand much more pressure than the gentle touch that most women use when handling it) will turn off the ejaculatory urge. Then the process can be repeated four or five times.

Masters and Johnson advise that the same scenario be played out over a period of days, until the man feels that he's gained some ejaculatory control. Then intercourse should be tried in the female-superior position, with the woman kneeling above the man. Any time that he feels he's nearing ejaculation, the squeeze should be reapplied. Used regularly for six months to a year, this technique is one of the most successful that has been developed in recent sexual research.

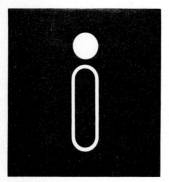

mpotency and fertility

Every man is likely to experience impotence at some point in his life. It can be trying even if it only happens once,

and if it happens regularly it can be devastating. Technically there are two types of impotence, primary and secondary. In primary impotence a man has never achieved an erection, either in anticipation of masturbation or in intercourse. In secondary impotence, he's lost the ability to get an erection. In 90 percent of cases, the problem is psychological. Primary impotence has been blamed on an overly strong maternal influence during childhood, strict religious orthodoxy, or a traumatic sexual shock. Secondary impotence, which is far more common, can be caused by fatigue, in which case it lasts only until a man's energies return, or by a variety of states of mind, including fear of failure, change in attitude toward a woman, stress, and deep-seated concern about his life.

In treating impotence, Masters and Johnson and other sex clinicians found that the causes, not the symptoms, have to be addressed. This means opening up blocked channels of communication between a man and a woman rather than teaching a man how to have an erection.

Why not teach him how to have an erection and be done with it? Well, even though such mental processes as anxiety, fear, and depression can sap a man's ability to get an erection, there is no mental process that he can learn to use to achieve an erection. Thinking about sex, thinking about or even seeing the things that used to arouse him, don't do a thing for a man who is suffering impotence. In fact, these thoughts and visions only make him more self-conscious. Treatment usually requires professional help, and the process takes time and patience on the part of both partners.

For the occasional incidents of impotence, you should remember that a man is only human; his libido can wax and wane as easily as yours. What's more, a man can have an erection without any sense of being aroused, and in such circumstances the likelihood of premature ejaculation is increased. Arousal is a state of mind that results in a number of bodily changes, not just erection. So having an erection doesn't necessarily mean that a man is aroused.

A man can be impotent yet still fertile, and he can be infertile and have no problem getting an erection. Potency and fertility are not the same thing. For a man to be potent, he has to manufacture a certain number of healthy sperm, he has to be able to get an erection, and he has to be able to ejaculate. The first requirement of potency, the production of sperm, is called fertility. Any problems in this area make it impossible—or improbable—that he'll be able to father children, and this is called infertility. Men who produce less than 200 million sperm per ejaculate are said to be infertile. The average sperm count per ejaculate is close to 500 million.

Of this number ejaculated into the vagina, it has been estimated that only 100,000 reach the oviducts, less than 1,000 reach the vicinity of the ovum, and less than 100 adhere to the outer surface of the egg. Only a single sperm penetrates the egg to fertilize it. The lower the sperm count, the less chance there is that a sperm cell can succeed in fertilization. A spermatozoon—an individual sperm cell—is only 1/500 inch long, and it has to make a journey of up to 12 inches against gravity and through the mucus currents in the vagina and uterus. For up to 30 seconds after sperm are ejaculated, they are inactive. Then, as they are stimulated by enzymes in the prostatic fluid, their tails begin the whiplike motion that will propel them along like tadpoles at about 3 to 7 inches an hour. On the average, sperm can reach the oviducts (Fallopian tubes) in about an hour.

Some 200 million sperm are manufactured daily in the seminiferous tubules of the testes. They undergo a four-stage maturation process that takes from 64 to 74 days, during which they lose half the number of chromosomes—from 46 to 23—and change from a rounded to an elongated shape. Each

Impotence—100 Years Ago

In the male, the cases are by no means rare where inability to cohabit exists. As a general thing, it is the legitimate fruit of masturbation.

The evils of excessive sexual indulgence are like those of self-pollution. Barrenness, debility and consumption often follow from excess.

—HARMON KNOX ROOT,
The People's Medical Lighthouse,
1854

mature sperm has three sections: a head, which contains the chromosomes and enzymes necessary for fertilization; a body, which contains enzymes to supply energy for motility; and a tail.

The mature sperm are stored in the epididymides, which are coiled tubes in the testes. There they remain viable for about 60 days. If they aren't ejaculated within this time, they degenerate and are reabsorbed. Once they are ejaculated, however, their lifespan is considerably shorter. Sperm can remain alive and capable of fertilizing an egg for 24 to 48 hours, depending on the conditions of acidity or alkalinity within the female reproductive tract. The fluid that sperm are ejaculated in—the semen—helps to buffer the acidity in the vagina. Sheer numbers of sperm alone don't assure fertility. Enough have to be normally shaped and motile to reach the egg and penetrate it. If more than 25 percent are abnormal, a man will be infertile.

Men who don't produce enough sperm can still father children with the help of artificial insemination, though they are technically infertile. The sperm from several ejaculations can be stored frozen and then thawed out and injected into the prospective mother's vagina at the time of ovulation. Storing sperm at −169°C. for five years and longer doesn't seem to hinder their capacity to fertilize an egg. Sperm banking, as this is called, has been used to store sperm from some men who've undergone vasectomy yet want insurance that their sperm will be available should they ever want children again.

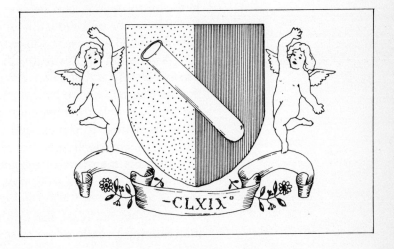

-CLXIX°

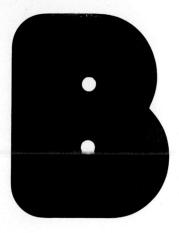

irth control

But maybe you're not interested in fertility just now. One way to achieve infertility is by vasectomy—a relatively simple surgical procedure in which the vas deferens from each testis is cut and tied off so sperm are blocked from traveling out of the testes during ejaculation. A man is still able to ejaculate afterward, but the semen contains no sperm. In some cases the surgery can be reversed and the tubes rejoined, but not always. So, for all intents and purposes, this procedure permanently sterilizes a man. Some inventive urologists have toyed with miniature faucet-type contraptions that are meant to be surgically inserted into the vas deferens and then turned on or off depending on whether a man wants children or doesn't. The problem is that live sperm can be present in the semen for up to six weeks after vasectomy itself, so turning off the faucet doesn't mean instant contraception. Thus far none of these vasectomy devices has gotten further than the animal testing stage. Unlike castration (removal of the testicles), a vasectomy doesn't deprive a man of the hormone testosterone, so his ability to get an erection and to ejaculate is not impaired.

Aside from vasectomy, the other birth control techniques and devices available to a man all leave something to be desired. Coitus interruptus—or withdrawal—is the oldest trick in the book. To make it work, a man has to withdraw his penis from the vagina before he ejaculates. Withdrawal is an all-or-nothing technique. If the penis isn't removed a safe distance from the vagina, the consequence, technically called birth-control failure, can be an unplanned pregnancy. The best that can be said about this technique is that when it works it works; when it doesn't, watch out.

A variation on this technique is coitus reservatus. The theory behind it is that a man can control himself to the point that he doesn't need to have an orgasm or ejaculation at all. He simply is able to engage in intercourse for as long as it takes his partner to climax, and then allow his feelings and erection to subside. In practice, coitus reservatus has among its adherents members of religious sects and experimental communities that have strict proscriptions on wasting one's seed.

Last, but not least, there's the condom. The idea of a man wearing a condom for any sexual activity from fellatio to intercourse may seem unappealing at first, because condoms have been associated with prostitution and protection against venereal disease. But condoms are effective contraceptives, rating about equal with the diaphragm and IUD, and they can be integrated into an arousing sexual sequence, particularly if you help him put it on.

The first condoms date back to the 16th century when the Italian anatomist Gabriel Fallopius (who gave his name to the Fallopian tubes) devised a linen sheath to protect men from syphilis. Now they are made out of thin latex. They are about 7 inches long and can be purchased dry or prelubricated. While they do transmit heat and sensations, some men complain that they make sex about as enjoyable as taking a shower wearing a raincoat. They do reduce sensitivity, but there are a lot of other places a man can be touched and turned on besides his penis.

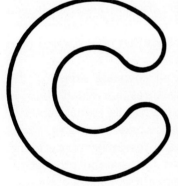

astration

Castration literally separates a man from his manhood, and, from written accounts when the operation was done before puberty, the lack of manhood extends far beyond a man's genitals. His voice remains high-pitched, he grows no beard, and he develops subcutaneous fat in the typical feminine pattern behind the breasts, over the thighs, and in the lower abdomen. Hair does grow in the pubic and underarm areas, but it, too, sprouts in the female pattern. However, the absence of testosterone, which is responsible

for these alterations, does prevent male-pattern baldness.

Eunuchs were thought to be asexual, and even if their brains had fleeting sexual flashes, it was believed that they could do nothing about it, since they were unable to achieve an erection. Needless to say, eunuchs themselves probably did nothing to discourage this view. But it is a misconception. Not all eunuchs suffered sexual apathy, nor were they all impotent. Sexual feelings and the capacity for arousal are dependent more on a man's thoughts than on his hormones. The nearer to puberty that a boy was castrated, the greater the likelihood that he had experienced sexual feelings. Once his brain had been imprinted, so to speak, with the memory of these feelings, he could recall the memory and rekindle an erection. This also goes for men who have been castrated after puberty. The ability to ejaculate wanes fairly quickly, within a matter of days, because it is more dependent on hormones than on sexual thoughts. But sometimes the ability to get an erection can last for years after the operation. In fact, some castrated men continue to have "dry-run" orgasms with all the corresponding sexual feelings that noncastrated men enjoy.

In ordinary circumstances, an adequate supply of the testosterone the testes produce assures that a man's body is prepared to respond whenever his mind's sexual center is stimulated. This mechanism also works in reverse. From studies on the physiology of coitus, researchers have found that sexual stimulation increases testosterone production. Even sexual arousal, without intercourse, causes a measurable rise in the level of testosterone circulating in a man's bloodstream. No one's yet done similar studies on women, so it's not known whether or not your sexual activity raises your estrogen levels.

Testosterone not only keeps a man's sexual apparatus in peak condition, it also keeps his muscles from wasting, his skin from wrinkling, and his bones from losing calcium. In this sense, sex—and its concomitant stimulation of testosterone—is good for a man's health. Besides being a good form of exercise, sex can improve a man's mood and relieve his psychic tensions. Whether or not these things are directly attributable to testosterone isn't clear to scientists yet, but from all evidence, sex apparently provides a man with numerous benefits aside from the obvious one.

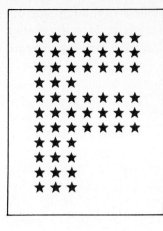

anciful facts

A marathon night of sex may sap a man's strength because of the energy he exerts in muscular activity. But short of an all-night session, there is no biological truth to the myth that a man should abstain from sex before he has to climb in the boxing ring or compete in a race or confront his boss. A brief encounter may be just the thing to lower his tensions so by morning he can focus his attentions more clearly on the goal at hand. Indeed, many professional athletes report that sex is a help, not a hindrance, in their endeavors on the playing field. No less a sage than Casey Stengel phrased it this way: "It's not the catchin' which causes the problem, it's the chasin'."

Morning erections

For most men, one orgasm with ejaculation is enough to relieve sexual tensions. Others sometimes prefer to make love two, three, or more times a night. It all depends on the man and the mood he's in. Younger men usually have a greater physical capacity for repeated ejaculations. The older a man is, the longer his refractory period—the time between erections.

But what about the man who wakes up in the morning with an erection? Does it mean that he's still filled with sexual longing? Or does it mean that he's been dreaming of something that's turned him on? There's not a woman—or a man—who hasn't wondered about this. If you ever were intrigued enough to ask, the answer you probably got was that morning erection is an indication of urinary urgency, nothing more. Most men believe this to be the case—they're not intentionally misleading you.

This excuse didn't seem to be reasonable to at least one scientist, Dr. Ismet Karacan, a professor of psychiatry at the University of Florida. Since he was director of the university's sleep laboratory, and had access to sleeping men, he decided to find out the cause of this common phenomenon. He found that erections occur during the periods of sleep when men dream. REM periods, as these dreaming intervals are called, are associated with rapid eye movements (hence REM), as well as an increase in blood levels of testosterone. In approximately 80 percent of the REM periods, a man spontaneously develops an erection independent of the nature of his dream.   Since dreaming—and REM—periods lengthen the longer that a person has been asleep, the chance that a man will wake up with an erection increases toward morning.

Semen

Morning erection, as a gauge of a man's desire, is about as inaccurate a measurement as calculating the amount of semen a man ejaculates. Yet some women persist in believing that when a man really empties himself out by ejaculating copious amounts of semen, he is giving all of himself, or not holding anything back. They equate volume of semen with intensity of feeling, but in actuality, this equation comes nowhere close to balancing.

Just as a man has no control over waking up with an erection, he has no way of consciously influencing the volume of his semen, other than by abstinence. The volume of semen in an average ejaculation after three days of abstaining from sex is 3.4 milliliters, or approximately a small teaspoonful. This amount can dwindle to 1 milliliter on the second go-around in a night, and it can increase to as much as 13 milliliters after long continence.

The volume of the ejaculate is primarily dependent on secretions of the prostate and seminal vesicles, and not on the number of sperm. That's why a man who has had a vasectomy still produces semen in normal amounts. Once the prostate and seminal vesicles have been squeezed nearly empty by the muscular contractions during ejaculation, the secretory cells within these glands have to begin producing more fluid. It takes about 72 hours to bring the level up to a volume that's considered necessary for reproduction, from the point of view of neutralizing the acidity of vaginal secretions, which gives the sperm the best chance of surviving long enough to fertilize an egg. If getting pregnant is not what you have in mind, then any amount of semen a man ejaculates should be considered normal. During ejaculation itself, the first fluid that appears is the milky prostatic secretion, which usually contains few if any sperm. This is followed by the sperm, which account for about only 2 percent of the entire volume of semen. Then the final component is the gelatinous, tapioca-like seminal secretion. The temperature of semen is the same as that of the body, 98.6°F.

Pre-Mature Ejaculation

The sex organs actually secrete into the blood material that makes a boy manly, strong and noble. Any habit which a boy has that causes this fluid to be discharged from the body tends to weaken his strength, to make him less able to resist disease, and often fastens upon him habits which later in life he cannot break. Even several years before this fluid appears in the body such habits are harmful to a growing boy.

—BOY SCOUTS OF AMERICA,
Handbook for Boys, 1911

The smell

The prostatic fluid contributes the odor and the somewhat bitter, slightly salty taste to semen, although this varies with the amount of prostatic fluid ejaculated. Any residual urine not washed away by the cleansing action of the fluid from Cowper's gland—which is released seconds before ejaculation—will impart a harmless ammonia odor to the semen. While odor and taste do vary among men, only an infection will create an obviously unnatural odor.

The only other substance that can cause an unpleasant odor or taste on a penis is smegma, a whitish secretion of the sebaceous glands on the penis that accumulates under the foreskin or prepuce, a loose fold of skin that covers the glans of an uncircumcised man. This substance probably has no valuable function other than to keep the foreskin from adhering to the glans, but it has been linked to cancer of the penis in men and cancer of the cervix in women. Daily washing is sufficient to keep smegma from becoming a problem.

Circumcision

Men who have been circumcised, of course, have no problem with smegma accumulating, because there is no place for it to accumulate. Circumcision, or removal of the foreskin, is the most frequently performed surgical procedure in the U.S., but its value is still open to question. Most doctors say the benefits outweigh the possible problems. They point out that circumcision reduces the chances of getting cancer of the penis and eliminates phimosis, a disorder in which the foreskin cannot be retracted, as it must be to attain a normal erection. The operation's opponents claim that the possibility of hemorrhage, infection, and surgical trauma occurring during or after circumcision outweighs any dubious benefit.

In any case, most men don't get an opportunity to decide for themselves, since the operation is ordinarily done within a day or two after birth. Circumcision, though, can be done at any age. Some men who have had the operation as adults for medical reasons (usually to correct phimosis) do indeed report that the sensitivity of the glans diminishes. But this change, they hasten to add, doesn't interfere with arousal, intercourse, or ability to achieve orgasm. In fact, the loss of sensitivity goes unnoticed after a while. (Circumcision is not restricted to men. Some women have an extra fold of skin covering the clitoris, and its removal, in the female variation of this operation, restores clitoral sensitivity.)

ouching and arousal

Contrary to prevailing folk wisdom, a man's penis isn't his only erogenous zone. The notion that men are relatively unresponsive to being touched over more of their body than their genitals has begun to wither under the weight of contrary evidence that has come out of sex research. Masters and Johnson were the first to show in any scientifically conclusive way that men who were overly sensitive to penis stimulation, and therefore extremely likely to be premature ejaculators, could retrain themselves to become sexually aroused from general body stimulation.

When it comes to erogenous zones, men have traditionally had a tough time abandoning the single-zone idea. It seems that they've mostly denied having powerful erotic feelings from anything but direct penis stimulation, because this was—and is—the area they themselves learned to concentrate on in their earliest sexual experience with masturbation. Once they got in the habit of focusing their sexual stimulation on the penis, they shut the door, so to speak, to wider tactile sensation.

The common sexual stereotype that most of us grow up with is that men primarily get pleasure from genital stimulation while women get erotically stimulated by being touched over their entire bodies. Sex researchers have found no biological or physiological reason for this distinction, and they blame misguided early sexual experiences for the persistence of the attitude. They suggest that men open themselves up to becoming aroused by nongenital contact and that women do likewise with genital stimulation. For your part, the idea is to help him learn that his ears, his neck, the small of his back, the interior of his thighs, and his palms are erogenous zones if he lets them be. Even the nipples, which many men consider to be strictly feminine territory, are emerging in the enlightened sexual '70s as the new male erogenous zone. Neither a man's body nor a woman's is biologically programmed to respond to any specific pattern of touching. So, beginning at the top and working down may make sense aesthetically, but anatomically the body responds just as well from warm, loving touches on the top, bottom, back, or anywhere.

.The middle ground is that almost any area of our bodies can be used for sexual stimulation if we're willing to experiment and explore. Paying too much sexual attention to a man's penis, even though he may encourage this, often backfires in the sense that it gets him too aroused too soon, and then he's done when you're barely half started.

Under these circumstances, if he comes too fast it's not entirely his fault. You owe it to yourself to get to know his body better, and this will open new doors of sensual awareness to him.

Touching isn't the only way men—or women—are sexually stimulated. Erotic material, both pictures or movies and written descriptions of sex, can be highly arousing. In studying the physiology of erotica, sex researchers used mechanical devices to measure vascular changes in the genitals of both men and women. They confirmed that men are turned on by seeing or hearing about sexual episodes, which comes as no great surprise. But they also found no difference between the sexes. Women, it turns out, are just as turned on by visual stimulation.

If your first response is to disagree, you'd be echoing what Kinsey found out in the 1940s and 1950s when he did his studies. He discovered that fewer women than men were turned on by erotica, and this view had been accepted until fairly recently. The impetus of sex research in the late 1960s and early 1970s led scientists to test this assumption in the laboratory. But first they had to develop a way to measure physiological changes during arousal, and they had to decide which changes were the best to measure.

The sign of arousal they chose was genital vasocongestion—blood-flow changes in the penis and vagina—which is the common denominator of sexual arousal in both men and women. As a man becomes aroused, the blood flow into his penis increases and he gets an erection. As a woman becomes aroused, her labia and vagina swell with extra blood. To measure blood flow to the penis, the researchers constructed a mercury-filled strain gauge in the form of a hollow rubber band that could be slipped over the penis and wired to an ink-fed pen that would chart the erection on graph paper. In its final assembly, the device was essentially a lie detector for the penis, and it was called a plethysmograph.

The device to measure a woman's state of arousal presented a few more technical problems, and it wasn't developed until 1974, when researchers hit upon the idea of measuring the diffusion of light as it passes through blood. It works on the same principle as holding a lighted flashlight against your fingers in a darkened room. A reddish hue will show up on the opposite side of the light, as the beam passes through the blood vessels in your fingers. The amount of light that passes through will vary with how much blood happens to be in your hand.

To do this same thing internally, the researchers constructed an acrylic cylinder a little less than 2 inches long and ½ inch in diameter. They fitted it with a photocell and a light source and placed it just inside the entrance to the vagina. A wire ran to the same type of graph that they used to record erection. The one limitation was that it could not be used during menstruation, since the extra blood distorted the reading.

After doing their tests, they found that while men could not ignore the obvious sign of an erection as a visible indication of arousal, some of the women tested said that they did not feel aroused even though the photoplethysmograph (as the female indicator is called) registered otherwise. Why the discrepancy? Well, it turns out that some women simply don't think that it is right for them to be aroused by erotic material, so they deny the bodily response.

That's just one example of the power of mind over matter. Men confront problems in this arena as well.

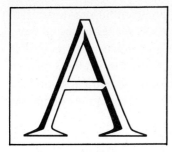**ging**

Men think that their sexual vigor will fail entirely as it begins to wane in their thirties, forties, and fifties. Indeed, the fear of sexual failure is so pervasive among men as they encounter the first signs of aging in their body that it's the most common cause of psychological impotence.

Signals

Actually, the first signs of aging begin long before most men are aware of them. The lens of the eye, which is used to focus vision on near and far objects, begins to lose some of its elasticity and is less able to focus from age 10 onward. This hardening process continues, and in many men—and women—results in cataracts, which is the name given to the lens when it has become opaque and obscures vision. The only way to improve sight is to undergo an operation for removal of the degenerated lens.

Hearing loss, in the upper ranges of sound, also begins around age 10. But most men don't notice that they're getting older until they are in their thirties. By then, they've already undergone about a decade of decline in testosterone production and their brains have shrunk about 10 grams, and will continue to lose an average of a gram a year.

According to the latest evidence on aging, IQ and memory can remain pretty much intact throughout most of life, and the picture of the brain as an ever-expanding sieve through which recent events and memories leak away is being revised in the light of new research in gerontology, the science of aging. Nonethelesss, aging does exact a toll, and scores of examples can be cited to bolster the argument that creativity and intellectual flexibility decline when a man strides into his thirties.

Diminishing testosterone

The decline in testosterone production, which continues at a slow but steady pace throughout a man's life, begins to sap his muscular strength ever so slightly when he's still in his thirties. By that time, he's already had to get used to the fact that he needs more time to get an erection and that he needs more stimulation to reach orgasm than he did when in his twenties. He'll likely attribute this to being wiser, not older; but in truth, his sex hormones are on the downhill slope when yours are still at their peak. So he'll have to be less dependent on his hormones and more dependent on his frame of mind to get aroused and to stay interested. Most men make this subtle adjustment naturally, without giving much thought to it. They take the gradual loss of testosterone in their stride, and make up for it by becoming better at the techniques of making love.

Other changes have also begun to take place when a man is in his thirties. The amount his muscles can be strengthened by training or working out decreases. The elasticity of the aorta and other major blood vessels decreases, causing blood pressure to steadily increase until the fourth decade of life, when it levels off again.

Cartilage lining joints begins to degenerate during the decade from age 30 to 40, eventually leading to arthritis, from which all old people suffer, some more than others. A little stiffness in his joints, a slight paunch around his waist, a bit of huffing and puffing when he climbs a few flights of stairs—these are all signs of aging. Yet the one that's paid the most attention, that's given the most homage as a sure indicator of advancing years, is the hair turning gray. The first gray hairs may appear anywhere on a man's head, but the ones that confer a sense of aging are those that sprout on the temples. The gray results through failure of an enzyme system within the color-producing cells in a hair follicle. The genetic clock within the cell simply runs out of color. This clock is timed to wind down at different ages in different men, which is why we don't all go gray at the same rate even though we all age at chronologically the same rate. Hairs on the face, chest, arms, and legs also lose their pigment-making ability with age. Those under the arms and in the pubic region usually—but not always—retain color.

Wearing and tearing

The body's ability to ward off the wear and tear of age and repair itself turns for the worse when a man reaches the age of 40. The only part of his body that continues to grow is his head and face, whose dimensions expand slightly for two more decades. The weight of gravity pressing down on a man's body for 40 or more years gradually compresses his spinal column. While he may increase his fortunes or his standing in the community, his actual stature decreases.

Cells don't regenerate as quickly in a 40-year-old body as they do in a younger one. Bones take longer to mend, cuts and bruises don't heal as rapidly. Sperm production takes longer. The heart loses its capacity to pump at a peak rate under exercise and stress. Reserves throughout the body diminish. The thyroid shrinks, slowing the metabolic rate and signaling a subsequent decline in other hormones. The prostate usually enlarges, foreshadowing a health problem that's all too common among aging men.

Middle years

Still, a man in his forties is in the prime of life. His endurance is at its peak, because the oxygen-carrying capacity of his blood is at its maximum. His muscles are as strong as they'll ever become. Then these peaks begin to waver. Strength and the ability to maintain maximum muscular effort drop off as the muscle cells themselves decrease in number.

Men in their late fifties can do only 60 percent of the physical work they were capable of in their forties. The strength of a man's back muscles declines over 90 percent after age 50. The walls of the air sacs in the lungs thicken with age, making it more difficult to breathe and hindering the passage of oxygen into the blood. To compensate, the chest muscles work harder to bring in more air with each breath. But the sheathing around muscles also thickens, slowing down the passage of oxygen from the blood into the muscles themselves. On top of this, the amount of oxygen the blood can carry declines and the amount of work muscles can do with inadequate oxygen falls by half between the ages of 20 and 50. About the only change a man will notice from these physiological declines is that he won't be able to sustain hard physical work for as long as he used to, and he'll need longer and longer periods to recover from his labors. The time it takes him to carry out complex movements draws longer the older he gets, not from any muscular or skeletal rigidity, but because his nervous system takes longer in initiating and guiding movements.

Male climacteric

Near the age of 50, about the time you enter menopause, his body will be undergoing somewhat similar hormonal changes, but not nearly as dramatically as yours. Where you lose three-quarters of your estrogen production in the first year or two of menopause, a man's testosterone production goes merrily along, declining only about 1 percent a year. What has been called the "male menopause" has less to do with hormonal supply than with the psychological adjustments men have to make when they're faced with the prospect of diminishing returns for their energy. They see younger men enjoying the things they still enjoy, but they're able to recognize a difference in the level of enjoyment, with the younger men having the advantage.

Getting over this middle-age hurdle means that a man has to make certain allowances. He can't expect to sprint as fast as a younger man, or box as long and as hard. His brain won't be able to handle complex, unfamiliar information as quickly as it once did, so his reaction time when he's driving a car, for instance, will be slower than when he was younger.

The lines of expression, when a man frowns or smiles or looks surprised, become the wrinkles of aging skin. And the contour lines, which form at the junctions of the cheek and the nose, the scalp and the ear, and the cheek and the ear, to name a few, also deepen with age as the skin loses its elasticity.

The deterioration of the elastic fibers in the facial skin combines with the loosening of its subcutaneous fat and muscle to produce the telltale signs of the aging face. Crow's-feet flare at the corners of the eyes. The eyebrows droop like hoods from their natural position on the superior orbital rim. The transverse lines in the forehead deepen. Fatty deposits in the lower eyelids cause bags to form under the eyes. Vertical frown lines groove the inner aspect of the eyebrows. The nasolabial folds, between the nose and the cheeks, thicken and sag. Creases deepen at the corners of the mouth. Transverse lines ring the neck. And fat accumulates between the mandible and the hyoid bone, producing a double chin.

By the time a man is 75, the strength of his forearm muscles is no greater than that of a nine-year-old, and his testosterone level is about the same too. The older a man grows, the longer it takes him to achieve an erection, but the longer he's able to maintain it. Thus what he loses in speed, he makes up for in ejaculatory control. During the plateau phase of sexual excitement, the testes of older men don't become engorged with blood as they do in younger men, and the sensation of inevitability that is the signal of the orgasmic phase in younger men can vanish entirely in older men. Here, too, there is some variation—some older men report that these sensations actually lengthen rather than disappear. The amount of seminal fluid ejaculated and the force of ejaculation invariably decline with age, but all the other physiological changes, from muscle tension to heart rate, reach almost as high a peak as in younger men. After orgasm, the older man usually loses his erection quickly, and he may need as long as 24 hours, depending on his age, before he is able to get another erection.

Much of aging is a process of give and take, with a good side often counterbalancing the bad. This doesn't mean that there is an equal benefit for every decline. There's no way an old man can make love as often as one who's decades younger. But then again, he doesn't need to. He can express his emotions in ways only time can teach.

SENSUALITY & SEXUALITY

SENSUALITY & SEXUALITY

he sensual man

Ideally, he'll be honest about his needs and open to yours; he'll be ready to stop "performing," willing to discuss any problems he or you might have, and able to accept the fact that he doesn't have all the answers just because he was born male; he will express and accept physical affection even when nonsexual in intent; he will not only share himself with you but encourage you to do the same with him; he will rid himself of the orgasm-as-holy-grail trap; he will not define masculinity with his sex organs; he will acknowledge—even embrace—the feminine side of his nature; he will be capable of displaying emotions openly; he won't approach sex as a contest but rather as one of the better ways to connect with another person; he will never mistake sexual agility for sensual pleasure; he won't neglect his body by devoting all his energy to yours, nor will he neglect your body by devoting all his energy to his; he will always regard himself as a human being first, a man second.

This, of course, describes an ideal that no man can completely fulfill. Today, men are poised halfway between self-discovery and self-concealment. But although their eventual direction is still uncertain, one thing is definite: The more a man allows himself sensual feelings, the better chance he has of experiencing a full life.

Sensuality and society

Sensuality is as natural to men as breathing. As a matter of fact, sensuality *is* breathing. And eating. And thinking. And experiencing emotions. And, of course, perhaps more than anything else, it is sexuality—not the starkly mechanical aspects of sex but rather the totality of sexual appetites. According to Dr. Eric Berne, of all such appetites "the one preferred by most people is contact with another human skin. This does not so much reflect a hunger for copulation as it does a need for reassurance, comfort, nurturing, and intimacy." But if the need for human contact is natural, why are men so often incapable of expressing it?

Men have fitted themselves into a societal restraint. This restraint consists of all the taboos, myths, fantasies, and plain wishful thinking inherent in the concept of masculinity. Some men wriggle free, some men are forever trapped, but most spend their lives in a shifting battle between what society tells them to feel and what they actually do feel and want to feel.

We are all of us—man and woman, Episcopalian and pagan, Democrat and Republican—born into this world *hungry.* Once arrived, however, we are submitted to a process of socialization that teaches us to repress many of our hungers for emotional gratification. Some of this repression—"You can't stab your baby brother with the fork"—is essential. Some—"Big boys don't cry"; "Little girls don't climb trees"—is arbitrary. First we're taught that we can't do some things and must do others; soon we take it a step further and learn that we can't want to do some things and must want to do others.

You've experienced how socialization affects your

growth as a woman. But you have been allowed to express a certain amount of sensuality. Indeed, the very word "sensual" has feminine connotations to many men. A man who freely expresses his own sensuality is viewed by most other males (and often females, too) as not completely masculine.

Most males, aware of their own needs but unwilling to rebel against social dictums, eventually create a public mask of self-denying stoicism. The mask is not always easy to penetrate. But if you stare at it long enough, you will begin to discern the face of the real man beneath. Not a superman, but a needy, flawed, credible, and wanting human being.

And what exactly does he want? Exactly what you want. Happiness… pleasure… love… comfort… the joys of the body and the joys of the spirit. In short, everything.

What is sensual?

"Sensual" simply means "pertaining to the senses." Sensual feelings are healthy. A sensual person is someone who is open to the pleasures that the senses afford, willing to experience the wealth of joyful sensations that the world offers.

Men and women are both born sensual—what's more sensual than a baby?—but men especially are eventually forced to live a dual existence. They have a physical capacity to savor pleasure, but a social responsibility to maintain a mask of stoic invulnerability, of indifference to sensual pleasure. This duality is particularly true of the sexual aspects of sensuality, and in no other area of human endeavor do men suffer so much confusion, struggle, and pain. He knows that he is not what he wants to be.

he way he wants to be seen

In his book *Compassion and Self-Hate,* Dr. Theodore Isaac Rubin notes that "too many men think of themselves as *men,* rather than as *human beings*...The inevitable result is [that] they are unable to see beyond the confines of the male myth and become encumbered by impossible and confused notions about masculinity. Because their perceptions are diverted away from reality, many of their humanistic charac teristics and assets are repressed to such an extent that vital caring emotions are numbed."

It begins in early childhood. All infants, regardless of their sex, enjoy a sensual response to their own bodies. However, soon a young boy learns to identify himself as male. His body (he is told) is not meant to be viewed as beautiful in any aesthetic sense but rather as a direct expression of masculinity. He is taught to disregard most aspects of his physical (and emotional) being in order to devote attention and concern to those few features that society has declared will define his maleness.

Strong

Typically, by the time a boy is around four, he's already learned how important muscles are to his self-image. His parents, his playmates, the books he reads (or has read to him), the television programs he watches—all inform him that the more muscular he becomes, the more admired he will be.

You can tell by the way I use my walk, I'm a woman's man; No time to talk.

—"Stayin' Alive." from *Saturday Night Fever*

This is not, of course, solely due to external influences. Boys, being boys, have a natural interest in physical prowess. Much of their physiological makeup—the combination of glands, hormones, and frontal-brain impulses that C.G. Jung has termed "the biological self"—urges them to strive for muscular coordination and display. After all, what little boy (or, for that matter, big boy) has not at least occasionally posed, biceps flexed, in front of the bathroom mirror? Men do find a certain amount of sensual pleasure in well-built male bodies. They are interested in their own builds—and not just because they want to be attractive to you. They are admiring of other men's good builds. And as long as this pleasure is a direct and uncomplicated satisfaction of a natural appetite— that is, as long as the pleasure *is* pleasure—there's no problem.

The problem, however, is the limitation that is placed on

men when biceps and pectorals become the primary features that they are allowed to appreciate in their own bodies. Men are not encouraged to admire other, less "manly" aspects of their physiques. You can tell him you like his broad shoulders and he'll be pleased, but if you've ever told a lover how much you enjoy his body—the line of his legs, the curve of his rump, the texture of his skin—he may very well have responded by turning several shades of red and ducking his head in embarrassment. A man isn't supposed to be beautiful. And he doesn't know what to say when he's told that he is.

Forget Michelangelo's *David;* forget David's *Marat;* forget Grecian sculpture and Renaissance art; forget, too, the evidence of your own senses. No matter how attractive a man seems to you, chances are he will deny—or, at least, refuse to acknowledge—his own beauty. Refuse, even, to acknowledge the *possibility* of male beauty.

He may really know—from experience—that his gangly (or squat) body and spidery (or chunky) limbs are appealing to you and to other women, and he may be secretly quite pleased with them. But he's not going to be comfortable about any compliments from you unless they imply that it is masculinity and strength that you admire in him.

Enviable

With all due respect to Sigmund Freud, it now appears that it's men—not women—who suffer the most from "penis envy." In his book *Male Sexuality,* Dr. Bernie Zilbergeld states that so much of masculine myth is centered on phallic size and performance that "the humanity of the penis has been lost. The mythical model makes it quite clear that the sexual measure of the man is a direct function of the size and power of that magical toy between his legs. Real men with real penises compare themselves to the model and find themselves woefully lacking. Most men believe that their penises are not what they ought to be. This isn't surprising. The penises in the model are products of fantasy, and the real always loses when compared to the creations of the human imagination."

By puberty, a boy has picked up the idea that the true he-man has the true he-penis. The male names given to the sexual organ reflect all too well a heroic model: shaft, tool, staff, rod, ramrod, battering ram, weapon, pole, joystick. No wonder, with images such as these, that the typical boy will typically develop a nonsensual attitude toward sex—toward, in truth, his own capacity for sex. There's no way his own appendage can match such images of cruel and formidable power. Although there's sufficient (and easily available) evidence that most penises are approximately the same size when erect and that in any case size has little to do with function, the boy will grow up believing that the bigger the penis the better, and that his penis is not large enough.

It is both fascinating and depressing to learn how timeless are the myths surrounding the male sexual organ. In ancient Chinese calligraphy, the rank of a particular man was indicated by a symbol signifying the length of his penis—the more exalted his membership in society, the more exalted his member. In the *Iliad*, Helen of Troy is identified as "men's curse made flesh—the woman never satisfied with the archer's arrow." And on a wall of a half-preserved brothel in the ruins of Pompeii can still be discerned an advertisement for a primitive penis extender. The caption reads, "Realize your dreams and become a giant among men."

Men who feel inadequately endowed also feel inadequately masculine. And so many will approach sex not as a joyful experience but rather as a test (sometimes an ordeal) of their manhood. One of the chief complaints women make about their husbands and lovers is that they're insensitive to a female's needs in bed. Well, sometimes, they're preoccupied with needs of their own that they don't want you to know about. It's not that males have less interest in tenderness and warmth but that they want that shaft, rod, joystick to be at its best. Sometimes they can be thinking too hard about their own bodies to relax and enjoy yours.

It's easy to say, as sexologists do, that men devote too much time and place too much importance on the functional aspects of what is, finally, only one aspect of sexuality. The male organ is not the male's sole erogenous zone, and not the sole instrument of your pleasure. But indoctrinated with the belief that he must prove his virility by having and then sustaining a (preferably huge) erection, he may simply not be relaxed enough for the more gentle arts of lovemaking when he's first making love to you. The better you know him the more casual he'll feel—"Ah, I just can't get it up tonight. I'm sorry, dear."—but by then a hard quick performance may have

Eureka! I Found it!

Love is not in the brains.

Love is not in the loins.

Love is in the temperament as centering upon the solar plexus.

—THOMAS W. SHANNON,
Nature's Secrets Revealed, 1914

become a habit. Too bad—because if he were really comfortable with sex it would happen so naturally and easily that he wouldn't have to worry about it.

Invulnerable

The heroic-man is not only epically strong and virile but also impenetrable. Generation upon generation of boys (and girls) have been presented with male role models who have an inexhaustible capacity to withstand not only pain but *any* feeling. The face of the heroic-man changes, as does the world he lives in, but the nature of the heroic-man is as immutable as the world's rotational orbit. It is but a short hop, skip, and swagger from Achilles to Beowulf to Lancelot to John Wayne to Clint Eastwood. Logic, if nothing else, tells us that humans are emotionally vulnerable, that men are human, and so men are also vulnerable. But the Male Mystique isn't logical. It is more like a religion, and it has a list of commandments that make the vengeful Jehovah of the Old Testament seem more like a benevolent Santa Claus. If he wants to be a man, then:

He shall not cry.

He shall not display weakness.

He shall not need affection or gentleness or warmth.

He shall comfort but not desire comforting.

He shall be needed but not need.

He shall touch but not be touched.

He shall be steel not flesh.

He shall be inviolate in his manhood.

He shall stand alone.

These commandments aren't nonsensual as much as they are *antisensual*. And it follows that any man who attempts to obey them would be as sealed off from human warmth as an astronaut circling the dead moon. Except for three saving factors.

First there is his own imperishable spirit. No one can survive without emotional release. Regardless of what they've been told, regardless of what they believe (or want to believe), a man is never able to completely suppress his inner self. He can hide it, or rationalize it, or diminish its importance, but he isn't able to banish that self permanently. Of course, the continual struggle between what he wants and what he thinks is required of him makes his emotions erupt in fits and starts. A brief explosion of inexplicable tears, an outburst of sudden affection, a late-night confidence—these are the humanizing cracks in his mask, the inevitable fractures of the commandments.

INVULNERABLE
THE SECOND

Second there is the ever-changing face of society. The current view of man as a sober-sided, slit-eyed, tight-lipped lone ranger—an estranged ranger—is a relatively novel one. Throughout most of history, and within most societies, men have been allowed to express themselves more freely. The primitive tribesman bedecked in feathers and paint, the Greek epicurean, the Elizabethan brigand, the Renaissance artist, the Restoration fop…there's a long line of men who danced, and pranced, and strutted their emotional stuff. And, keeping in mind the mercurial nature of our present cultural scene, there's no reason to suspect that men won't be given that chance again. The fact that long hair, jewelry, and stylish clothes are now acceptable to men may be signs that the he-man image is fading.

And the third saving factor? It's you.

ere's looking at you, kid

When you were a young schoolgirl, they'd court you by putting frogs in your desk drawer, or relentlessly teasing you on the playground. When you were a little older, they'd slowly cruise back and forth along the main drag, four or five to a car, whistling and catcalling after you and your girlfriends. And now that you're a woman, they voice their appreciation by following you on the streets, all the while strutting and boasting and murmuring sweet obscenities into your outraged ear.

> On my block we call it "running the gauntlet." Construction workers, businessmen, even little kids—you walk past them and they act like all they see is meat on the hoof.

The public man's response to women does not come close to resembling the private man's view. If male strangers are sometimes rude, crude, or downright lewd in their comments to you on the street, it's mainly because they've been brought up to believe it's not only a masculine privilege but even a masculine *duty* to greet each new feminine presence as raucously as possible.

But this type of verbal machismo is only the pose. In his book on sex and marriage, doctor Allan Fromme writes: "Our sexual behavior is essentially the result of our attitudes towards sex; and these attitudes, in turn, are a product of how we've been brought up." Noting that men are particularly affected by attitude training, Dr. Fromme observes that what men say or do does not necessarily reflect what they want or need. You see that beefy construction worker as the archetypical chauvinist cynic, but he sees *you* through the eyes of a genuine romantic.

Marshall McLuhan once said that "interior desires are best articulated through exterior mediums." Man's true feelings about Woman can be most clearly viewed in the way he presents images of her. Male-oriented literature, art, music, and even commercial advertisements depict women as symbols. Although there are several popular feminine stereotypes—the Mother, the Whore, the Companion, the Bitch—by far the most prevalent is the Salvation. Most men see most women as chimeric, mysterious, glorious, and always slightly out of reach.

Which doesn't do either men or women much good. For one thing, this idealization puts a strain on almost any involvement between the sexes. You are, of course, not a symbol but a person; and more than a few relationships have been shattered because of the impossible image women are expected to live up to.

Fortunately, it doesn't end there. For men also see you as their entry into a world otherwise forbidden to them. A man who'd never dream of buying *himself* flowers or reading a book of verse, for example, may be pleased to buy flowers for you and read verse to you. The prototypical bachelor's apartment may be decorated—if it's decorated at all—in early Cro-Magnon, but he can enjoy—without any damage to his male image—the changes you make when you move in. And as for that lover who thinks his chest isn't hairy enough or his arms thick enough, telling him how attractive he is might embarrass him but will also free him to see himself in a more positive light.

Looking back at him

Until recently, women played a rather small part in releasing the sensual inner man. Women have been as controlled as men. If he's been told that rough-and-tough was masculine, you've been told that rough-and-tough was sexy. The Women's Movement, however, has challenged all that.

Are Times Really Changing?

It may well be that expressions of a new era in dating are based more on wishful thinking than in behavior.

The very real possibility exists that what has changed dramatically is the male "line," but not the male perspective.

—D.H. BERG,
Adolescence

Since the masculine posture is at least partly designed to spark feminine interest, it is highly probable that more and more men are getting the message that women are attracted to the inner self. However, probably many men will continue to view you as a means to achieve the sensuality otherwise forbidden them. As one man put it: "When I look at a woman, I see the only poetry I can permit into my life."

ites of passage

A shy little girl hiding behind her mother or father is considered adorable; a shy little boy who does likewise is considered a sissy. A girl child who cries in the dark is comforted; a boy child is admonished to "act like a man." Two young female friends embracing, or kissing, or even dancing are looked upon benignly by society; two young male friends who touch each other had better be wrestling.

These are just some of the ways children are trained to differentiate between "proper" and "improper" behavior. Although the distinctions between the two modes are mostly imaginary (that is, it's as natural for a boy or man to cry as it is for a girl or woman), society still insists on labeling certain responses as "feminine" and others as "masculine."

"Neither men nor women are born with a specific preference for sensual activity," writes Dr. Rubin. "No matter what parents, clergymen, or teachers may say, a child is actually a very pliable individual, devoid of any taboos, and unable to differentiate between what his elders consider 'right' or 'wrong.'"

But adults, having had sexual prejudices imposed upon them when they were young, will usually pass them on to their children. In a 1970s study commissioned by the United States government, it was revealed that the majority of tested parents would not hug or cuddle their sons (after the average age of five) as often as they did their daughters (regardless of age), would not kiss male children at all after a certain age (usually the onset of adolescence), and would discourage even the youngest boys (four years old in one case) from weeping by calling them cry-babies or telling them to "act their age." When asked to explain, the most common response from the parents was: "I don't want my son to grow up to be a sissy."

Boys, of course, need as much reassurance, comfort, and physical demonstration of affection as girls do. Not only do they not receive it, however, but they are also directed to view any emotional display as unhealthy. With the exception of athletic pleasures, sensual feelings of any kind, whether sexual or nonsexual, are actively discouraged. And even athletics are approved more as a show of competitive spirit than as a way of enjoying the body—which may be why adult joggers are so stunned by discovering that exercise is pleasurable that they make a religion out of it. The discouragement of sensuality doesn't stem from cruelty but from ignorance: Parents actually believe they're helping their children grow into manhood or womanhood.

And it's not just parents. Teachers, ministers, TV and film heroes, siblings, other children, even some child psychologists also teach youngsters that crying is "for girls only," that emotional demonstrations and physical touching are mostly limited to the female world, and that aggression, competition, and physical dexterity are reserved for the male world.

First encounters

As a general rule, a boy's *direct* sex education isn't very helpful, either. He is warned about exploring his own body ("If you play with yourself it'll ruin your health"). And he is discouraged from exploring other members of his age group's bodies (with a sharp slap if he's caught with a girl, with hysteria if he's caught with another boy). And even if he's given a correct explanation of the sex act, most parents and teachers (unless they're either specially trained or especially sensitive) tend to emphasize the clinical details without discussing the accompanying emotional ones. In addition, the young boy must also contend with conflicting social attitudes toward sexuality. His parents warn that sex, unless sanctioned by society (i.e. marriage) is wrong, even evil (though a confession of pre-marital sex would likely earn him his father's relieved respect rather than condemnation); at the same time, his male friends are indicating to him that having sex is the best way to elevate his status. He's also told that sex is somehow nasty, shameful, and funny; his schoolmates giggle and whisper about it, laugh tracks are turned all the way up whenever it's mentioned on TV, and even his father might pull him aside to share a "dirty" joke. Further-

Then he showed me these books, and he give me 1 that he believed I could whip, and I took it home and read it through. It turned out you didn't get a baby from kissing, but from intercourse (fornication), and a load was lifted from my mind. The book was quite helpful in many other ways as well. I was about 10 at the time, and my mind settled down a good bit, and I just went on growing and not worrying. It said in the book that when we was at the age of fornication there would be new worries crop up. As it turned out, when I come to it it all went off rather pleasant.

—MARK HARRIS,
The Southpaw

more, he's exposed in various ways to the he-man version of lovemaking: ruthless, selfish, coarse, and with little apparent emotional content. Any man who is a man, he determines, must treat women as merely disposable proof of his manliness.

This is hardly the most fertile soil for sensuality to flower in. And yet the boy does, thankfully, have access to the opposite point of view. His own rapidly developing physical and emotional systems—not to mention his rapidly developing interest in girls—are informing him that there's more, much more, to sex than what society has taught him.

Close encounters

There's no way anyone can ever be prepared for his or her first complete sexual experience. Even so, a woman (or young girl) does have certain advantages over her male counterpart. Tactile sensations, emotional interactions, are feelings she's comfortable with. A man (or young boy) has little, if any, advance anticipation of the moment we all discover that, to quote Walt Whitman, "if anything is sacred, then the human body is sacred."

Given our predilection for exaggeration (at best) regarding our sexual lives, polls and surveys about the first sexual experience must be approached with more than a grain of salt. As the first lovemaking can take place in a bedroom or the back seat of a car, or on the beach, or thousands of other places—we're an inventive race—there's little purpose in discussing any details. Except, perhaps, to note that no matter how good, bad, or indifferent the actual act, *everyone* remembers his or her first time with a mixture of amusement, bemusement, embarrassment, affection, loss, poignancy, and mystery. For most men, the joining of their body with another's is the first time they've ever had an *opportunity* to discover complete sensuality.

Shoulder to shoulder, bolder and bolder

When a young man removes himself, either physically or spiritually, from his family's influence, he will often move next into a male-oriented world. This could be the military (not as usual any more since the draft ended), a college dormitory, or an office. Here he will find the same separation of sexes, with all the accompanying prejudices, that existed in his childhood.

Already trying to duplicate the heroic-man image, the young man now has more reason than ever to wear a mask. Not only is he judged on how well he can conceal any emotional frailty, but he also is encouraged to adopt a cavalier attitude toward the opposite sex. For no matter how much lip service the Male Mystique pays to fairness, it really celebrates the "love 'em and leave 'em" approach to women. Sex, thus, becomes a score card, and the sensual aspects of it are lost in the general scramble for points. Although individually he may be sensitive to the nuances of sensual pleasure, the young man is informed by his peers that the more aggressive and ruthless his behavior toward his sexual partners, the more manly he is.

Dr. Havelock Ellis once observed that "the danger is twofold. First, by giving males a stylized common cause, [the aggressive pursuit of females], it diminishes the possibilities of any true friendship between men. Second, and more evident, it interferes with the man's eventual attempt to form a more lasting relationship with one woman."

Discouragement and disillusion

If a couple can't be open to each other outside of bed, what chance does candid communication have in the bed? Instead, the man will act out the age-old habits of masculinity: undemonstrativeness, abrupt and intermittent sexuality (instead of the continual flow of sensuality), and stoical repression of emotion.

And the woman, too, must share responsibility for this. A young woman who's been exposed to little, if any, male emotionalism tends to panic if her husband or lover expresses any. Rather than constructively using marriage (or any relationship) to break through the barriers of myth and stereotype, many people use it to perpetuate the disguises that hide real feelings.

> *We were married right after high school. The first six months were fantastic: We couldn't keep our hands off each other. But we didn't grow. I mean, neither of us had much experience with sex, and we just didn't have any idea how to go about gaining any more. More my fault than my wife's. I didn't even know how to talk about sex. After a while, we both started playing around. I don't suppose it was better with other people, not for me anyway, but at least it was different. Finally, we split up.*

In most urban centers now, for example, many men and women will spend a period of time—anywhere from six months to several years—involved (if that's the word) pursuing quantitative instead of qualitative sex. The results of all this disengaged coupling appears to be a growing disillusionment with the possibilities of long-term relationships.

Variety may well be the spice of life, but too much variety—like too much spice—ruins the taste buds. Consider singles bars. They seem a perfectly reasonable solution to the problem of meeting people in a large city. But, as anyone who's ever spent an evening in one can testify, the atmosphere in such bars is usually one of desperate hostility. Everybody wants to connect, but only briefly; the next night, most will return to the bar stools looking for new connections.

Why? Probably because a one-night stand, exciting as it can be, nevertheless offers very little in the way of genuine human contact. "Why should I commit myself to one woman when there are so many around?" asks the man behind the he-man mask. But the real question is: "Why can't I find a woman who can keep me home nights?" Sensuality requires mutual trust, mutual regard, and a mutual desire to share. Carnality is never a satisfying substitute.

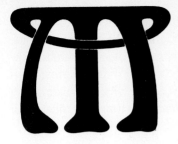

yths

In the introduction to *Beyond the Male Myth*, the first nationwide study of sexual behavior in the human male since Kinsey's 1948 report, Dr. Anthony Pietropinto writes that "modern man has been depicted in a variety of ways, most of them unflattering, all of them sketchy and simplistic." Some of the examples he cites are the bungling husband of TV situation comedies, the violent predator of popular adventure novels, the exploitive chauvinist enemy of the more strident feminist manifestoes, the noncommunicative cipher of "pop" psychology books, and the macho brute of man's own tradition. Myths can force men to hide their real selves from you. Nowhere is a man more tempted to disguise himself than when he is lying naked with a woman.

What follows are five of the pervasive myths regarding the sexual nature of men. These myths, widely accepted by males and females alike, can be held responsible for much of the misunderstanding and disappointment you may have experienced with the males (particularly the male lovers) in your life. As myths tend not only to conceal reality but to become a twisted kind of reality, it is essential that all of us learn how to distinguish between fact and fiction.

Male sexuality is not a complicated matter. If this were true, why do so many men complain about their sex lives? In one recent survey conducted by *Psychology Today* of some 52,000 people, approximately 55 percent of the men said they were sexually unhappy, and 39 percent of the men said they had specific sexual problems. Nothing simple can generate such discontent. Why, then, this assumption that sex is an uncomplicated word to the male species?

Well, for one thing, men don't like to discuss sex. They do brag about it, and joke about it, and lie about it. They rarely talk honestly about it. To reveal sexual ignorance or doubt or concern is to violate the image of absolute self-confidence. And so, writes Dr. Zilbergeld, "men learn to fake it." They fake confidence when they're unsure, they fake comfort when they're uneasy, they fake knowledge when they don't know what comes next, they fake interest when they really couldn't care less, and they fake enjoyment when they're actually miserable.

This deception goes in circles. Although a man may be dissatisfied with his sexual experiences, he's nevertheless reluctant to share his worries with fellow men—who, in turn, will be just that much more reluctant to share *their* troubles. And so it goes, on and on, each man convinced that *every* other man is having a better time in bed than he. Most men feel they're singularly lacking in some skill in lovemaking shared by all other males. They feel, too, that they must at all costs hide this deficiency from the rest of mankind.

Men are even more hesitant about confiding in women about sexual doubts. At its best, sex can be the ultimate sensual adventure, one in which a person can discover both his own emotional depths and his partner's as well. Instead of opening himself to this shared and privileged moment, however, a man will often go to great pains to mask himself from his lover. Any hint of a less than totally rapturous acceptance of him on a sexual level may trigger off a wild volley of counteraccusations. "It's your problem, not mine." "You don't want a man—you want a goddam vibrator." "If you really loved me, you'd be satisfied with what I can give you." After a while, women learn it's better just to grin and bear it, or pack up and move out, or do anything *but* try to have a candid discussion of problems. It's sadly ironic that the times of greatest intimacy can also be the times of greatest communication gaps.

Another reason for the myth about men's sexual simplicity is to be found in the great scarcity of written material on the subject. There's no dearth of information about women, especially in these more liberated times, but as one noted sexologist puts it, "since much less has been said and written about men, the impression is conveyed that women have many more problems than men and that it must be very easy to be male in this society, especially when it comes to sex."

A man can't get enough sex. Unfortunately, this myth has resulted in a serious dilemma for most men. Although they have long accepted a woman's right to say no to a sexual advance, they are often not able to extend the same privilege to themselves.

The real man is not a sex machine. His physical system is much too complex to shift smoothly into high gear each and every time he's presented with an opportunity for sex. Feelings, too, play an essential part. A man is not all that different from you. They also need the proper emotional climate—and this includes not only who he's with but where

Men and Masturbation

More than 200 college men from the New York area were asked about masturbation. Here are some of their answers:

Do you continue masturbating when you are having other sexual activity?

Not at all	45%
The same as before	19%
Less often	18%
Only occasionally	17%
More often	1%

Why do you masturbate?

Feeling horny	48%
Pleasure	21%
Loneliness	12%
Mental strain	11%
Other reasons	8%

Are your orgasms more intense during masturbation or intercourse?

Intercourse is better	51%
About the same	40%
Masturbation is better	9%

How do you feel after you masturbate?

Satisfied	68%
Guilty	13%
Depressed	11%
Perverted	5%
Afraid of going insane	2%

and when he's with her—to respond in a completely sensual (thus, completely successful) manner to lovemaking.

Needless to say, this sex-equals-manhood mentality puts a lot of pressure on the man. For one thing, it demands that he always be capable of sustaining an erection. But the penis isn't the hydraulic drill celebrated in folklore. And since a penis isn't a machine but is rather the physical demonstration of a man's desire, there is no way it can demonstrate desire when desire is not present. Many men worry about being impotent when what they really are is just uninvolved.

A man can smile when he doesn't want to, but he can't get an erection by willpower alone. He can often get one by physical stimulation when he isn't really in the mood—and can then perform, almost mechanically, and may even get into the mood after all. But that's hardly the same or as satisfying as feeling a frank desire to start with.

The sex-on-demand myth puts as much wear and tear on a man's spirit as it does on his body. When sex becomes a duty instead of a pleasure, he will be too busy performing to enjoy the show. Copulation becomes just that—a cold-blooded medical term rather than a warm-blooded binding. There's something particularly degrading about separating body from soul during sex. In fact, it's just as damaging for men to be treated as sex objects—either by themselves or by their lovers—as it is for you.

It was to release men from the nonsensual role that Dr. Herb Goldberg, author of *The Hazards of Being Male*, drew up his guidelines for the emancipated man. Among them:

Do not participate in sex unless you are fully aroused. Never fake involvement.

Learn to say no if you have no desire.

Respect, cherish, listen, and learn from your body's responses.

Do not preoccupy yourself with techniques.

These guidelines are for the benefit of women too. By following his own feelings, rather than those he's supposed to have, a man can free himself to be a lover instead of a lovemaking engine.

In the dance of sex, the man calls the tune.   It's an old story, and maybe it even happened: Christian ministers newly arrived in Tahiti were so shocked by the uninhibited behavior of the natives they felt called upon to spread the gospel that men and women are supposed to do it only in marriage, only in the dark, and only in one way. Thus, the "missionary" position: man on top, woman on bottom.

Now, the joys of sexual diversification have been too widely heralded to be repeated here, but a few words may be in order concerning the joys of *sensual* variations.

Most men accept the idea that sex is a man's responsibility. He organizes it, he initiates it, he leads, and he *always* finishes what he's started. A man, in short, is responsible for the satisfaction of both parties—one can hardly call them partners.

This kind of approach to sex is damaging on several levels. First, it transforms sex from fun to hard work. And, in doing so, it also raises the specter of possible failure. For if a man takes sole responsibility for what happens between him and his lover, then he must take the blame for any problems that may occur in the process. And, as we have already witnessed, failing to please a woman is simply another way of failing as a man.

This also effectively cancels out any mutuality in the act, which makes lovemaking rather pointless. By definition, sex is (at least) a two-person affair—except, of course, for masturbation, but even then there is usually an image of another person in mind. If the man assumes he's general of logistics and strategy, the woman will feel like a powerless private—and the ritual of sex will become something like the ritual of war.

Finally, the take-charge attitude creates static in communication. He may have read *every* sex manual in print, he may be up on *every* late-breaking news item in sex research, he may have memorized *every* sexual variation in the *Kama Sutra*, and he may own *every* sex device ever dreamed up, but he still won't be able to please his partner unless he's first willing to allow her the opportunity to express her needs for herself. No two women are the same, and even the same woman will have different needs at different times. A sensual male is not a man who knows what to do beforehand but one who knows enough to ask his lover for information, advice, and, yes, even help.

Men only want one thing. This myth is a compendium of lesser myths. The first is that men are not capable of engaging in physical contact except when such contact leads to intercourse. (This, in turn, is related to the concept that men aren't capable of engaging in any *emotional* contact.) Pornography, dominated as it is by males, is an instructive reflection of the Male Mystique. There is little hugging, cuddling, or caressing in porno books or films, except as a prelude to the main event. Pornography, however, should never be mistaken for the real thing. Men may not always be comfortable about touching (or being touched), but this discomfort should not be confused with disinterest. You may find that if you initiate affectionate, nonsexual loveplay, such as kissing and nibbling, your man will quickly reciprocate in kind. With one nibble he'll destroy two myths: that men *always* want to make the moves, and that men *never* respond to affection. It's sometimes difficult for women, who since girlhood have been not only allowed but encouraged to ask for and demonstrate affection, to understand men's awkwardness about this.

All guys go to whorehouses for is to get kissed and hugged.

—LENNY BRUCE

A second sub-myth involved here is that men always have to perform in bed. Instead of approaching sex as a shared experience, men often feel compelled to regard it as a goal-oriented test. "Did you come? Did you come hard? Did you come more than once?" Even if he can get beyond the idea that sex equals manhood, he will still be trapped within the idea that sex equals orgasm.

But good sex does not necessarily require an orgasm. This is something women, as well as men, need to learn. In the sex-manuals, cuddling and kissing and touching are all lumped together under the heading "foreplay." This suggests that any physical form of intimacy must be directed toward penetration, intercourse, and orgasm. This may be a valid point of view if sex is considered solely a means of conception, but sensuality is recreation more than procreation, and should be welcomed as such.

The problem isn't that men want anything different, or less, than you want in bed, but that many men have never learned to see sex as anything but sex. Only by ridding himself of goals—erection, performance, and orgasms—can he free himself to appreciate and savor the range of sensual possibilities between the two of you.

Never trust a man in bed. Your mother's warned you, your father's warned you, your girlfriends all have warned you: Men are not to be trusted. They will promise you undying love to get you into bed, and then swear undying gratitude if you'll only get out of the bed—and their lives—come the dawn.

True, there are men whose mentality has never much progressed beyond the Great Hunter. Most, however, are looking just as hard as you for the unique someone to make him happy. To be suspicious of every man who looks your way is to diminish any chance either of you have for genuine contact. Besides, it clouds another issue: Men don't trust you in bed, either.

So here we are. Filled with distrust, in bed and out of bed. And since sensuality is simply not possible without trust, we've all got a major problem. The solution? That same word you might have noticed popping up throughout this chapter: communication. Men and women have to learn how to talk to each other. They cannot remain encapsulated within myths and suspicions and still hope to experience genuine joy together. In one of his classic comedy routines, Bill Cosby is reminiscing about his first sexual encounter. It was, to say the least, a mess. The woman tried to help, but, says Cosby, "I never thought of her showing me, because I'm a man and I don't want no one showing me nothing—but now I'm older and I'm beginning to wish somebody would at least kinda slip me a *note*..."

Until we begin slipping each other lots of notes, until we begin communicating with each other, sharing wants and fears, strengths and weaknesses, until we stop playing roles and start playing seriously—until that time we'll all remain trapped.

antasies

Fantasies of success, fantasies of power, of wealth, and fantasies—naturally—of sex. Everyone has them. And, writes Dr. Rubin, "there's nothing wrong with fantasies themselves, as long as fantasizing doesn't get out of control by distorting one's approach to real life. If they do, however, they produce much self-deprivation."

This is precisely what happens to some men. They create an idealized woman in their minds, one that reflects images of

themselves as he-men, one that can never be found in reality. It's not possible to discuss the literally thousands of shapes male sexual fantasies can take. But as men—unlike women, who, again according to Dr. Rubin, have daydreams that are less sexual and more romantic—tend to fantasize in the same general way, it *is* possible to discuss what seem to be the two most prevalent types of fantasies.

Hi, I'm Barbie. Fly me. For some reason, certain "feminine" occupations—like stewardess, nurse and waitress—turn the masculine dream machine on overload. Perhaps it's because these jobs can be perceived as service; perhaps it's because popular media have placed sexual connotations on them. At any rate, these women play a large part in men's dreams.

Too familiar to need much elaboration here is a typical scenario: meeting one of these women, taking her home, and then having her provide all kinds of sexual favors without her asking for anything in return. Often, the woman simply lies there passively while the ardent man turns her this way and that. Often, too, she submissively obeys all commands. Sometimes, the fantasies include bondage, physical punishment, or rape. But whatever the variation, the result is always the same. The woman, somehow both completely humiliated and completely sated, swears undying fealty to the man who's abused her (and usually swears, too, that he's the greatest lover she's ever had).

In itself, this fantasy is merely titillating. In real life, a man's unlikely to find a woman who will give everything and ask nothing. Far easier, and far less threatening, is the fantasy woman who not only requires little attention but is also filled with undiluted worship for the man using her.

It's not that men are selfish. It's just that any woman who asks a man to provide her with what *she* wants is—inadvertently—challenging him to demonstrate his manhood. Should he fail in some way, his already tenuous grasp on the masculine image becomes just that much weaker.

Hi, I'm the Dragon Lady. I'm going to fly you. In this fantasy, a man is abducted by an exotic (usually foreign) woman who ties him up and uses him in much the same fashion as he's used the Barbie doll. Men aren't as candid about this one, mainly because it places them in a nondominating—and therefore nonmasculine—position.

But although the two fantasies seem to be opposite, they are actually only opposite sides of the same dream. Both reflect a man's inner dissatisfaction with his limitations. And although they both require submissive and dominant role-playing, they represent—in at least one sense—liberation as well. In the first fantasy, the man is freed from all responsibilities to please the woman. (Not that he objects to pleasing women—it's the fact that he feels *duty-bound* to please them that's so much a restraint.) In the second, he reverses his usual role by having the woman use him.

Neither of these fantasies is particularly harmful. But if a man is extremely insecure in sexual reality, he may find himself retreating deeper and deeper into sexual fantasy. If he retreats too far, he may never be able to come back to reality. To quote an old folk song:

If one day too many a dream he'll make
Then dreaming he's alive, he may forget to wake.

No one enters the world automatically equipped with sexual know-how. And as problems faced in many men are products of misguided training, the *solutions* to the problems can be learned.

our ecstasy, his agony

Because men are conditioned to deal with life from behind an emotional mask, they tend to be more conscious of role than of content. A vast chasm tends to open between sex and sensuality. Sex concentrates solely on the physical; sensuality respects physical contact but places an equal amount of importance on emotional reverberations as well. Sex is limited to the buildup and release of tension; sensuality appreciates that tension for its own sake.

> It's like my husband's the pilot, and I'm the airplane. Push that lever, and it's a high-altitude climb. Press this and that switch, and it's wheels down, nose up, and another perfect landing. He makes me feel like my body's a control panel.

Most men, believes sexologist Dr. Mary Calderone, "don't approach lovemaking as participants out to share an enjoyable experience; they're *performers*, forced to prove to themselves that they are very, very good. They want—they need—victory, gold stars, the genuine applause and response of their audience of one. Their partner's orgasm is the sexual gold medal they are after and the key to their own sexual self-acceptance."

No other life form on this planet has as many external cells so pleasurably responsive to touch as humans. And yet—or perhaps for this very reason—we live in a society where skin-to-skin contact is highly regulated. If many men are reluctant to initiate or accept physical embraces out of bed, they are just as reluctant to go beyond purely functional (that is, sexual) embraces in bed.

Getting him to enjoy it

Men involved with sex as performance are men uninvolved with just about everything else: their sensuality, your sensuality, sensual behavior in general. This does not mean, however, that they're happy with the results.

Can this attitude be corrected? Luckily for everyone, the answer is a definite yes. Although they are not the most homogeneous group in the world, sex therapists generally agree that the male can easily unlearn performance-oriented habits by learning how to take a more passive role. In *The New Sex Therapy*, Dr. Helen Singer Kaplan suggests that "a simple 'just lie there and enjoy it' approach on the part of the

female partner usually guarantees that the male partner, if at all willing, will quickly learn how to stop acting and start *being* sexually involved." Not all male sexuality problems, however, can be so easily resolved.

In the rotten old days, all a nice woman was expected to do was lie there, stare at the ceiling, and think about putting up the preserves. Today, the role is considerably more active. But although men are no longer completely blind to the fact that women have needs, they continue to feel they must take responsibility for those needs. In a sense, men have co-opted the female orgasm—that is, they've tried to take control of the occurrence, quality, and number of orgasms a woman might have. Inevitably he is forced to two conclusions: The more you reach orgasms, the more a man he is; and your failure to attain orgasm reflects his failure as a man. Actually, it's rather ironic—virility, once the highest expression of a man's sexuality, is today defined by many men as the ability to produce a full sexual response in a woman.

Although today most men assume the attitude that "it's about time women did more than just lie there," they are in truth threatened by assertive women. The modern paradox is that he wants you to be sexually available and sexually competent, but he's terrified if you should openly express specific needs and desires.

There are several reasons for this reaction. An insecure man cannot accept the slightest intimation that there's something he could be doing other than what he *is* doing. The deceptively simple request, "Touch me here," has shriveled many a male ego.

Another reason he may fear an assertive sexual partner is that he may be uncertain of his own capabilities. If he lets you take the initiative, maybe you'll make demands on him he can't meet.

Men are frightened that if they fail to satisfy a woman, she'll sneer at him and turn elsewhere for her pleasures. Even a woman's well-publicized capacity for multiple and/or continuous orgasms is a fearsome threat to many men. Maybe once won't be enough for you. Thus his fears about sexuality are directly related to his fears about male sexuality. He can't accept yours if he fears his own is lacking.

exual dysfunctions

When pressure, fears, myths, and unrealistic expectations of sex become more urgent than sex itself, a man will typically develop a dysfunctional reaction. Although sometimes sexual problems are physical in cause, more often they are a manifestation of what is basically an emotional problem.

If a man lacks confidence, has trouble expressing feelings, or fears rejection, he may experience so much anxiety that he's unable to perform sexually. This may show up as premature ejaculation, the inability to reach orgasm, or the inability to achieve or sustain an erection. These are mentioned in Chapter 5. These problems, more than anything else, *embarrass* him, and they will probably embarrass you, too. However painful this is, what you both need to do is talk about the problem. Talking is the only way he'll be able to push through the fear (and perhaps guilt) he has about having sexual difficulties—and the only way he'll get the reassurance he needs to be able to deal with them.

Premature ejaculation

There is no known mechanism in the male body that can malfunction so as to cause premature ejaculation. Both physicians and psychiatrists agree that it *always* arises from emotional stress (and also that it has the highest cure rate of all sexual dysfunctions). The essential problem here is that the man is an "unaware" ejaculator. This means that he is oblivious to the physical signals that indicate he's nearing ejaculation. Treatment of premature ejaculation—usually by the "stop-go" masturbation technique—is simple and almost always successful.

Nonejaculation

Also known as retarded ejaculation, this is a man's inability to ejaculate while inside a woman's vagina. Although the incidence is not nearly as high as premature ejaculation, it is also thought that this condition usually results from psychological problems. Although sex-therapy techniques have sometimes proved successful, a man suffering from nonejaculation must also revise his entire approach to sex if he hopes to gain a complete cure.

Low sexual desire

If your lover has not been too interested in you lately, don't just immediately assume he no longer finds you sexually attractive. Considerably more likely is the possibility that he's lost interest in sex in general, and it isn't easy for a man to admit to this. The most common emotional reason for this is tedium. Many couples overschedule their nights (or mornings or afternoons) for sex. A break in the routine, or some spontaneity, can work wonders.

Often, low sexual desire is the result of physical problems. Persistent backaches, migraines, habitual drinking, and certain medications can also induce a disinterest in sex. Or sometimes there may be no known reason. In *Becoming Partners*, psychotherapist Carl Rogers tells of this experience in his own marriage:

During my forties there was a period of nearly a year when I felt absolutely no sexual desire—for anyone. No medical cause was found. Helen was confident that my normal urges would return and simply "stood with me" in my predicament. It is

Glossary

amatory instincts: interest in sex.

apathy: almost total loss of interest in sex.

atrophy: total loss of interest in sex.

—JAMES THURBER and E.B. WHITE,
Is Sex Necessary?

easy to think up possible psychological causes, but none of them "clicks" as far as I'm concerned. It remains a mystery to me. But her quiet continuing love meant a great deal to me and probably was the best therapy I could have had. At any rate, I gradually became sexually normal once more.

Erective dysfunction

The popular medical term is "impotence," from the Latin for "powerlessness." No other sexual problem will produce so severe a reaction in a man. To him, failing to sustain an erection is failing to sustain his status as a man.

There are three basic forms of erective dysfunction: organic, functional, and psychogenic. Organic failure is from a defect in the genitalia, reproductive system, or central nervous system. Functional failure is due to physical problems that affect blood circulation, muscles, and nerves, usually resulting from intake of drugs or alcohol, exhaustion, or low energy. Psychogenic failure is a result of emotional inhibitions. The last form is responsible for some 90 percent of all cases of impotence.

Psychogenic failure tends toward self-perpetuation. If a man fails to achieve an erection he begins—unless he's very secure—to worry about it. The more he worries about it the more failures he has. This stage is called "spectatoring." By keeping constant vigil on his sexual performance, the man blocks any normal penile response, and each incident of failure diminishes the possibility of success in the next attempt.

The following stage is the "testing" period during which his immediate goal is to have his firm penis inside a woman. In his panic for reaction, all shared intimacy will be put aside.

If the problem persists, a man then enters the "acceptance" phase. This can be bad if he just decides he's a neuter. Or it can be good. Once he can admit to himself that his problem is not going to disappear, he will usually be able to seek out help. Sometimes professional help may be needed. Often, however, a supportive relationship, one in which he's assured that his sexual problems have not reduced him as a man, may be effective. At any rate, the only way he's going to be helped is by recognizing that the problem is an emotional one and that he's still a man.

The Don Juan complex

This is not a physical dysfunction, exactly—it is more of a hyperfunction. It is a form of keeping score in a competition that lacks opponents. Not every man who is involved sexually with several women is automatically suffering from a problem—except maybe exhaustion.

The Don Juan, however, is a man who cannot make an emotional investment in his relationships with women. Over-compensation for insecurity, an obsessive need to prove masculinity, even hidden hostility toward women—any or all can drive a man from bed to bed without ever finding any real satisfaction. The he-man mask is in absolute control here; the only way a man can throw it off is to release his internal self. This is rarely easy. Dr. Rubin writes: "It is particularly difficult to make even initial inroads in a man who is very immature and full of macho confusions. It must be remembered that an undeveloped infantile mentality is essentially a selfish one, which desires all kinds of feeding and knows little or nothing of sharing or giving."

lternatives: homosexuality and dropping out

So far, we've limited the discussion of sensuality to its expression between men and women (and between men and themselves). Time now to examine some of the other available options.

With even the scientific term guaranteed to strike dread in the hearts of all upright citizens, homosexuals are among the most abused minorities in this country today. Doctors have submitted them to electric-shock treatments, lawyers and politicians have tried—often successfully—to make their private conduct a crime against the public, psychologists have described them as "abnormal," the media satirizes them, the police discriminate against them, adolescents (sometimes with their elders' blessing) form "queer-baiting" clubs to terrorize and physically assault them.

Until recently, homosexuality was widely regarded, by professional and layman alike, as a psychological disorder. But according to Dr. C. A. Tripp, author of *The Homosexual Matrix*, the most thoroughly researched and unbiased book on this subject to date, homosexuality is actually a *social* disorder. Despite all efforts to find it, there still exists no medical or psychiatric evidence that homosexuality is psychopathic behavior. In fact, many cultures have accepted homosexuality as a natural sexual alternative. But for reasons that would take an entire tome to explore, our society has decided that it is morally and ethically wrong for men to be each other's lovers. Calling homosexuality a neurotic response is just rationalizing society's decision to condemn it.

This may explain why so many psychology books persist in claiming that heterosexual men have an ingrained fear of being unconsciously, or subconsciously, homosexual. This is simply not true. Dr. Tripp points out that most males form their sexual preference before they reach their twenties. The discomfort they feel when exposed to homosexual men or homosexual activity is not a reflection of inner doubts but only of the discomfort society has trained them to feel.

In fact, it's probably a safe assumption that the majority of men have had at least one sexual, or quasi-sexual, experience with another man. (This has already been somewhat documented by the *Kinsey Report*.) This should not, however, be defined as a "homosexual experience." At the onset of puberty, a boy is bombarded with sexual needs. If he

Fear of Heterosexuality?

A homosexual young man was standing on a street corner and leisurely watching a Brigitte Bardot type of girl wiggling by. After watching her approvingly, he turned to his friend and said, "There are moments in my life when I wish I was a lesbian."

—MARTIN GROTJAHN

can't find a girl willing to experiment with these new feelings, or is afraid of girls, he may very well turn to other boys. Most men, although uneasy—to say the very least—about admitting it, have had by adolescence some physical contact with a member of their own sex. (And this is probably true for most women, too.) Mutual masturbation ("jack-off circles"), examination of each other's genitals, even limited sexual encounters (usually with an older man)—none of this is a "sin" but rather a natural part of budding sexuality.

Also, there have been some advances in the understanding and acceptance of true homosexuality. In 1880, Oscar Wilde was only able to refer to it obliquely as "the love that dare not speak its name;" in 1967, director Mike Nichols referred to it as "the love that won't shut up." But although more and more gay men are openly proclaiming their sexual nature, they are still being stereotyped by society. The most prevalent misconception of homosexuality, for example, is that there are two principal types of homosexuals—the masculine and the feminine—and that these two types act out the roles of aggressor and passive receptor when they are engaged in sex. In truth, all men have their masculine and feminine sides, and the true sensual man—whether straight or gay—explores both without guilt or misgivings. Sex between two men is as varied as it is between a man and a woman.

> I'm gay from choice, not need. My first sexual experiences were with women. The trouble with going to bed with a lady, though, was I always felt compelled to play one role. You know, the aggressive masculine lover with his helpless, admiring victim. Making love to another man gives me the chance to get into all parts of myself—not only the aggressive self, which is there, but also the passive self, the passionate self, the bawdy self, the loving self, the intimate self. Tell you the truth, I think hetero sex is dull.

Ironically, being ostracized has freed homosexual men in many ways. Because they're labeled "different," they feel free to dress more colorfully, show emotions more freely, express creative tendencies more openly. Gay men who worry less about living up to a "masculine" ideal may allow themselves to feel a natural sensuality still blocked out by many heterosexual males..

Bisexuality

If little is known about men who have sex with men, even less is known about men who have sex with both men and women. There are three main schools of thought on bisexuality.

The first states that it's an unnatural vice, a psychological abnormality—an emotional and physical reaction to confronting and accepting one's homosexuality.

The second is that bisexuality is the healthiest of all physical predilections. In *The Joy of Sex,* Dr. Alex Comfort writes: "All people are bisexual—that is to say, they are able to respond sexually to some extent towards people of either sex." He does warn, however, that "how far people act bisexually will depend on a great many things, including the society they live in, their opportunities, and how far the same-sex part of their responses worries them."

The most generally accepted point of view falls somewhere between these two extremes. James Leslie McCary, author of *Human Sexuality,* says that "bisexuality is rarely found in persons who strongly define themselves as heterosexual. Instead, it is those people who are homosexual who are most likely to experiment with both sexes. Usually, though, they remain primarily committed to their same sex, and only occasionally 'explore' heterosexual avenues of intimacy." But remember that McCary is talking about men who are committed to having experiences with both sexes— not about the many more men who merely have had occasional homosexual experiences.

Asexuality

In the winter of 1971, a New York City newspaper ran a half-column plea for "asexual liberation." It was meant to be a joke, but so many evidently sincere people responded that next week's edition ran an enormous headline: "Power to the Asexual!" But despite the deluge of mail the paper received in accord with its statement, medical science is still not sure whether asexuality actually exists. Assuming that it does, we can only regard it to be the antithesis of sensuality. Keep in mind that, strictly defined, asexuality is "complete and permanent disinterest in engaging in sexual activity." It should not be confused with either a physical condition that prevents sex or a purely conscious decision to abstain temporarily.

Celibacy

Celibacy here does not mean the lifelong vow practiced by Roman Catholic priests, certain Buddhist sects, or ascetics of any persuasion. Instead, it simply represents a temporary decision to withdraw from lovemaking. There are many valid reasons for making such a choice.

For instance, many believe that repressing their sexual energy releases other creative energies that they can then put into their work. If a man finds himself intensely involved in some project—a work proposal, say, or a term paper, or an art work, or the big game—he may discover that going without sex allows him to devote more time and concentration to the job at hand. Of course, there are probably just as many artists, athletes, and businessmen who believe just as fervently that increased sexual activity helps them get the creative juices flowing. Celibacy is basically a personal decision based on each person's specific needs.

Celibacy is also useful as a means to resharpen sexual desire, or as a means of dealing with a sudden loss of interest in sex.

Finally, a man can use celibacy to gain distance from a relationship so as to sort out his feelings, determine whether he wants to remain involved, consider how he can get more of what he wants and less of what he doesn't want.

Many men are reluctant to choose celibacy because "a man isn't a man unless he wants sex." But, writes Dr. Zilbergeld, "sexual abstinence can be helpful in many situations where a man wants to get to know himself better and come to some new understanding about where he is going." He also advises men not to worry about ill effects: "No matter how long you stay in the celibate state, you will never forget how to do it."

Celibacy—100 Years Ago

Protracted celibacy is a violation of physical laws. Where the secretion of the semen is not discharged through the natural passages, it must be absorbed into the body in a decomposed state, to clog up the system, impart impurities in the blood, and derange the actions of the lungs and the heart.

—HARMON KNOX ROOT,
*The People's Medical
Lighthouse,* 1854

FITNESS

194

& DISORDERS

FITNESS & DISORDERS

Nutrition

Ideas about what a man needs to eat to keep himself going range from the peculiar to the ridiculous. "Rocky" gulped raw eggs, Gandhi extolled the virtues of vegetables, the Abkhasians in the Caucasus Mountains of the Soviet Union swear by yogurt, farmers in Iowa love their meat and potatoes, businessmen reach their offices on a tide of black coffee and leave them in pursuit of crystal-clear martinis, Dr. J. H. Kellogg trusted in dry corn flakes, Napoleon had a penchant for truffles, Casanova praised the wonders of oysters, Ernest Hemingway wrote his books on a fuel largely consisting of peanut-butter sandwiches and margaritas.

Perhaps the strangest short-term diet of all time, though, belonged to a Cambridge, Mass., man by the name of T. J. Hicks, who vowed that the benefits of strychnine, raw eggs, and brandy propelled him to first place in the Olympic marathon of 1904. It was 90 degrees in the shade the day of the race, which was held in St. Louis that year, and the humidity was so high that spectators claimed you could reach up and wring it out of the air. Hicks was only one of the 27 who embarked on the 26-mile, 385-yard journey. He ran in grand style.

Running for gold

Whenever Hicks appeared to be flagging, his physician, following alongside in a new Oldsmobile, injected him with a few cc's of strychnine (which at the time was thought to be a stimulant) and handed him a draught of raw eggs and brandy. Reports of the race fail to record what became of the car or the doctor, but T.J. won. As he crossed the finish line he collapsed, and his prostrate body had to be carried into a nearby gymnasium. The heat and the strychnine, not to mention the grueling run, left him feeling none too well. Later that afternoon, he recovered sufficiently to emerge from the gym and claim his gold medal, but strychnine, needless to say, was on its way out as an energy booster.

By 1943, the Food and Nutrition Board of the National Academy of Sciences–National Research Council had published a list of calories and nutrients, along with the amounts of each, that a man needs every day to keep his body in good working condition. It turns out that although raw eggs are a source of protein they probably did Hicks little good during the race, since the energy needed to run his digestive system was diverted to his running muscles. With his stomach and intestines functioning at minimum efficiency, the protein wasn't broken down and absorbed, so it just lay there.

Calories

If anything helped Hicks at all, it was the brandy. Three ounces supplies nearly 600 calories, the same amount as a man burns up in an hour of running at the rate of 8 minutes a mile. The Food and Nutrition Board recommends that an average man (between the ages of 23 and 50) consume 2,700 calories a day. This number is more than adequate to run his basic life processes such as brain activity, heartbeat, and the like—which take about 75 calories an hour during the time a man is awake and 55 calories an hour while he's asleep—and still leave extra calories to burn in his daily activity. The concept of calories in food—"That piece of cake contains 500 calories"—is somewhat misleading from a nutritional point of view, because food contains carbohydrates, fats, proteins, minerals, and vitamins with nary a calorie in the lot.

Calories actually are a measurement of the amount of energy that it takes to run a man's (or a woman's) metabolic machinery. A man gets about 85 percent of the calories his

How Many Calories Is He Burning?

Activity	Calories per hour
Sleeping	55–100
Watching TV	75–100
Eating	150
Driving a car	170
Shivering	300–400
Walking	300–350
Bicycling	350–500
Swimming	300–700
Handball	600–800
Running	700–800

body needs from the carbohydrates and fats in his food. The remaining 15 percent come from proteins (which also supply essential raw material for growth, repair, and maintenance of his tissue).

Energy sources

Carbohydrates from sugar in plants and animals, as well as from starch in plant seeds, are a man's chief source of energy, fueling his central nervous system, his muscles, and all of his organs. A man can usually get all the carbohydrates his body needs from natural—which in this sense means unprocessed—foods. Fruits, even those canned but packed in their own juices, provide sugar in the form of fructose. Meat has glucose, the primary animal sugar. Corn, potatoes, rice, and wheat contain starch. The sugar a man spoons into his coffee or sprinkles on his breakfast cereal is refined from sugar cane and sugar beets, and has found its way into many of the processed foods that line supermarket shelves, leading to an overabundance of carbohydrates in the normal diet.

Socrates got along fine without ever tasting as much as a granule of refined sugar. So did Jesus, the Roman Legionnaires, and the Egyptian pharaohs. Nowadays, a man consumes about 125 pounds of sugar a year. Most nutritionists believe this to be excessive, and they blame the sugar for causing the most widespread degenerative disease in the United States—dental cavities. Aside from that, though, there is no persuasive evidence implicating sugar in any other disease.

Fat

Whatever excess sugar the body doesn't burn up, it converts into fat. The equation is roughly 3,500 stored calories to 1 pound of fat. But if for some reason a man (or a woman) doesn't get sufficient carbohydrates in his diet for all his energy needs, or if he simply burns up more than the amount his food supplies through exercise, his body will draw first on its reserves of carbohydrates stored in the liver. When those are expended, it will start burning stored fat, which is the key to losing weight.

Fat, either from foods or from around a man's waist, is the most concentrated energy source that the body can use. Ounce for ounce, it provides slightly more than double the

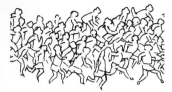

calories of carbohydrates. There are two types of fat in the ordinary daily diet: saturated and unsaturated. The difference lies in how the molecules of carbon, hydrogen, and oxygen are arranged. Animal fats, such as those in butter, meat, fish, and eggs, are saturated, and most, but not all, vegetable fats are unsaturated. (Corn and soybean oils are unsaturated; palm and coconut oils are not.) This distinction is important, because saturated fats have been linked to high cholesterol levels in the blood, which many doctors believe sets the stage for arteriosclerosis, heart attacks, and strokes. About two-thirds of the men in the United States are thought to have blood levels of cholesterol and triglyceride (the major component of the body's fat tissue) that are undesirably high.

By not eating foods high in cholesterol and saturated fats, a man can reduce the level of these chemical culprits that float in his blood, but there's no scientific proof that this alone will prevent him from getting a heart attack. Obesity, stress, high blood pressure, and smoking have all been associated with heart attacks, as has a hereditary predisposition. Nutrition undoubtedly plays a role, but a man's body does complex things with the food he eats, and most of the nutrients contained in his diet—or your's—work in concert with one another, not independently, to give him energy and keep his internal wheels, so to speak, well greased.

Vitamins

Vitamin C, for instance, has been shown to cleanse cholesterol deposits off arterial walls, at least in laboratory tests on animals, when it's administered in dosages of 500 milligrams or more a day. The cholesterol apparently is moved from the sites where it can hinder blood supply to the adrenal glands, where it is put to use in the manufacture of, among other things, male and female sex hormones. When a man doesn't get sufficient cholesterol out of the food he eats, his liver will synthesize it for shipment to his adrenals and subsequent conversion into testosterone and progesterone. In other words, if a man—or for that matter a woman—doesn't take in enough dietary cholesterol for his body's needs, then his own cells will manufacture it for use in the assembly of numerous hormones.

As if this isn't complicated enough, scientists have found that too little vitamin A in a man's diet can lead to a vitamin C

Old Wine in a New Bottle

The latest approach to vitamins is not the orange-flavored variety you may remember from your childhood. Now you can buy them in a hip flask with a jigger cap, mixed with 36-proof sherry. Recommended daily dosage: one shot, swallowed before dinner.

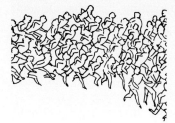

deficiency, and a man who doesn't have enough vitamin C in his system will have trouble absorbing iron. Too little iron, and he becomes anemic. The point is that a man must have an adequate supply of all the "essential" nutrients—those that his body cannot manufacture—in order to keep healthy. If one or another is in short supply, his internal balance can be upset and he'll suffer some disorder as a consequence. Nowhere is this more apparent than in the vitamin deficiencies, such as rickets (vitamin D deficiency), pellagra (niacin deficiency), or scurvy (vitamin C deficiency), to name a few, but it is just as true for protein deficiency.

Proteins

Proteins contain combinations of 20 amino acids, which are the building blocks for the growth of new cells and repair of old ones. Of the 20 amino acids, eight are essential for adults (nine for children); without all eight, cells in the body cannot assemble the proteins they need. The best protein source comes from animals. Plants do contain protein, but they often don't contain all the essential amino acids that the body needs, and that is why vegetables are a poorer source of protein than meats or dairy products.

Digestion and absorption

Once foods have been broken down into their component elements by the digestive processes in the stomach and intestines, the nutrients are absorbed and the wastes eliminated. The whole digestive process takes about 15 hours, and in that time, carbohydrates, fats, amino acids, vitamins, and minerals find their way to the tissues and organs that use these raw materials to construct all the hormones, enzymes, juices, solutions, and numerous chemicals that keep a man from running down and wearing out.

Fats, proteins, and carbohydrates supply the energy and raw material. Vitamins and minerals provide the oil to lubricate the machinery. A deficiency of a certain mineral or vitamin and one or another chemical process can grind to a halt. In the case of vitamin C, though, scientists suspect this wasn't always so. At one point in evolutionary history, man's ancestors probably manufactured their own vitamin C from sugar, as most animals still do. But then some millions of years ago this chemical attribute was apparently lost, and man—along with the Indian fruit-eating bat, the Oriental red-vented bulbul, and the guinea pig—still retains this hereditary handicap of having to find his vitamin C growing on trees or cropping out of the ground.

The role of vitamins

Vitamins have a primary role in facilitating certain chemical reactions within cells. Nonetheless, scientists discovered what vitamins actually did in the body by studying people and animals that had been naturally or experimentally deprived of certain essential substances which were later determined to be vitamins. Thus the disease beriberi, which was rampant among people in Asia who lived on a diet mainly of polished rice, was found to be a deficiency of vitamin B_1 (thiamine). This vitamin was stripped away with the rice husk when the grain was polished. Other vitamins were similarly discovered through studies done on people who were thought to be suffering some unusual type of disease restricted to their locality.

By trial and error with various vitamin dosages, scientists over the last 50 years have determined what they believe to be a generous allotment of vitamins that will keep a human body well-stocked, and food manufacturers have done their share by including supplemental vitamins in everything from soup to nuts. Thus most men or women needn't worry about missing their fair share. Still, there are nagging questions about whether or not extra amounts of certain vitamins can improve sex life or prevent the common cold. The verdict of scientists is far from being conclusive. Some contend that large doses of vitamin C—a gram or more a day, which is, at the least, 20 times the Food and Nutrition Board's recommended daily allowance—not only ward off the common cold but also alleviate its symptoms should a cold-causing virus be so callous as to settle in a man's body despite his efforts to make his system inhospitable to the germ. A number of scientific studies have been done to find out if vitamin C really can combat the common cold, and the results, though mixed, seem to indicate that the vitamin does indeed help.

Such experimental studies done with other vitamins, though, have not substantiated the sometimes outlandish claims made for them. The notion that vitamin E can, for example, boost sexual prowess is totally erroneous. The way

Sniffles Got You Down?

The best way to get rid of a stuffed nose, recommends an Indiana home remedy, is to breathe deeply nine times from a dirty sock.

that claim came to be made illustrates how nutritional fads can derive from pseudoscientific misinformation. In the search for what vitamin E does in the body—a search, by the way, that is still going on—a group of laboratory rats, males and females, were fed a diet that contained none of the vitamin. They gradually weakened, their muscles turned flabby, and some became paralyzed. The males' sperm-producing testicular tissue degenerated, leaving them sterile. The females, on the other hand, were capable of ovulating and, when mated with fertile rats, succeeded in conceiving. But the embryos disintegrated. When vitamin E was restored to their diet, the ill effects disappeared.

Out of these laboratory experiments grew the speculation that vitamin E might somehow improve reproductive function in humans and alleviate muscular weakness, and so appropriate test subjects were gathered and administered the vitamin. Alas, the magical effect that had been hoped for never turned up.

eight

About the only thing that influences how much a normal man should eat is the amount of physical activity he engages in. The average man, for whom the Food and Nutrition Board designed its recommended dietary allowance (RDA) table, is 23 years old, stands 5 feet 9 inches, and weighs 154 pounds. He also engages in only light activity during the day, burning between 120 and 239 calories an hour in an environment that averages 68°F. If a man is older or works in an office where he is sitting most of the day or works outdoors doing heavy manual labor, his energy needs are going to be different from the so-called "average man's," and he'll need to adjust the number of calories in his diet either up or down depending on the level of his activity. Other than that, he needn't modify any specific nutrient, because the recommended daily allowances are ample for anything he does.

This isn't true for you, though. You need more iron than a man to replace that lost in menstrual blood. (Iron is an important component of hemoglobin in red blood cells.) And your vitamin, calorie, and calcium requirements, among others, increase during pregnancy—and afterward, if you decide to breast-feed. (Obstetricians have calculated that

having a baby takes an extra 40,000 calories, or nearly 200 a day over the 2,000 that are recommended for nonpregnant women between the ages of 18 and 35. Breast feeding requires an additional 1,000 calories a day.)

Calories are burned in lots of ways—making love, for one, uses about 150 calories—but mental activity, surprisingly enough, burns up virtually none. An hour of intense thought figuring out how to fill in his income tax forms may leave a man dripping with nervous perspiration, but his brain gets by during that time with as few calories as there are in one oyster cracker. To put a sizable dent in the calories his food supplies him with, a man has to move his muscles in more strenuous activity than pushing a pencil across a sheet of paper.

Overweight

There are only two ways for a man to maintain his desirable weight, and they work best together. The first is to watch what he eats, limiting the number of calories to those he expects to burn up. And the second is to exercise.

The realization that he's a few pounds overweight usually sneaks up on a man in his late twenties or thirties. He's been concentrating on making a living, settling down, perhaps starting a family, and he hasn't paid much attention to what he's been eating or to the fact that he hasn't worked up a good sweat since college. Then one day he notices that his pants are getting a little tight around his waist, his belt has no more notches to let out, and he has sprouted what are euphemistically called "love handles," those bulges between his hips and his ribs.

Some men are bothered by what they call "going to seed," and some aren't. A man can be happy, well adjusted, and comfortable with himself a few pounds overweight, just as a woman can be. But the transformation of a man who takes his weight and physical fitness for granted into a man who eats cottage cheese and jogs can be quite startling.

It is as difficult for a man to ignore the pressure to trim down (with the implication that he'll simultaneously become vigorous and attractive) as it is for a woman. The propaganda for dieting and exercising is everywhere—in advertising, in the movies, in magazines, on the best-seller lists.

The stigma of being overweight is further reinforced by evidence that extra pounds can lead to high blood pressure, varicose veins, heart disease, hernias, gall-bladder disease, diabetes, and arthritis. An extra 40 pounds can also cut four or more years off a man's life expectancy.

Unless a man has had overweight problems from an early age, he's usually at or near his ideal weight a few years after adolescence, or by about age 20. A man is at his ideal weight when he is within the "pound boundaries" for his frame size and he can grab no more than an inch of fat between his fingers when he pinches the skin overlying his upper arm, thigh, or stomach. His relaxed waist measurement should also be at least 2 inches less than his deflated chest measurement.

Desirable Weights For Men Aged 25 and Over

Height		Weight (in pounds, wearing indoor clothing)		
Feet	Inches	Small Frame	Medium Frame	Large Frame
5	1	112–120	118–129	126–141
5	2	115–123	121–133	129–144
5	3	118–126	124–136	132–148
5	4	121–129	127–139	135–152
5	5	124–133	130–143	138–156
5	6	128–137	134–147	142–161
5	7	132–141	138–152	147–166
5	8	136–145	142–156	151–170
5	9	140–150	146–160	155–174
5	10	144–154	150–165	159–179
5	11	148–158	154–170	164–184
6	0	152–162	158–175	168–189
6	1	156–167	162–180	173–194
6	2	160–171	167–185	178–199
6	3	164–175	172–190	182–204

—according to the Metropolitan Life Insurance Company

Weight increases of 5 to 10 pounds over a man's ideal weight are not unusual for men in their thirties, but when the gain approaches 20 pounds that's the danger sign defined by doctors as the beginning of obesity. Twenty pounds or more of excess fat puts a measurable burden on a man's—or a woman's—cardiovascular and respiratory systems. He tires more easily than he would if he weighed less, he runs short of

Rules for Dieters

No matter what diet a man (or woman) chooses, it should meet these criteria:

It must reduce the number of calories eaten.

It must be adequate in all other nutrients.

It must be a diet that can be eaten over a long period of time.

It should not stress rapid weight loss (more than two-to-three pounds a week).

It should include some form of physical exercise.

It must be different from your previous diet.

It must form the basis of permanent new eating habits.

–T. P. LAUDA and
A. ELIZABETH SLOAN,
Food For Thought

breath with less exertion, and the decline in the amount of physical activity he's capable of takes a toll in his level of fitness. His muscles weaken, his joints lose their flexibility, his heart pumps less efficiently.

The number of fat cells in a person's body—man's or woman's—doesn't increase appreciably beyond age six. Instead, the individual fat cells enlarge as weight is gained. They keep enlarging as unused carbohydrates and fats in the diet are converted into fatty globules and stored in adipose, or fat, tissue. Men tend to add extra pounds to the abdomen, developing the familiar potbelly, or middle-aged spread. In a woman's body, though, excess fat gets distributed more widely. Hips, upper arms, breasts, and thighs are the likeliest spots for fat to accumulate on a woman.

Dieting

Dieting, to most men, means cutting out snacks, sweets, extra helpings, maybe skipping a meal here and there, or switching to light beer. Those who take their diet more seriously, or who are following their doctor's orders, may have to pay more attention to such things as saturated fats, salt, and carbohydrate-rich foods. To them, a prudent diet is not a weekend affair, and it's not something to be done once a month when the bathroom scale gets dusted off and stepped on.

Eating sensibly is a matter of attitude. Some men have the right attitude, some don't. Others are forced by ill health

or dwindling energy to learn about eating right. The best guideline is for a man to stay clear of fad diets, those that proclaim "Instant Weight Loss" or "Two Weeks to Health," and follow instead a prudent course recommended by nutritional authorities. This means that he shouldn't overdo fats and sugar. And he shouldn't eat anything that he knows from past experience will disagree with his stomach.

As a man gets older—and that doesn't mean sixties, it means mid-thirties (by the time half of his expectable life is over)—his digestive system can no longer tolerate the abuse it could when he was younger. Of course, this is true for you too. Greasy foods, highly spiced foods, hard-to-digest foods all cause gastric and intestinal flux. A slice of pepperoni pizza or a chili dog may go down as easily as it ever did, but once it hits bottom, his stomach may feel queasy.

Exercise and Fitness

Watching what he eats may help a man lose weight and protect his digestive tract, but it won't keep him fit. The only thing that improves fitness is exercise. Even if a man doesn't increase the number of calories he consumes, he will begin gaining weight just by the normal decline in physical activity and the metabolic changes his body undergoes as he ages. The number of calories burned by the metabolic processes that run a man's heart, lungs, digestive system, and other internal organs declines by 2 percent a decade. Thus a 40-year-old man needs about 50 calories a day less to fuel his basal metabolism than he did when he was 20. What's more, unless a 40-year-old man makes a concerted effort to exercise regularly, he'll retain more of the calories his food supplies than he did when he was younger and more physically active.

That's not to say there are no 40-year-old men who are physically active. More and more of them are every year, simply because the benefits of exercise are hard to ignore. Over the last 20 years, and particularly during the last five years, scientists have documented the changes a human body undergoes during regular exercise. Although there is no proof that these changes will lead to longer life, the presumptive evidence supports the idea that the more fit a man or woman is, the better the body will be at warding off the deleterious effects of stress and disease.

Once a man's growth is completed, his physical condition won't improve unless he places increased physical demands on his body through exercise. Almost any activity can be considered exercise, but some things a man does—or can do—are more productive than others in terms of conditioning his body. Walking burns about 200 calories an hour, rhythmically contracts and relaxes muscles in the legs and back, gets the blood moving by squeezing the veins in the lower extremities. But it is not as good a form of exercise as running or jogging, swimming, cycling, skipping rope, or rowing a boat. When these types of activity are sustained for 20, 30, or more minutes at a stretch, they raise a man's body temperature, increase his heart and breathing rates, induce sweating, force his muscles to use more oxygen and burn more calories, and increase his blood flow.

Effects of exercise

Regular, vigorous exercise over a period of weeks can make significant changes in a person's body. Besides causing fat to be burned—initially at the rate of 1 to 2 pounds a week (provided the calorie intake doesn't increase)—exercise can lower the resting heart rate, decrease some types of high blood pressure, and increase the ability of muscles to consume oxygen without producing lactic acid, which is the chemical that's responsible for feeling fatigued. As a person continues to exercise, his or her body will make other adjustments. The resting metabolic rate will decrease and, concomitantly, energy reserves will go up. The diameter of the capillaries that feed muscles and the heart will widen. Blood chemistry will change, causing—at least in some men—a decline in high cholesterol and triglyceride levels.

On top of all this, exercise is the best way to work off nervous tension, the steam that accumulates from stress. There's also evidence that exercise improves mental functioning by making a man more alert. Men who are used to regular running or swimming say that it clears the fuzz out of their heads. When they miss their exercise routine they feel sluggish and out of sorts. Some men even report a heightened consciousness—a sort of clear-headedness—when they are exercising, and this can be attributed in part to the increased blood flow to the brain that occurs during a good workout.

Starting an exercise program

Just as there is no ideal diet, there is no single form of exercise that will suit all men. How he chooses to exercise will depend on where he lives, how much spare time he has, and what he enjoys doing. If a particular type of exercise is looked on as a chore, a man will quickly tire of it. All his good intentions won't mean a thing if he doesn't exercise regularly, either every other day, or better yet, every day, for a minimum of 20 minutes at a stretch. There are no short cuts to getting, or staying, in shape. No one's body can store the conditioning effects of exercise. A muscle has to be used every 48 to 72 hours to stay conditioned.

Experiments conducted by NASA showed that muscles deteriorate at a phenomenal rate if they're not regularly exercised. Of course, they don't waste away entirely because they're used in routine daily activities. But for every five days a man doesn't exercise, his muscles lose one-fifth of their maximum strength. They not only get weak, they get flabby and they tire quickly when they aren't used. This is the condition most muscles are in when a man decides that it's time for him to embark on a personal crusade to get himself back into shape. He purchases a pair of jogging shoes, digs out his old sweatshirt, and takes to the road.

A man simply cannot expect that his unconditioned body will announce to him that he's done enough for one day. The internal warning system works only when a man overreaches the absolute limits of his capacity. Then something is bound to give. In horses, that's when a bone shatters or, at the very least, the horse comes up lame. A man's body usually doesn't respond so dramatically. All it takes is a severe cramp for a man to acknowledge that it's time to quit. (Cramps are a form of muscle spasm caused when the cells are starved for oxygen.) If he doesn't listen to his body, but tries to "run through" his pain, then he may really injure himself by tearing a muscle or overstretching ligaments.

Short of actually doing damage to himself, a man has no way of knowing that he's done enough on his first day out unless he heeds the adage, "Train, don't strain." And that goes for any new exercise regime he may be embarking on. This means warm up first and start out slowly. A few minutes of stretching and limbering exercises let the muscles and joints know what they're in for. He should start out at a slow pace until the rest of the body has a chance to warm up. At the beginning, 15 or 20 minutes is plenty. As his body becomes conditioned, he should lengthen the time spent exercising as well as the intensity of the exercise.

During strenuous exercise, the heart can pump eight times as much blood as when it is resting, or some 12 gallons a minute. The body temperature can shoot up from its normal 98.6° F to 105° F, without causing any harm. To counterbalance such overheating, sweat glands can pour out as much as 2 quarts of fluid an hour. A runner can lose 10 percent of his or her body weight through sweat loss over the course of a marathon. But the sweat that's worked up in the average half-hour or one-hour jog doesn't help a man—or a woman— lose weight, nor does it "clean out the pores." From all available evidence, sweating doesn't remove any toxic substances from the body, all it does is cool the blood off and lower the body's temperature, similar to what a radiator does in a car. Nor does the amount a man sweats have anything to do with how fit he is getting. On a hot, humid day he can work up a sweat while reclining in a hammock. A man becomes fit only by exercising his muscles, not his sweat glands.

Any kind of exercise will—over time—condition the muscles and melt fat off a man's body. But the fat won't come off any specific area, it will come off in small amounts everywhere at once. (Fat is lost as it is converted into glucose for the muscles to use during contraction.) So spot-reducing by weight-lifting exercises and calisthenics doesn't work any better for a man than it does for a woman, which is not at all. Nonetheless, these exercises will contribute to overall weight loss. And even if a man gets most of his exercise by running or jogging, he'll get additional benefit by doing calisthenics, such as push-ups, sit-ups, and the like, because these activities exercise muscles that don't get much use in running.

Effects of flabbiness

Why does a man let himself get out of shape? He may have always thought of himself as unathletic. So anything that smacks of sports turns him off. Repetitive calisthenics may not produce fast enough results for him, so he loses interest. And, of course, after he's married, he may think that there's no longer any reason to impress anyone with the flatness of his stomach or the tautness of his biceps.

The Two-Legged Diet

Is running a good way to lose weight? Yes, according to the editors of *Runner's World*. Of their readers who started running as adults, two-thirds lost weight.

Here are the results of their readers survey:

Under 10 pounds lost:	11%
10–20 pounds lost:	26%
20–30 pounds lost:	14%
Over 30 pounds lost:	15%
Little or no change:	34%

When a man is out of shape, he puts additional strain on parts of his body that can least afford the burden. The excess fat that gathers around the abdominal organs puts a strain on the abdominal muscles, eventually weakening them so much that the internal organs sag out of position. This can hamper intestinal movements and otherwise interfere with digestion. Weakness in the abdominal musculature can also lead to hernia, a condition in which a loop of intestine gets pushed through into an area it doesn't belong. Hernias usually occur where blood vessels or part of the digestive tract pass from one anatomical region to another. The most common site for hernia in a man is the inguinal canal, a passageway in the pelvis through which the testes descend just before (or sometimes just after) birth. The spermatic cord and blood vessels that supply the testes are the only structures that normally remain in this canal. However, a weakness in the muscle that covers the top of the canal, between the pelvis and abdomen, can lead to an inguinal hernia. Sometimes a truss is enough to push the misplaced loop of intestine temporarily back into place. Usually, though, the hernia has to be corrected surgically.

Lack of muscle conditioning can also place undue strain on a man's spinal column. Backache, which is the second leading cause of pain after headache, is frequently the result of asking too much from an unconditioned muscle. When a man stretches awkwardly to flail at a tennis ball or lifts a heavy carton out of the trunk of his car, he's liable to overstretch a muscle in his lower back. The muscle responds by going into spasm, actually knotting up into a tight ball. Painful as this is, it serves a purpose in that it prevents a man from further exertion that might damage his spine or the nerves that branch off from his spinal cord.

A man bending over to lift a 50-pound weight puts over 600 pounds of pressure at the juncture of his spine where it curves into the small of his back. Without the muscles that support the spinal column, his backbone would snap like a matchstick. Even weak muscles provide a certain degree of support. But the stronger a muscle is, the more strain it can take. One of the best ways for a man to improve the condition of his back muscles is by improving his posture. Chin up, shoulders back, hips tilted forward (by contracting the buttock muscles) are the three movements that align the spine into a position that takes extra tension off the back muscles. But posture is something most men forget about after third grade, scout camp, or the army.

rugs

The average man slouches toward 40 with fits and starts of exercise here and there. When he's tired and it looks as though he's going to drag himself through the day, does he exercise to get his blood going again? No. He grabs a cup of coffee and relies instead on the stimulating effect of caffeine to give him energy. The caffeine in one cup of coffee can measurably increase a man's heart rate and blood pressure.

All stimulant drugs, including caffeine, nicotine, amphetamine, and cocaine, increase the activity of the central nervous system. Electric impulses fire at a more rapid pace, and in some sections of the brain, the stimulation enhances one function, but, paradoxically, inhibits others. Stimulants make a man more alert, but depress his appetite.

Amphetamines as appetite inhibitors were once widely prescribed for people who wanted to lose weight without effort. But these drugs have unwanted effects as well. They are habit-forming and they make sleeping difficult. To counter these effects, some men resorted to taking barbiturates or other central-nervous-system depressants, especially alcohol. These drugs inhibit electrical activity in the nervous system, and they make a man feel calmer and sleepier. It's not too difficult to see how uppers and downers could be easily abused. Amphetamines could be taken during the daytime to increase productivity, by boosting self-confidence and strength. In the evening, barbiturates could be taken to put a damper on the flow of nervous energy.

Any drug that a man takes, no matter if it's obtained legally or illegally, will affect one or more of his body's functions. Aspirin, for example, will reduce body temperature, ease inflammation, and lessen pain by affecting different regions of a man's body in different ways. A single 5-grain aspirin will also increase the time it takes his blood to clot by a minute or more for as long as a week after the tablet is swallowed. That is why aspirin isn't recommended for a man if he has bleeding ulcers or any blood-clotting disability. The same goes for a woman.

Tobacco

The most frequently used drug in the world—tobacco—isn't ordinarily considered a drug by those who smoke it. But the nicotine, tars, and gases that are inhaled each have a specific effect in the body. Nicotine is the addictive substance. It's the substance that a man's body craves when he goes out at 11 p.m. to buy another pack. Nicotine gives cigarettes their "kick," and it also gives them their poison. At the rate that it's inhaled in cigarette smoke, nicotine can dull the sense of touch, increase the heart's rate, and constrict blood vessels in the brain. The tars in cigarettes have been linked to bronchitis, emphysema, and lung cancer. And the tars in a single low-tar cigarette can impair the lungs' ability to clean themselves. The gases, such as carbon monoxide, in cigarette smoke can reduce the oxygen content of the blood, putting a strain on the heart, which then has to pump more blood to get sufficient oxygen to all the cells in a man's body. Smoking is clearly unhealthy from a number of standpoints. More men take the habit up and continue it than women, though the statistics have been evening out for the past decade.

Marijuana

Marijuana smoking causes a number of changes in the body. It increases heart rate, dilates capillaries inside the eyelids, stimulates appetite, inhibits the salivary glands, and sedates some parts of the brain (it impairs short-term memory) while stimulating sight and sound centers. Marijuana has been around for thousands of years, and in that time it has been used to treat scores of ailments. In the 1800s, it was prescribed for rheumatism, migraine headache, and painful menstruation. Though it is no longer prescribed, marijuana is available, and, like other street drugs, it is used exclusively for its effects on mood and perception. A number of studies have been conducted by scientists looking for harmful effects of marijuana smoking, but none have been conclusively proven. Marijuana apparently doesn't cause brain damage and it doesn't lower immunity or testosterone levels. But it may damage lung cells, as does tobacco smoke.

Alcohol

Alcohol, like marijuana, removes inhibitions. But although a man may think he's being stimulated by the alcohol in a beer, or glass of wine, or shot of whiskey, he's actually being depressed. Alcohol slows down impulse activity in the central nervous system, and large enough quantities of it can anesthetize brain cells. It also temporarily impairs liver function, slows reaction time, irritates the lining of the stomach, and interferes with learning.

The effect that alcohol has on a man depends on the amount of it he drinks. An ounce and a half of 90 proof spirits, which is equal to two beers or about 6 ounces of wine, will give a man a sense of well-being. He'll begin feeling tranquil, and if he has any anxieties—and who hasn't?—they'll seem to vanish. With double that quantity of alcohol his muscular movements will become slower and less accurate. It will take him more time to react to visual stimulation, so if he's driving a car, he won't be able to get his foot to the brake as quickly as when he hasn't had anything to drink.

As a man's alcoholic comsumption goes up, he becomes increasingly intoxicated. His attention and concentration spans diminish. His movements become more erratic. Walking turns into a stagger as his ability to coordinate his muscles decreases. Fifteen ounces of 90-proof vodka (or whiskey) over a short time can make him lose consciousness.

The man who has a drink before supper is probably doing no harm to himself. The alcohol begins being absorbed almost as soon as it gets to his stomach. As it goes down, it stimulates his sense of taste and, once it enters his stomach, it stimulates gastric juices. Most of the alcohol is absorbed into the bloodstream through the intestine, not the stomach. Nevertheless, any food that's in a man's stomach when he starts drinking will slow the alcohol-absorption rate. Once the alcohol gets into his bloodstream, it will diffuse to all the tissues in his body. (In a pregnant woman, alcohol will pass through the placenta into the fetus.) His brain, though, will be affected more than any other organ.

Of the many claims made for alcohol, the most controversial is the one that says it will do wonders for a man's sex life. No one has yet found a drug whose aphrodisiacal powers are beyond a shadow of a doubt, but alcohol in small quantities comes close. The limitation to small quantities is important, because if a man consumes too much, he'll have a hard time resisting the urge to sleep. Alcohol doesn't directly stimulate the sex center in a man's brain, but if circumstances

The Effects of Alcohol

Macduff: *What three things does drink especially provoke?*

Porter: *Nose-painting, sleep, and urine. Lechery, sir, it provokes and unprovokes—it provokes the desire but takes away the performance.*

—WILLIAM SHAKESPEARE,
Macbeth

lead him to think about having sex, alcohol may strip away whatever inhibitions he ordinarily has.

Pound for pound, men are not better—or worse—at holding their alcohol than women. Their bodies metabolize it at the same rate yours does, and it produces the same effects no matter who is drinking it. It is true, though, that the more alcohol a person drinks over a period of time, the more he or she will need to produce the desired effects. However, large quantities of alcohol consumed over a long time can destroy brain and liver cells, and lead to a variety of ailments including nervous tremors and cirrhosis (which causes jaundice, weakness, and weight loss, among other things).

How drugs act on the body

Most drugs can be harmful to one or another type of cell in the body. That's why when physicians prescribe any medication, they are careful to note the amount that should be taken. Small doses of barbiturates can help a man fall asleep; large doses can kill him. Small doses of marijuana can make a man feel pleasantly high; large doses can cause frightening hallucinations. Small doses of opiumlike drugs (such as morphine or demerol) can suppress pain; large doses can inhibit breathing. The same goes for any drug, from nicotine and caffeine to amphetamines and alcohol.

The dose of a drug isn't the only thing that alters the effects it has on a man's body. His internal chemistry, even his mood, can modify the eventual effects of a drug. And drugs themselves can enhance or inhibit the effects of one another. Alcohol together with barbiturates can cause coma and death in much lower quantities than either alone. In certain situations, marijuana can heighten anxiety rather than inhibit it.

If you could watch what a drug does when it gets inside a human body, you'd see that it is absorbed by cells in much the same way nutrients are. But unlike nutrients, which cells utilize in fashioning all the substances necessary for normal function, drugs interfere with the cellular machinery. Some drugs stimulate internal chemical processes, others inhibit them. But in both instances, drugs upset the natural flow of chemical events inside cells. These normal processes are under the guidance of a man's individual genetic blueprint. Slight variations in the genetic message cause specific chemical processes to be faster—or slower—in one man than another.

So some men are able to metabolize certain drugs faster than other men. And, by the same token, certain drugs cause wider—or lesser—fluctuations in one man's internal chemistry than in another man's.

iseases of men

Most diseases are common to men and women, though the incidence may vary. The ten leading causes of death among men, in order of frequency, are diseases of the heart, cancer, stroke, accidents, pneumonia, diseases of early infancy, diabetes, arteriosclerosis, cirrhosis, and emphysema. A man has about a one in five chance of having a heart attack before he's 60 years old. Before menopause a woman is three to five times less likely to have a heart attack, but afterward her chance of dying from heart disease is equal to that of a man. Women also have a lower death rate than men in 57 of the 64 specific causes of death listed by the major insurance companies. The diseases in which the mortality of women leads that of men include diabetes, pernicious anemia, uterine cancer, and specific abnormalities associated with childbirth.

A man's genes can apparently make him more, or less, susceptible to certain illnesses, including diabetes, heart disease, stroke, and many other major killers. Men can also inherit about 60 disorders that rarely affect women, including colorblindness, hemophilia, and one type of muscular dystrophy. The genetic abnormalities that account for each of these inherited conditions are located on the X chromosome, which a man inherits from his mother.

The transmission of these conditions is governed by the laws of inheritance that have been discovered by geneticists over the last two centuries. In studying how certain traits are transmitted from generation to generation, they've learned that some genes are dominant and others are recessive. The dominant genes are the ones that function in determining traits, while the recessive genes remain inactive. Among the genes that control the iris color, the one that causes brown eyes is dominant over the one that causes blue eyes. Since most genes work in pairs, the dominant member always gets preference over its recessive counterpart. But if a man inherits two recessive genes, one from his mother and one from his father, the recessive trait will show up.

Defective genes

This arrangement answered a number of questions about inheritance, but it left one problem unsolved. What about those conditions that seemed to affect only men? Geneticists discovered the genes that determine these conditions in a man work alone, and unlike most other genes, a single recessive gene will cause the disorder. Furthermore, they found that the genes for each of these "men-only" conditions are carried on the X chromosome. Its partner, the Y chromosome in men, carries genes that determine male sex, but little or no other active genetic material. So if a man inherits an abnormal gene on his maternal X chromosome, he will develop whatever condition the single gene causes.

For a woman to get any one of these disorders, her mother would have to be a carrier—that is, have a single defective X chromosome—and her father would have to be afflicted with the condition. Even so, her chances would be 50-50 that she would inherit her mother's normal X chromosome, not the defective one, and thus only be a carrier herself and not have the disease. A single, normal gene for blood-clotting, or for the ability to distinguish between red and green, or for any other X-linked traits, is sufficient to mask the defective gene. However, a woman can still pass the abnormal gene on to her children. Half of her daughters, on a statistical basis, will be carriers, while all of her sons will be afflicted with the condition.

The defective gene, though, doesn't stop causing trouble with the first generation that inherits it. The daughters who are carriers can pass it on to their children, both male and female; and the sons who are afflicted can pass it on to their daughters. Queen Victoria of England was a carrier of the hemophilia gene, which either arose spontaneously as a mutant gene within her cells or was inherited from one of her parents. She transmitted the hemophilia gene to at least two of her five daughters and to her only son. They, in turn, transmitted it through marriage and subsequent children to many of the royal families in Europe.

Gout

Besides being more vulnerable to certain genetic diseases, men also suffer more frequently than women from gout, ulcers, and accidents. Gout is a potentially crippling

Premature Heart Attacks— Genetically Caused?

Twenty percent of all heart attacks occurring in men before the age of 60 are caused by one of three genes that regulate the body's fat metabolism. (Approximately another 5 percent is attributed to polygenic causes.) These single-gene abnormalities predisposing to heart attack were estimated to occur in one in every 160 Americans, making them the most common disease-producing genes in our population.

—U.S. PUBLIC HEALTH SERVICE,
What are the facts about genetic disease?

form of arthritis in which crystals of uric acid, from the breakdown of protein in the body, are deposited in the cartilage of joints. The favorite lodging places of these crystals are in the big-toe, ankle, and finger joints. The poet John Milton suffered from the agonies of gout, which supposedly helped him find the right words to depict the horrors of Hell in *Paradise Lost*. But he wasn't the only famous sufferer. Gout afflicted Benjamin Franklin, Charles Darwin, Henry VIII, Michelangelo, Isaac Newton, and Alexander the Great, to name a few. Nowadays gout still afflicts more men than women; about 95 percent of the 1,000,000 people with gout in the U.S. are men, most of whom are over 45. Women, if they do develop gout at all, get it after menopause. The throbbing pain of a gout attack—which usually starts at night—can be lessened with anti-inflammatory drugs and painkillers, and the levels of uric acid can be reduced with still other drugs and dietary restrictions.

Ulcers

Ulcers are most common in men between the ages of 20 and 50. They can form and disappear without causing any symptoms, so some men never know that they had an ulcer. An ulcer occurs when digestive acids erode away a small patch—usually no larger than three-quarters of an inch in diameter—of the lining in the duodenum, or in the stomach's lining. Stress, spicy foods, and alcohol have all been linked to causing ulcers, as has a genetic predisposition. Even when an ulcer does cause pain or bleeding, it can heal without surgery if a man (or woman) adheres to a bland diet, keeps himself away from too many stressful situations, and takes antacids whenever he feels a twinge of trouble.

Accidents

The first known automobile casualty in the U.S. occurred in 1899 when a man by the name of Mr. Bliss was struck as he was trying to cross what he probably thought was a quiet dirt road. Ever since then, men have been killed and injured more frequently than women in automobile accidents, either as drivers or passengers or as pedestrians. Men also die more frequently than women in accidental falls, drownings, and fires, and from accidental bullet wounds. This doesn't mean that men are more accident-prone than women. No one has yet shown that men have any stronger unconscious impulse to harm themselves than women. Why then do men make up nearly 70 percent of all accidental mortality victims? The answer probably lies in their fondness for proving their manhood in foolhardy ways.

Prostate problems

As a man ages, his body becomes more susceptible to a variety of ailments, but one that plagues the majority of men over 50 is prostate enlargement. The prostate gland lies at the base of the bladder, and as it enlarges it constricts the urethra (which passes through it), leading to problems with urination and, possibly, bladder and kidney infections. Normally, the gland measures 1 to 1½ inches in diameter, but it can enlarge to 10 times that size. No one knows precisely why the prostate enlarges with age, but the best guess is that it has to do with the decline in male hormone production.

In the early stages of prostatic enlargement, a man may notice that it takes longer to start urinating, and that the stream is not as full or as forceful as it once was. As the degree of enlargement increases, he'll have trouble stopping his urine stream. By this time, the enlarged prostate has prevented the bladder from emptying fully each time a man urinates, so he'll find himself having to go to the bathroom more frequently, and dribbling urine for several minutes afterward.

The prostate gland can become infected at any time during a man's life after puberty. The treatment for this involves antibiotics and a disconcerting procedure called prostatic massage. The fluid that accumulates in an infected or an inflamed prostate can be dislodged if the gland itself is gently pressed. A urologist does this by inserting a finger into a man's rectum and applying forward pressure toward the region in which the gland lies. Digital examination is also the way a urologist is able to examine the prostate for evidence of enlargement that's due to normal aging or cancer. The prostate is nearly as common a site for the development of cancer in men as the breast is in women. However, not all lumps or enlargements in the prostate (or the breast, for that matter) are malignant.

When the prostate is found to be cancerous, the best thing a man can do to halt the malignancy from spreading is to undergo prostatic surgery. The gland can be removed in two ways: from the rear, through the rectum, which can leave a man impotent because some nerves necessary for erection are unavoidably severed; or through the penis, in an operation that is technically called a transurethral resection, or TUR for short. In performing a TUR, a urologist first passes a narrow tube or catheter into a man's urethra. He is able to remove the gland piecemeal through this tube, using a surgical instrument that allows him to both shred the gland and watch what he's doing at the same time. After a man recovers from a TUR, he is able to achieve an erection and have an orgasm, but his semen is not ejaculated from his penis. Instead, it is propelled backward into his bladder. The sensations, nevertheless, are much the same, and if a man is prepared in advance for this occurence, his sex life can be entirely normal except that he cannot father children.

In ordinary circumstances, the normal secretions of a man's prostate not only ensure the motility of his sperm, but also kill off at least some harmful bacteria that may enter his urinary tract. This is one of the reasons why men suffer far fewer urinary-tract infections than women. The antibacterial property of prostatic fluid has no effect, however, on the organisms that cause venereal disease.

Venereal diseases

Gonorrhea, which is the most common venereal disease, was named nearly 18 centuries ago by the Greek physician Galen, who mistook the discharge caused by the disease in man for an involuntary flow of semen. The confusion was cleared up in the intervening centuries, and now it's known that gonorrhea results from infection with a coffee-bean-shaped bacterium that is transmitted through sexual relations.

Three to seven days after a man is infected with these bacteria, he feels some discomfort in the tip of his penis. The next symptom will be a thick, yellowish discharge from his urethra, followed by a burning or stinging sensation during urination. If the bacteria aren't stopped by appropriate antibiotic medication, they can spread upwards (causing scarring in his reproductive tract that can lead to sterility) to his prostate and bladder, and from there the bacteria can infect his joints and even the valves of his heart.

Syphilis, which is less common than gonorrhea, is a more serious disease that, left untreated, will damage a man's

It Only Hurts When I . . .

Allergies come in all shapes, sizes, and forms. The most unpleasant must be the allergy reported by a 30-year-old woman, who said she suffered from vaginal itching, swelling of the eyes, hives, or difficult breathing after sex. Since this occurred no matter whom she made love with, doctors believe she is allergic to male sperm.

heart, blood vessels, and brain. The first sign of syphilis is a painless sore or ulcer, usually on the tip of the penis. It will disappear without treatment, but that doesn't mean the disease is over. The second stage makes itself known a few weeks later when a rash erupts over much of a man's body. This can be accompanied by fever, swollen glands, and general achiness—all the same symptoms as the disease causes in women. If the disease still goes untreated, the bacteria will go into hiding, or a latent phase, as it is called. Over a period of years the bacteria will slowly but irrevocably destroy a man's cardiovascular and central nervous system. Penicillin, as well as a few other antibiotics, is the recommended treatment for syphilis and gonorrhea.

Another prevalent venereal disease is genital herpes, which is transmitted by a cousin of the virus that causes the common cold sore. The virus causes painful blisters to erupt on a man's penis, glands to swell in his groin, and general fatigue. At present there is no treatment to combat the virus. The blisters can take weeks or months to clear up, and then, for no apparent reason, they recur. Once a man is infected with genital herpes he may harbor the virus for life, but he won't always be infectious. The virus can only be transmitted in its active phase, when blisters are visible.

Surviving

Medicine has made substantial inroads into many of the illnesses and ailments that men are heir to, and the lessons of nutrition and exercise have produced ample documentation about the things a man has to do if he expects to get the most out of life. But, despite all this, some men are bound to get sick once in a while, and some will die young. On the whole, a man's body wears out more quickly than a woman's. The wonder of it all, though, is why, with everything that he does to himself, he lasts as long as he does. If anything, a man's longevity is a testament to his body's amazing resiliency. It can bounce back from nearly all the trials he puts it through and still manage to dance a step or two, to laugh, and to hug well into ripe old age.

WORKING MEN

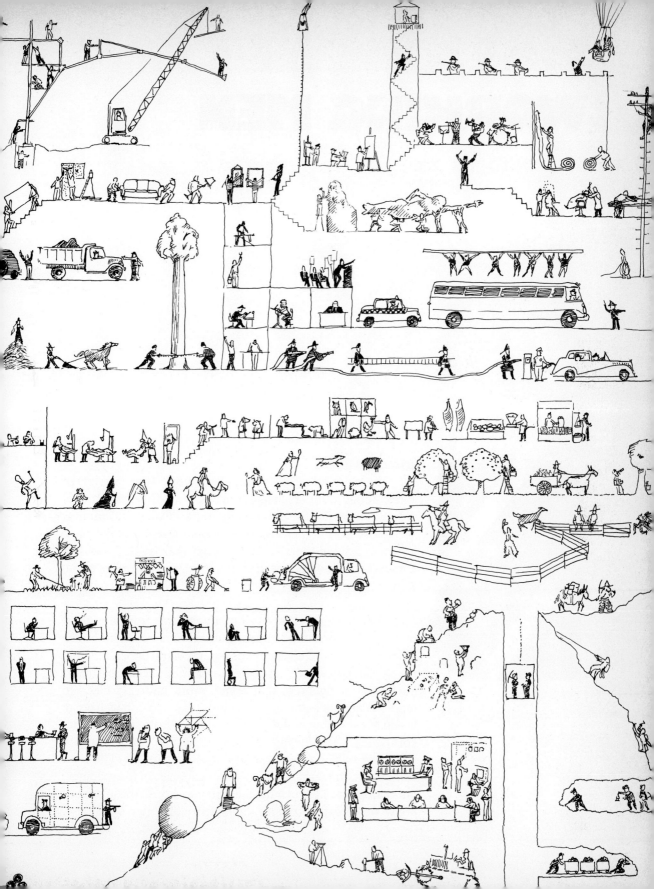

WORKING MEN

erious business

    There are few, if any, jokes about work. There are lots of jokes about mothers-in-law, politics, and Brooklyn; about droughts and floods; about plague, pestilence, and famine; about love (lots and lots of jokes about love); about marriage (lots and lots and lots of jokes about marriage); about life, about death, about taxes. But there are very few jokes about work. And why, after all, should there be? Work is not a joking matter.

    Man has indeed received many rewards from the sweat of his brow. Some of these rewards cannot be so much defined as *felt*: the challenge of a particularly difficult task ... the satisfaction when that task is successfully accomplished... the sense of rightness that comes from having a place to report to at nine in the morning and a place to depart from at five in the evening ... the respect received from, and given to, colleagues... the feeling of community that's inherent in a job... the fulfillment that arrives at the end of an eight-hour work day...the particularly pleasant exhaustion from doing a good job regardless of what that job may be. All these strands are woven inextricably into the tapestry of a man's life.

Work also happens to be the major reason why we've managed to survive—so far, anyway—as a species. Ever since he first stood on his two hind legs and discovered the advantages of his two opposable thumbs, man has felt it necessary to impose his will on the environment. Fortunately, he was able to channel that aggression into (mostly) constructive activity. If he hadn't, we'd have long been an extinct race, and the world would now belong to the insects—who are not exactly slackers when it comes to hard labor, either.

Work has helped keep man from becoming prey to his worst self-destructive instincts. Work has also kept man from being prey—period. In *The Origin of Species*, Charles Darwin stated that man had to liberate himself from nature so as to best withstand nature's law. "The big shall eat the small" is the harsh but natural order of things, an order which should have made us a particularly frequent entree on many another life form's menu. But it hasn't. For good or for evil, we have endured and persevered and conquered. And it is our ability to work that has put us on top of the biological heap.

Why work?

Work is an essential element of the "Male Mystique." Competition, the winner-loser syndrome, aggressive behavior above and beyond the call of duty, implausible idols, impossible ideals—men's work attitudes are symptomatic of the compulsion men feel to match themselves against an archetypical Worker (part Muhammad Ali, part Neil Armstrong, part Howard Hughes) they can never hope to resemble. Few are free of this compulsion. Your father, your son, your husband, your lover, the man you work for, the man you work with—all are influenced constantly by externally enforced myths regarding their jobs. And many are, as a result, anguished.

Men—that is, the majority of men—need to work. No use trying to understand the often passionate, often painful hate/love affair between a man and his job without first understanding that one absolute fact. Men *need* to work.

Maybe this irritates you. After all, women also work, in ever-increasing numbers, and at what were once exclusively "masculine" occupations. And you're working for many of the same goals that your male counterparts are: money, security, status, power, and creativity. Motivations such as these are

Work is our sanity, our self-respect, our salvation. So far from being a curse, work is the greatest blessing.

—HENRY FORD

common to both sexes. But there is, nevertheless, a primary difference between the working man and the working woman. The truth is, you generally have a more pragmatic (thus more realistic) approach to work. For most women, employment is a means to an end. For most men, employment *is* the end.

And it's not difficult to see why. There's nothing in a man's world that isn't in some way connected to his job. Ask a woman who she is, and she'll most likely respond by describing her relationship with the world (and the people) around her. Ask a man, and he'll probably reply with a list of what he does and of the things he owns. His house, his car, the associations he belongs to, the titles (including, of course, his

career title) he's managed to garner, his duties and his responsibilities—by such stuff is a man's identity realized. Putting aside for the moment the fact that his work in and of itself is possibly the major part of his sum total, a man's job is also the way in which he can maintain these things and thus, too, himself. From the outside looking in, the intensity a man brings to his work may often seem either realistic ("If I lose my job, I won't be able to pay the rent") or simply trivial ("If I lose my job, I'll have to give up golf"). But if you consider that his home, his golf clubs, his clothes, his whatever-else aren't just possessions but rather the means through which he knows who he is, it should then become more apparent how men and men's work are inextricably entwined.

The job he hates to love

In a government-sponsored study of men's attitudes, approximately 5,000 married men were asked to name the single most important element of their lives. More than 75 percent replied: "My job." (The study also asked 5,000 married women this question; 75 percent responded: "My family.") Yet when the same 5,000 men were asked to name the one element of their lives they most hated, again more than half responded: "My job."

I guess we're what you'd call a typical '70s family. Translation: We need money. My husband works, I work, and our two children have part-time, after-school jobs. Everyone does his share. For the rest of us, it's just a question of priorities. Work means money means a decent life. But for my husband— well, it's not the same at all. He puts in a 9–10-hour day, takes stuff home with him nights and week-ends, is always worrying himself sick about the job. He says he hates it. But that doesn't seem to mat-ter. And the money doesn't matter either. If we woke up rich tomorrow, he'd still get dressed, gulp down his coffee, and head for the office. He'll always work. There's no way he'd ever give it up. It's like he's, I don't know, hooked on his job.

This strange contradiction is indicative of the modern working man's plight. On the one hand, he views his job to be central to his life; on the other, he is increasingly less satisfied

If They Could Do It All Over Again, Would They?

These are the percentages of workers who said they would choose the same work they now have:

Mathematicians	91%
Lawyers	83%
Journalists	82%
Skilled printers	52%
White-collar workers	43%
Skilled steelworkers	41%
Textile workers	31%
Blue-collar workers	24%
Unskilled autoworkers	16%

with the nature of his job. The contradictory characteristics of work will often result in confusion and pain for the male worker. The following account is from one of the men involved in the study.

> *I don't know why I have to work. I used to think it was the money, but that's not it. I mean, it is the money—I've got a family to feed—but money isn't the basic thing. For instance, last year I woke up one morning wanting to quit my job. I was bored, tired, the usual crap, so I figured—Why the hell not? Me and my wife are careful folk, and we managed to put away a nice fat nest egg. Besides, I'm an ironworker, and there's always plenty of demand for guys like me. So I decided to treat myself to a three- or four-month vacation. Just lay around the house and take my ease. At first, I felt this incredible freedom. That lasted exactly one week. Then, this weird laziness set in. Stayed in bed later and later every day. No reason to get up. No place to go if I did get up. By the end of that month, I was some sort of vegetable. And it just got worse. By the end of the the second month, I didn't feel like me any more. I stopped talking to everybody—the old lady, the kids, everybody. Didn't even drop by the neighborhood bar any more. It was like I was ashamed in front of the guys, like somehow I wasn't a man any longer, like I didn't exist...*

Like I didn't exist. Work, in the male context, is synonymous with identity. And the more important the work, the more important that identity. Which is why so many men judge themselves, and each other, by their careers. It is, in fact, an essential tenet of the Male Mystique: A man is what a man does.

is job, his self

The belief—the typically male belief—that one is no better than what one does has been examined by sociologists, psychiatrists, anthropologists, economists, political scientists, theologists, and just about every other "ist" in the dictionary. It's been variously labeled: sometimes respectfully, as the work ethic; sometimes bitterly, as the rat race. It's been damned, it's been praised, but it is not—at least not yet—fully comprehended.

My boyfriend used to be this real laid-back dude. Just scuffled around, doing odd jobs whenever he needed some bread. But he's got expensive hobbies—cars, scuba, me—so he made up his mind to get some steady work. He didn't care what. It was just for the money. Finally, he found one of those executive trainee programs. And all of a sudden, it's Dr. Jekyll and Mr. Hyde time. Total transformation. Three months ago, ask him who he was and he'd say, "Well, my name is Jack, and I'm into this and I'm into that, and I like this stuff and I hate that stuff, and so on." Ask him now, he says, "I'm a junior executive." No more. No less. And he's miserable. Not because the job's shitty—which it is—but because the job's not "important" enough. I used to love this complex human being. Now I'm going out with a career.

It is clear that the job-identity equation has caused men untold anguish for thousands upon thousands of years. One of the most popular poems of the 19th century, embroidered on countless samplers and hung on innumerable schoolhouse walls, ends with these lines:

*I hold that a man had better be dead
Than alive when his work is done.*

It's a savage motto. And the fact that it was written by a woman, Alice Cary, only demonstrates how prevalent was—and, for the most part, still is—the myth that men's worth begins and ends with their jobs. Men should do important work. Men should succeed at important work. And if a man's work is neither important nor successful, then what kind of man is he anyway? This code not only separates most men from most work, but it also separates most men from most women.

Somebody—a man, no doubt—once wrote: "It's a man's world." But is it? Is it *really?* In his book *Man: The Fallen Ape,* Branko Bokun postulates that the reason magic and myth are so male-oriented (in, that is, male-oriented cultures) is that men are so much more insecure about their place in the great scheme of things than are women.

Although it's true that most civilizations have, in one way or another, subjected women to second-class citizenship, it is also true that women tended to know precisely the cultural definition of their position in society. Keep in mind that the idea of careers for women in the outside world is new —*very new*. Until recently, your ideal *career* was to maintain home and hearth. It might have been boring, it certainly was limiting, but at least it was consistent.

But men—especially men who have worked at highly specialized jobs—have not always been as sure just what their contribution to society is. This insecurity has resulted in many myths surrounding men and work: Man the Seed Bearer; Man the Empire Builder; Man the Adventurer; Man the Conqueror.

Well, it's great work if he can get it. The problem is, he rarely does. What happens when Great Works become mere jobs?

Life on the assembly line

Most work is work for wages. A century ago, more than half the work force was self-employed. Today, 90 percent of all employed people work for someone else.

I've worked both sides of the street—first on the assembly line, then in the front office. There's no difference. Same setup behind a desk or on the line, it's just work for wages, work for wages, but I'm here to tell you that anything's better than working for wages.

Freud has defined revolution, whether political or religious, as a movement toward a completely classless society. If this is true, than all revolutions must be marked as failures. All, that is, but one: the Industrial Revolution.

For where God, banners, and good intentions have faltered, work has marched steadily onward. Indeed, work has proved to be the Great Equalizer, leveling many of the boundaries that once separated the traditional social strata. And nowhere is this more apparent than in the most heavily industrialized countries, such as the United States, West Germany, and Japan. Poverty, racial bigotry, and elitism are not absent from these nations, of course, but the majority of their citizens are now firmly, if not always comfortably, ensconced in the middle class. There is still a tendency to distinguish between the blue-collar and the white-collar workers, but such distinctions reflect snobbery rather than reality. There is little actual difference—not in economic standards, not in social aspirations—between the assembly line and the office with a view.

But the price for this equality has been a high one. Equality demands a common denominator, and the common denominator here is that much work today offers little in the way of either challenge or satisfaction.

For example, in New York City, there is a Department of Transportation. Within that is a Division of Roads and Highways. Within that is a Bureau of Traffic Control. Within that is a Board of Public Transport Safety. Within that is an Office of Street Maintenance. Within that is a Section of Pothole Repairs. Within that is a group of Pothole Repair Teams. Within that is one foreman (to supervise operations), one driver (to handle the truck), and three workers (one to pour the filler, one to tamp it down, one to smooth it over). This is the essence of job specialization. It's also the essence of the modern man's workday.

There's nothing particularly new about the specialization of jobs. What is modern, though, is the reduction of men to units of labor. It's no longer necessary for a worker to have a unique talent; now, it's only necessary that he is trained to perform a simple operation in a simple way. The key to this reduction is the production line.

Whether they fill holes, initial corporate memos, or turn three screws on a gasket, the majority of men no longer work on a product but rather on a component of that product. Hard enough to find self-worth in the results of most modern work; impossible to find it when that work represents only a fraction of the effort needed to complete the entire job. But self-worth and self-identity are not the only reasons men work. For regardless of their uncertainty concerning their place in the world, they must still survive in the world. And *that*, at least, is still a tough job.

The fight

At the end of the day, five days a week, he returns home, grunts a hello, fixes himself a drink, fixes himself another drink, finishes the newspaper he began on the Commuter Special, eats dinner, then settles down for a three-to-five-hour

Sign on a Factory Wall

It's not my place
To run the train,
The whistle I can't blow;
It's not my place
To say how far
The train's allowed to go;
It's not my place
To shoot off steam,
Nor even clang the bell;
But let the damn thing
Jump the track
And see who catches hell!!

session of brain-numbing TV before falling into a fitful (and often heavily sedated) sleep. His attention span is alarmingly short when you try to tell him about your day, and he is reluctant to tell you anything about his own. Ask him what's wrong, and he'll say: "Nothing." Ask him again, and he'll turn up the volume on the TV set. If you're persistent, and if you're lucky, you may eventually get a reply: "What's wrong is I'm tired, and why I'm tired is that I work, so leave me alone because I work in a jungle."

Some jungle. Even the minimal benefits of today's typical job would give Karl Marx reason to reassess the advantages of capitalism. Short hours and good money, and that's just for

starters. Albert Camus once observed that "when work is soulless, life stifles and dies." So, he might very well have added, does the productivity rate. Most modern jobs offer little in the way of psychic nourishment. To compensate for this—or, more accurately, to improve the poor work performance that this creates—many companies (prodded, it's true, by the unions) now routinely offer all sorts of "perks" to keep their workers working at peak efficiency. Besides the old reliables like health insurance, pension funds, profit sharing, and incentive bonuses, some businesses have gone so far as to provide, free of charge, adult-education courses (in everything from Administration to Zeitgeist), psychiatric counseling (both individual and group), and even gymnasium facilities (the extreme example of which is one Japanese firm that has also pasted photos of its top executives onto the employees' gym punching bags).

However, there's a strange paradox at the very heart of the working world. He still does have to fight—fight to feed his family, to shelter them, to clothe them. And there are new, but no less lethal, predators to fight off, too. Bills outstanding. Mortgages due. And always another man, with the same incentives, waiting to replace him if he should falter.

Which is why the commuter is so exhausted at the end of his day. For despite the glass-and-steel framework, despite the modernistic decor, despite the air conditioning and the carpeted halls and the comfortable furniture, despite the office with a view, despite the secretaries with a view, despite the coffee breaks and the lunch breaks and the break breaks, despite all the matter-of-fact luxuries of the daily grind, the

world he works in—the world most men work in—forces him to use the same skills his hairier forefathers had to use when downing a mastodon or defending the cave.

It's perhaps a comical idea that beneath Industrial Age Man's three-piece suit beats Stone Age Man's brute heart—but it's only comical if you ignore the pain that comes from dealing with life in such a consistently aggressive and competitive manner. The myth is that men do it because they enjoy doing it. The truth is that men do it because they believe it's necessary. And they might, just might, be right.

I like to think of myself as one tough lady. But I'm Rebecca of Sunnybrook Farm compared to the men in my office. Sometimes I can't believe those guys! Always out for the main chance, always hustling, always at each other's throat. That's the worst. I mean, there are days when they're up to their knees in blood. Of course, I'm not saying they like it.

"Survival of the fittest" was our tribal ancestors' law. Is it any different in these more civilized times? If men today still insist on acknowledging primitive instincts it's because they still, in a very real sense, feel they're in a jungle, even if it's a jungle with a paid vacation and pension benefits.

Like father, like son

At the climax of *Death of a Salesman*, Willy Loman—that synthesis of the American working man—stands alone on-stage. His dreams lost, his life proved meaningless, his family

The Office In Which I Work

In the office in which I work there are five people of whom I am afraid. Each of these five people is afraid of four people (excluding overlaps), for a total of twenty, and each of these twenty people is afraid of six people, making a total of one hundred and twenty people who are feared by at least one person. Each of these one hundred and twenty people is afraid of the other one hundred and nineteen, and all of these one hundred and forty-five people are afraid of the twelve men at the top who helped found and build the company and now own and direct it.

—JOSEPH HELLER,
Something Happened

scattered, his own suicide just moments away, he can still shout after his departing son: "That boy—my boy—is going to be magnificent!"

The most advanced civilizations are always those that provide the most upward mobility. And this mobility, in turn, is always achieved through work. All of history is marked by one persistent pattern: A culture begins, prospers, grows, opens itself to waves of immigrants eager for the chance to better themselves, prospers even more, grows even more, and continues to do so as long as it continues to provide equal opportunity through equal work.

The most recent example of this pattern is, of course, the United States. By the end of the 19th century, countless thousands of Europeans and Asians had immigrated to her shores. Welcoming them all was the Statue of Liberty: "Give me your tired, your poor, your huddled masses yearning to breathe free... " Noble words. And like all noble words, something less than completely accurate. But even though America's immigrants found that the streets of their adopted country were not paved with gold but with concrete, even though they had to pound that concrete in search of jobs that weren't much different from the ones they had at home, they discovered that here—as in any young country in need of an expanded labor force—work meant an improved way of life. Better yet, work allowed immigrants a chance for advancement unheard of in more rigid, less work-mobile societies.

To give our children the advantages we never had, to watch them climb to heights we never could attain—doctors, lawyers, artists, scientists... How much of us owe our careers to parents or grandparents who worked in sweatshops, lived ten to a room, and spoke only broken English (if they spoke English at all)? We happen to call it the Great American Dream. We might as well call it the Great European Dream. Or, for that matter, the Great Samoan Dream. So let's just call it *the* Dream.

It's mostly because of work that the Dream has so often become the reality. And it's mostly because of work that the Dream has so often become the Nightmare.

It gets to me. Sometimes it really gets to me. I lay
in bed and stare at the ceiling and think about
tomorrow at the plant. How I'll punch in at 9:04, go
to my place on the belt, say hello to the guy on my

left, say hello to the guy on my right, say yessir, yessir, to the foreman, turn the same goddam screws every 15.6 seconds, take the coffee break at 11:00, lunch at 12:30, back to the belt, sneak a cigarette in the john at 3:00, back to the belt, knock off at 5:00 whistle, home again, supper, TV, bed, starts all over the next day....Sometimes, late at night, I get so miserable it scares me. When that happens, I just tell myself it's for the kids, it's all for my kids. And then I can sleep.

In his book *The Seasons of a Man's Life*, Dr. Daniel J. Levinson writes that "every father, usually in his mid-to-late forties, must come to terms with the fact that, contrary to expectations, he cannot live through his children. This can be a devastating experience, especially when it involves a father-son relationship." Many men justify their dissatisfaction with their work by assuring themselves of the satisfaction they'll eventually receive from their children's, particularly their son's work. Often, of course, a boy will reject outright his father's plans for him. But even when he accepts them—whether by following in the old man's footsteps or by taking a more prestigious path—he will not be able to supply the answer to his father's needs.

When I was a kid, I dreamed about being a pilot. Excitement. Adventure. New worlds to conquer. But love's old sweet song: I got married, had kids, found a job in an insurance company. Not much adventure, but it paid the bills. And I'd come home nights, and look at my son, and tell myself that I was giving him the chance to enjoy everything I couldn't. And the hell of it is, that's exactly what happened. He became a lawyer, which might not be as exciting as being a jet pilot but is still a bunch better than being an insurance agent. So now he's got the things I used to dream about: interesting work, important work. And I go to the same lousy office, shuffle through the same lousy pile of papers, think of my son, and say to myself: So what? Don't get me wrong. I love my boy, love all my children, and I'm proud I was able to help them, but—but it's not enough. What about me?

And if it's hard to be a man who's just learned his son's success, however great, is not going to make up for his own years as a less than happy worker, then it's just as hard—perhaps harder—to be a son who's been conditioned to believe his career must be his—and his father's—life.

But the conditioning continues, and so the job-identity myth is perpetuated from generation to generation. As soon as a male child is born, his proud parents scrutinize him for any special characteristics. Does the kid have a strong grip? Then perhaps he's destined to become a great athlete. A loud voice? An opera star. Sensitive hands? A surgeon. All through childhood and adolescence the pressure will build—family pressure, peer pressure, school pressure. In the pressure cooker of society, it is not enough to be a boy—one must be a boy with a future.

But the future will often prove as disappointing for the son as the father's present is for the father.

ituals of our tribe

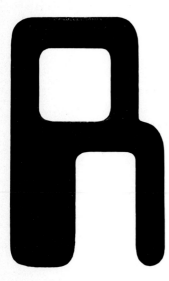

In 1972, the Secretary of Health, Education and Welfare appointed a special task force to examine the life of workers in present-day society. The result, a 262-page book entitled *Work in America*, begins with the following statement:

> *It is both humbling and true that scientists are unable, in the final analysis, to distinguish all the characteristics of humans from those of other animals. But many social scientists will agree that among those activities most peculiar to humans, work probably defines man with the greatest certainty. To the archeologist digging under the equatorial sun for remains of the earliest man, the nearby presence of primitive tools is his surest sign that the skull fragment he finds is that of a human ancestor, and not that of an ape...*

So from our earliest emergence as a species, work has been all-important. Perhaps by considering early and primitive human societies for a moment, we can gain more understanding of why this is so.

In her classic, *Coming of Age in Samoa*, Margaret Mead pointed out that male adolescence in any society is essentially a series of initiation rites, each bringing the initiate one step closer to final absorption in the male community. She demonstrated, too, how that community was actually a series of interlocking groups also controlled by ritualized behavior. Clubs, fraternities, lodges, even bowling teams—men, elsewhere uncertain of their position, are able in groups to find a well-defined hierarchy that lets them know precisely where they stand in relation to those around them. If you've ever seen such a group in action, you could not help but notice the importance of formal rituals—secret handshakes, elaborate private jokes, clothes, language, and general conduct.

Work is a primary group for men. There's considerable power and reassurance available to a man when he can perceive himself as part of the "team," reassurance he cannot always experience as an individual. Thus, work offers many ritualized rewards.

But, as Claude Levi-Strauss has written, "rituals tend to mask reality." A young man who's spent much of his early life being prepared for a career via initiation rites—being taken to the office by his father is one, another is learning team spirit at sports, a third is the high school Career Day—rarely has enough breathing space left to evaluate just what it is he's already getting himself into.

Employers often not only encourage rituals but institute their own as well. Although jeans are becoming a more common sight in some businesses (and are, in fact, almost uniforms in others), a formal dress code is still *de rigueur* for much of office life. Such codes can reach absurd proportions.

One of the most popular books of recent years was John T. Molloy's *Dress for Success*. In reviewing it, one critic lamented the author's "whole-hearted endorsement of the very meanest of bourgeois values" and went on to say: "We can only watch in absolute horror as Mr. Molloy's Stalwart Youth sheds Levi's for sports blazer, blazer for suit, and so on and so on, until merging perfectly with the corporate image. It reminds me of nothing so much as the feathers and paint sported by a primitive making his way up the tribal ladder of success. Haven't we progressed farther, at least, than this?"

Yes and no. Men are, as you will shortly see, beginning to rebel against the constrictions of work-imposed codes. But ritualized conduct is still very much a part of their working

Successful dress is really no more than achieving good taste and the look of the upper-middle class, or whatever is perceived by the greatest number of people to reflect these qualities.

—JOHN T. MOLLOY.
Dress For Success

world, especially when that world is a corporate one. In the tribe, symbol and reality were bound together; in the corporation, symbol—clothes, language, conduct—not only fails to represent reality, but will often overwhelm it. Again, it's comical to think of a group of IBM executives, all dressed in Brooks Brothers suits, all equipped with customized attaché cases, dancing around a campfire—but, again, it's only comical if you can ignore the pain hidden by the fantasy.

Give us this day . . .

Samuel Johnson once wrote an essay in which he rhapsodized, "What is more proper, more fitting, more joyful than the busy drone of familiar work?" Not much, it would seem. For in yet another of those contradictions, the same daily routine that makes men feel so constricted in their work also provides them with some of work's main rewards.

My father was a salesman. A damn good salesman, too. Won a lot of those incentive bonuses, won a lot of plaques, even once won a free junket to Hawaii. But what really excited him was all the day-to-day small stuff. Topping the office comic's best line. Being called on to referee some squabble between other workers. Getting the last word with the boss. He seemed more excited when he was presented with his own inscribed coffee mug than when he landed his biggest account. All those little wins, those little victories. I couldn't understand it. Not then. Not until I got a job of my own.

The pleasure of winning battles, no matter how small, is not something to be dismissed out of hand. Dr. Theodore Rubin has, in fact, characterized a man's typical workday as a series of brief crises, each with its own loss and its own gain. Separately, such crises are often trivial. Combine them, however, and they may very well offer a man the same kind—if not the same degree—of triumph he might experience breaking the bank or winning one for the Gipper.

Some of this, it's true, is an overreaction resulting from frustration. Yet a great deal more is a genuine response to successfully meeting a challenge. And it doesn't make much difference if the challenge is less than epic in scope. For while men may have become increasingly disenchanted with their jobs, they still get considerable satisfaction from putting in what is simply a good day's work.

> *It's easier explaining what I do than why doing it should make me feel so good. I come to work in the morning, and first I make a list of things to be dealt with that day. I straighten up my desk, make my calls, drink my first cup of coffee, sharpen my pencils, and then I'm ready for TCB—you know, taking care of business. By the end of the afternoon, I check over my list again. Usually, there's nothing all that major on it. But if I've done more things than not, I feel like my day's been worthwhile. Tell the truth, I feel like I'm worthwhile.*

Stability, too, is a reward. No matter how adventurous they like to think themselves, no matter how often they stare out the office window and dream about the Spanish Main, most men are comforted by the daily grind of work *because* it's the daily grind. Again, this would seem to indicate the gap—chasm, even—between male fantasy and male reality. Although loath to admit it, men are not at all comfortable in a disruptive world. What they crave most is what they most deny craving: the patterned and structured life. As you've already seen, men are continually besieged by changes they're not ready for—actually, not been readied for. Work, with its nine-to-five symmetry and its nonsurprising environment, acts like a gyroscope to stabilize an otherwise often topsy-turvy existence.

And then there's the reassurance that comes from being with their fellows. There's nothing very startling about this. For example, have you ever had a really good summer vacation and yet still been happy—and relieved—that first day back in school? If so, you can appreciate the strength men draw from each other's presence at work. As the poet Rilke said, we are solitary beasts. And it's the very routine of office companionship—the same tired jokes, the same petty conflicts, the same old confidences—that helps dissipate, at least for an eight-hour stretch, the solitude that can be so frightening to men (and, admit it, to you, too).

Last but by no means least is the thrill of the bona-fide major victory. Pride, prestige, personal gratification, and business advancement—it's self-evident that winning the Big

One is the crest of the wave. But, still, it is not really the main reward most men derive from their jobs. Partly this is because winning hard means playing hard, and the effort is just as exhausting as the result is rewarding:

> *I'll bust my butt for six months to make a major contribution to the business. Then I'll coast on it for the next six months. Going at top speed all the time is just too much like—hell—like work.*

Also, many men—due to either their own or their job's limitations—are never going to reach the crest. But that doesn't have to matter—for, as we have seen, work can be its own reward.

inners

"Nice guys finish last," said baseball manager Leo Durocher, and he's now celebrated as a hero in male folklore not only because he managed to finish first so often but also—perhaps mainly—because he was quite definitely not a nice guy. The winner—or, variously, the Champ, Numero Uno, the Successful Man—has the position of honor in the Male Mystique. The nice guy barely squeezes in at the bottom. Thus, the two concepts are rarely reconciled within the same man.

A little elaboration is in order here. There's a wealth, an embarrassment of wealth, of self-help literature on the best-seller lists. Recently—perhaps because the Male Mystique is wearing thin—such books have become blatant in their support of aggression. Just a quick peek at some of the titles—*Winning Through Intimidation, Looking Out for Number One, Power! How to Get It! How to Use It!, On Becoming a Corporate Ace, The Gamesman*—is an indication of the qualities deemed essential for work success. And if that's not proof enough, an equally brief peek into any one of these books should suffice. Here's an excerpt from *Success*, by Michael Korda, listing the winner's major qualifications:

It's OK to be greedy

It's OK to be ambitious

It's OK to have a good time

It's OK to be Machiavellian (if you can get away with it)

It's OK to recognize that honesty is not always the best policy (provided you don't go around saying so)

Notice that this list doesn't include work skills or company loyalty or good old-fashioned fair play. Not that these attributes aren't important (at least the first two); it's just that the winner's prime directive is to reach the top, and then stay there.

> *What makes me run? I've been asking myself that a lot lately. When I was younger, it never much bothered me. I just assumed it was for the money, the prestige, the need to—well—to conquer. Nowadays I'm not so sure. I've got prestige, but no friends. And as for conquests: I'm divorced, my kids talk to me maybe once every two months, and I'm never sure whether a woman is interested in me or my position. Some conqueror. I guess I'm not all that concerned with what makes me run. I'm really trying to find out what will make me stop.*

Of all male handicaps, the win/lose syndrome is the most debilitating. A man may enjoy a wonderful family life, good working conditions, a comfortable lifestyle, and still be judged a loser, by both himself and others. A man may have no family life and a job that is killing in pace—and just how killing will be made apparent soon—that leaves him little time for *any* lifestyle and still be judged a winner.

Nor does the nature of his job have anything to do with it. The company president and the company janitor are likely to share the same need to win in their respective jobs. It is not position but rather commitment that determines whether or not a worker is to be called a winner. Although there are exceptions, winners are not usually innovative, rebellious, or destructive of systems. On the contrary, they are the epitome of the system.

They have no choice in this. Winners, in truth, probably have less freedom of will than any other type of worker. It is part of the Male Mystique that the more "masculine" the man, the more power-oriented and emotionally repressed he must be, and that winners, by nature of their work, are masculinity personified. The result? A rule stark and cruel in its simplicity: Winners are condemned to perpetuate the structure that traps them. It's not enough for them to learn how to become kings of the jungle. They must also learn how to love and maintain the jungle.

A winner is not to the purple born. Instead, it's a matter of training and social conditioning. "Winning isn't the most important thing," declared Vince Lombardi, "it's the *only* thing." Most boys are exposed at an early age to some form of this philosophy. And those best able to adopt it will be encouraged to follow it throughout life. They're assured that they're expressing positive masculine attitudes, such as healthy competitiveness, strong motivation, and honest self-interest, but what they're really being congratulated for is their ability to be as cold-bloodedly manipulative as possible. And these same boys will be admired and envied by the "weaker" boys, who will feel even less adequate than they already feel.

The boss

On a practical level, the relationship between employer and employee is so clearly defined that it needs no explanation here. Any functioning system requires a specific chain of command. This is not only inevitable but all-encompassing.

I've been working at the same place for some six years now. I know my job, I know my company, but I don't know my boss. And I like it that way; I don't want to know him. But a few weeks ago, he asked me out for a drink after work. Turned out that he had some personal hassles he wanted to get off his chest. Here I've been working all these years with this guy, and suddenly, for the first time, he's become real. Too real. His alcoholic wife, his screwed-up kids, his debts, his troubles with his girl-friend—I just didn't need to hear all that stuff. I don't want to look at him and see just another poor slob with problems—I want to see the Boss.

In a reasonably large company, almost *every* worker is some other worker's boss. And if it ended here—if most workers were bosses and vice versa—there would be little need for any discussion. But there happens to be another level, a symbolic level, a level in which boss and working man are distinctly separate entities.

Note that we are talking about symbols, not caricatures. The boss is not Mr. Dithers, the worker is not Dagwood Bumstead. Even so outspoken an advocate of ruthless power as Robert Ringer admits that "today's employer, whether he be company president or office manager, can no longer indulge himself in the pleasures of Absolute Rule." There's precious little room in the modern work world for martinets. Now a boss is required to be part counselor, part psychiatrist, part confidant, part general and part private, part teacher, part priest, part (a very small part) buddy, and part (a very large part) parent.

As Dr. Levinson writes in his book *The Season's of a Man's Life:* "The mentor relationship is one of the most complex, and developmentally important, a man can have in early adulthood. The mentor is ordinarily several years older, a person of greater experience and seniority in the world the young man is entering." The most common form this relationship takes is the one created between a worker first starting the job and his immediate—that is, most visible—superior. It's complex because it involves many subtle interactions of instruction and reward; it's important because it

reinforces and encourages the younger man's absorption into
the working world.

> I've had a long successful career, met a lot of high-
> powered people, but the guy who made the biggest
> impression on me was the foreman of the plant I
> once worked in. It was my first real job, and Mac—
> still remember his name—was the one who taught
> me the ropes. I don't just mean the job per se; I
> mean the whole thing about being a man, and
> doing a man's work, and being accepted by other
> men, too.

Nor is this limited to instruction. Comments Levinson:
"Mentoring is best understood as a form of love relationship.
It is difficult to terminate in a reasonable, civil manner." But, as
he further points out, end it must. At some point in the
worker's development, it is necessary that he reject his former
role as junior trainee and attain seniority. The struggle
between teacher and pupil, boss and bossed, is again
symbolic; a man doesn't have to quit his job in order to quit
this relationship. Instead, after a usually painful severing of
emotional ties, he and his former mentor enter into a new
involvement as adversaries.

Of course, they're friendly—or at least polite—adversaries. Once the worker has gained enough confidence in his
ability to do the work, he begins to view his boss as an
obstacle on the road to success. Unless he's particularly
aggressive, this, too, is more symbol than reality. But it does
goad him on, forcing him to extend himself as much as
possible and to learn, in the process, his own range of
competence.

> I once worked for this genuine son of a bitch in the
> Accounts Department. I really wanted to rise in the
> company, and I figured the only way to do it was to
> get his job. But no way. I mean, he used to run
> circles around me. That guy had a capacity for work
> that was unbelievable. And he used to drive my ass
> into the ground just trying to stay in the race. I
> never did get his job. Got my promotion, though. I
> worked so hard that people started noticing me. As
> a matter of fact, it was that same s.o.b. who recom-
> mended I be moved upstairs.

There are, to be sure, certain situations when the adversary roles are considerably more than symbolic. If, for example, a man happens to find himself working for a younger man or a woman, very real conflicts will almost invariably arise. Most men respond to a female boss by trying to reduce the impact of her power over them, often by placing the working arrangement within a sexual frame. The young boss/older worker problem, however, has no such ready-made solution. In *On Becoming a Corporate Ace,* the otherwise dauntlessly optimistic author advises: "If you should find yourself suddenly reporting to a man younger than you, you have but three choices: 1. Get his job. 2. Quit your job. 3. Grin and bear it." But, he adds, there is no way to escape the humiliation and anger that come from such a predicament. In the working man's eyes, to be subordinated to someone who is either younger or female (or, worse, younger *and* female) is an inversion of the natural order of things. No readjustment of symbols will help here. Instead, he'll either come to terms with his own prejudices (and so free himself of them) or suffer their consequences.

Anger against an employer does not always have to be the result of frustration, however. It can, instead, be a constructive, even necessary element in a job. A man who is unhappy with his work but unable to leave it may have a real need to find a focus for his pent-up resentment. In such instances, the boss becomes the personification—yes, we're back to symbols again—of the company. By directing his hostility against that personification, the worker is able to relieve himself of some of the pain of being a worker. (This may seem unfair, but most experienced employers accept it as part of their role.)

The Best Boss

He isn't necessarily the nicest guy, researchers are finding. Bosses who are more interested in companionship than power often get poor results.

Now, some bosses really are sons of bitches, or rather they're so competitive and aggressive that working for them becomes torture. But even if he's the most reasonable and even-tempered of men, the boss will generally be regarded by his employees as the enemy. There's no way to avoid this. And there's no reason to avoid this. It's better for a man to take out his resentment on his *boss*, who in turn can take it out on *his* boss, than on you.

The boss and work relationship may, in fact, be the only portion of the working world in which myth plays a benevolent—rather than harmful—role.

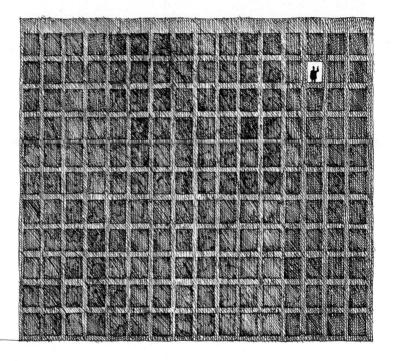

Workaholics

He puts in anywhere from 12 to 14 hours a day at the office. He doesn't recognize weekends, and he's never heard of vacations. He sleeps badly, when he can sleep at all. He has no family life. He often has no family. He is always restless, always active, and his mood is continually swinging from boredom to anxiety, but he never seems to have the time for exercise or relaxation. His only recreations are eating, drinking, and working. He drives fast. He drives himself faster.

Do you know what the single most dangerous occupational hazard is in this country? No, it's not on-the-job accidents, or black-lung disease, or any of the other work-related injuries and illnesses. It's workaholism.

Dr. Joan Gomez, who's made a comprehensive study of working conditions, has said that in 1974 "some 200,000 men between the ages of 15 and 55 died (as opposed to 121,000 women). And the most likely candidate for early death has proved to be the workaholic."

There is, currently, considerable disagreement regarding the causes of this illness. Some experts link it to aggression, some to thwarted sexuality, some to the code of manhood. A few psychiatrists, like Dr. Harry Levinson, have even suggested that it is a form of unconsciously willed suicide.

However, just about everyone now agrees on its effects. To put it bluntly, workaholism is a killer. Heart attacks and cerebral strokes are typical among men who work at an obsessive pace, of course, but there are other diseases connected to workaholism, too. To name the most common: peptic ulcers, alcoholism, arthritis, rheumatoid arthritis, gout, hypertension, drug addiction, schizophrenia, and impotence.

Interestingly enough, the incidence of these ailments among underachievers is similar to that among overachievers. This is no doubt because winners and losers are but two sides of the same coin—the Male Mystique.

Workaholism cuts across the board in other ways, too. It's not the nature of a man's job but rather his approach to it that determines this disorder. Assembly-line workers are as likely to fall prey to it as air-traffic controllers. In fact, stopping work will often not stop workaholism. Even if he manages to survive to retirement age, the workaholic will often find himself still trapped by ingrained work habits.

My husband retired two years ago, but he still doesn't know how to relax. All he does now is make himself sick with boredom. And all I can do is watch him grow older by the minute. I used to hate his job, hate it for what it was doing to him. Now I'd give anything if he could go back to work.

The most typical justification workaholics apply to their behavior is that they're "building for the future." But, cautions Dr. Gomez—who ranks it as one of the top ten killers of American men—"for the workaholic there is seldom any future at all."

oes it have to be this way?

Man is a rebel. He rebelled against nature's system by creating his own. And he rebels against his own system by constantly trying to replace it with others. Sometimes this rebellion is violently imposed, sometimes it's peacefully inevitable. Sometimes it's triumphant, sometimes not. But win or lose, gentle or strong, man has always refused to simply accept his lot in life. Lest you think men are hopelessly trapped in the working system, be assured that an increasing number are fighting back. The desire to hit back is reflected not only in the working man's job performance but in his job attitudes as well.

> We've always been autoworkers. My grandfather, my father, now me. But times are changing. It's like all the old bullshit is gone now, burned out, and good riddance, too. I mean, my grandfather worked for the union, believed in the union, believed all that stuff about the dignity of the worker, the need to stand together, the evil bosses. I'm not saying he was wrong, not then anyway, but look what happened. Unions get to be the same fat cats the employers are. So then my father fought to reform the union. A lot of good that did. The pension he's on now wouldn't fill a flea's pisspot. Which leaves me. My generation. We don't believe in anything. Except looking out for number one. And the only heroes we got are the guys who beat the house odds.

Not all working men want to be mutineers. Many instead prefer the role of reformers.

> I went over to Avis with Robert Townsend [later the author of Up the Organization, still one of the most effective books on work reform in—or out of—print]. He taught me how to push for change instead of disorder. When I later went out on my own, I found myself working for this really rigid organization. My first impulse was to quit, but then I figured why not at least try to improve things. And I did, too. Nothing really out-and-out revolutionary, mind you. Just things like campaigning for a looser dress code, streamlining bureaucratic chains of command, setting up dialogues between management and workers.... Small stuff, I guess, but when you add it all up, it can really get things going. I've learned that any system can endure as long as there's room enough to make adjustments for the benefits of its workers. As for me, instead of being a habitually unemployed discontent, I've managed to keep both a steady job and my own sense of identity and worth.

Changing expectations

And then there are the workers who neither fight nor change the system. Instead, they'd rather rearrange their own expectations of that system's reward potential.

I've been working for the same publishing house for some fifteen years now. When I first came aboard, I was one gung-ho jerk. My slogan then was: The more you put in, the more you get out. But I've wised up a lot since those days. There's just so much, and no more, that a career is able to give you. I like my job, like the money and prestige and even the work, but I no longer expect it to provide me with the reason for my existence. I've learned to be more realistic; and in the process I've also learned to value the rest of my life outside the office. My marriage, my children, my children's educations, my own education, hobbies, sports, the books I read, the movies I see, the community theater I belong to—these are the things really important to me. My job gives me some satisfaction in itself, sure, but mostly it provides me with the wherewithal to maintain the kind of world I'm most happy living in.

Another man spent more than a decade building up a lucrative career as a stock-market analyst only to suddenly quit one day in order to open a small leather-crafts store.

I just reached a point where I could no longer rationalize what I was doing simply because I was supposed to be doing it. One day, I said to myself: Time now to start doing what you want to do. So now I'm working 20 hours more a week, I'm making less than half my previous income, and I'm loving every minute of it.

And yet another dropped out of the work force completely. Joining what appears to be a definite trend, he's opted to become a "house husband."

For several years my wife and I both worked. She loves her job, I hated mine. We were having all kinds of marriage problems as a result. Just deciding whose turn it was to do the housework was an epic hassle. Then one day she suggested I quit my job. I laughed at it at first—actually, I was pretty insulted at first—but the more I thought about it, the better it looked. Finally, I agreed to give it a shot. It wasn't easy to get rid of all those masculine prejudices about cleaning and cooking, but gradually I started enjoying myself more and more. Taking care of the house hasn't only freed me from responsibilities as a worker that I didn't want, either. It's also put new life into my marriage. In fact, we've just decided to have a child because now one of us—me—can spend the day taking care of the kid. Friends ask me if I'm ready for it. Ready! I can't wait. I think it's going to be the best work of my life.

The change in work expectations can also be directly linked to the growing number of employed young people. Out of a work force of more than 85 million, approximately 23 million are now under the age of 30. More affluent and better educated than his parents, the young working man has taken the lead in demanding better working conditions. In fact, the President's Commission on Campus Unrest wrote that youthful workers tend to find their very identity "in rejection of the work ethic, materialism, and conventional social norms and pieties."

In 1971, Daniel Yankelovich conducted national attitude studies of college students and discovered that:

Only 36 percent saw themselves willingly submitting to "being bossed around on the job."

Only 39 percent agreed with the statement "Hard work will always pay off."

And almost 80 percent felt that a meaningful career is an important part of a man's life—more desirable than security and rapid promotion.

Researchers conclude that the 1960s were a watershed decade in the attitudes of young workers. The expectations that young people bring to their jobs have changed dramatically. Where once workers sought only a successful career, they now also want it to make their lives meaningful.

A campus headhunter for one of the largest corporations in the United States sadly concurs: "Ten years ago, all the kids I interviewed would ask about raise policies, opportunities for promotion, and pension plans. Now they want to know the value of the job in terms of their own personality. I don't know. I just don't know. Kids today don't want their jobs to make a living; they want their jobs to make a personal statement."

And if the workers are changing, then the work world finds itself forced to change, too.

Fifty years ago, for example, the typical work week was from 76 to 90 hours long. Today, it's 35 to 40 hours. And many businesses—both in this country and abroad—have already successfully instituted what many see as the next major alteration in the work system: the four-day week.

Companies are also actively searching out ways to make their workers feel more valuable in relation to their work. In Japan's Toyota Corporation, any assembly-line worker dissatisfied with any component on the line can demand that the belt be stopped until the problem is corrected. In Sweden, most corporate workers share in the company profits; the more productive they are, the more financial rewards they receive. And in America, certain firms have begun to hold a monthly "Reversal Day," in which employers and employees switch jobs for eight hours in order to get a better perspective on the responsibilities and problems each group has.

The open door

"Workers of the world unite! You've got nothing to lose but your chains" was Karl Marx's rallying cry. But if working men have been caged—and they *have* been caged—by codes of behavior, by restrictions, by constrictions, by myths, by taboos, by the entire cruel panoply of the Male Mystique, then that cage has one new and redeeming feature: Its door is unlocked. Its door, in fact, is wide open.

Some men have already discovered this and broken free. Others have begun to plan the break now. And as for the rest (still, it would appear, the majority), at least they've been given the opportunity to free themselves. Besides, help is on the way. Help from an unexpected quarter. Help from someone until recently even more suppressed than the working man. Help, in short, from you.

Space-Age Work Song —as sung by Johnny Paycheck

Take this job and shove it.
I ain't workin' here no more.
My woman done left
And took all the reason
I was workin' for.

— DAVID ALLEN COE,
©Warner-Tamerlane Publishing Corp.,
1977

qual rights

There are ten clerks in the billing department. Five are men, five are women. Each morning, the women take turns brewing coffee, watering the office plants, and phoning in orders for lunch delivery. One finally rebels, saying "Why can't the men share all this Mickey Mouse stuff?" A male co-worker snaps back, "The last lady who asked that found herself looking for a new job." The woman returns to the coffee pot.

If you've ever held a job—and, according to the U.S. Department of Labor, nine out of every ten American women will work outside their homes at some time in their lives—you already know about the pervasive male discrimination against the working woman. What men have been taught is that you have no business in their business. Not as equals, anyway.

In her book *Passages*, Gail Sheehy sums up the male vs. female work code thusly: "Men must. Women don't have to." No matter that you're as career-oriented, or as good at your job, or in as dire need of that paycheck as he. The typical working man not only believes that he *has* to work but also believes—just as fervently—that you do not. He believes that he has a career—and that at most you have a job.

The male animal has an instinctive response, usually termed a "territorial imperative," to defend his turf from any and all interlopers. This response, writes behavioral scientist Desmond Morris, is "as characteristic to an officeful of men as it is to, for example, a pride of lions."

It is not particularly difficult to understand how a woman at work will frequently trigger this male defense mechanism. As long as your job can be stereotyped as "feminine"—typing, filing, billing, etc.—and as long as you're willing to act out the feminine stereotype—making the coffee, tidying up the office—men will tolerate you as a co-worker. Any attempt to rid yourself of this subordinate role, however, still tends to be perceived as an invasion of masculine territory.

Anything goes

This invasion is both inevitable and (at least on the surface) friendly. Why is it so often received with such blatant, even conscienceless, hostility? Consider the following: Three colleagues are informed that they're all candidates for the same job opening. Two are men, the third is a woman. Although the men are rivals for the promotion and also have personal reasons for disliking each other, they unhesitatingly join forces against the woman. Innuendoes and condescending remarks are aimed at her. The two men then turn on each other. Their tactics and countertactics, however, are not nearly as destructive as those they previously employed against the female candidate. In fact, the competition results in the two men becoming friends. But neither one ever speaks kindly of the woman again.

Men at work tend to be fiercer and less ethical when competing with women than when competing with other men. When men are rivals, regardless of the value of the prize (more money, more power, more whatever), they often view each other with an almost game-playing sympathy. If a much-desired promotion represents better food and housing to one male, he can accept the fact that it represents the same to his male competitor. But even if the same is true, as it so often is nowadays, for a *female* competitor, the man feels no sympathy, no inclination to pull his punches. (Indeed, he's often actively *encouraged* by his fellow men to assume a no-holds-barred attitude in any work-related contest involving a woman.)

And there's another, not quite so openly spoken, reason why men will compete so relentlessly against women. It's easier, and considerably less risky, than fighting a man.

A man, most men believe, is taught to be aggressive, strong, and competitive. This, he is told, will help him become a success (a good career).

A woman, most men believe, is taught to be pliant, nonaggressive, and cooperative. This, she is told, will help her become a success (a good marriage).

Well, the fact is that women as a class have been unprepared for the upper-echelon business world. A man competing with a man is restrained by the knowledge that he's going to receive as much punishment as he metes out. A man taking on a woman feels no such restraint. There's little in your feminine training that's equipped you to deal positively with masculine aggression. Not only are you less able than a man to defend yourself from a man, but you are also less likely to do much damage in return.

Working like a man

And there's yet another reason why men respond so passionately to a female rival: fear.

Look, I'm beaten by a man, all right, it hurts, but at least it's a man. Maybe he's better than me. Maybe he's faster than me. Maybe he's smarter than me. Somebody wins, somebody loses. That's just the rules of the game. But to be beaten by a woman— that's gotta be a statement about my own weakness. I not only feel real bad about myself, I look real bad to all the other men. Losing to a guy is painful; losing to a woman is devastating.

That men are afraid women will use their sexuality to gain ascendancy over them in a working situation is often a fact. However, there's another side to this particular coin: Men are also relieved if they can believe that a woman's business success is *due* to her sexuality. Company gossip about a woman's sex life will sometimes rise in direct proportion to that woman's climb up the company ladder. Men are profoundly—no, *viscerally*—threatened by a woman's success. And so, what you may perceive as an attack upon your personal integrity is, in fact, a defense of men's validity as workers.

In *Winning Through Intimidation*, a book dedicated to the proposition that no man is created equal, author Robert J. Ringer advises his would-be corporate killers that "the best way to defeat a female [business] contender is to simply ignore the fact she's a contender in the first place."

This is true. Depressing but true. Under even the most benign—i.e., nonthreatening—circumstances, men seldom view women's work as seriously as they do other men's. If a proposal comes from a fellow man, an executive might feel compelled to consider it seriously (and probably would also feel just that less secure in his own job). But if the "contender" is a woman, he feels no need to take the proposal seriously. And he may further reduce the proposal's potential worth by: (1) asking the woman to discuss it over lunch, which has more social than business connotations; (2) listening to it attentively but noncommittally, which underlines his seriousness at the same time it cancels out hers; (3) changing the subject, as soon as possible, to more "feminine" concerns; (4) trying to transform the lunch into a sexual liaison; (5) shelving the proposal by simply never mentioning it to the woman again; and (6) allowing a story to start that he's romantically involved with her.

Now, none of these maneuvers need be calculated or even conscious. The man would simply be doing what comes most naturally to him. In all probability, he would consider himself a most liberal man and would be surprised—shocked—outraged—by any suggestion that he is prejudiced against women workers.

Open prejudice

In many work situations, however, there is no attempt to hide this prejudice. On the contrary, the prejudice is often the reason why women are hired at all. Any personnel manager, any *honest* personnel manager, will acknowledge that physical attractiveness is a major plus for female job applicants. But there's another issue involved in this, an issue summed up by Barbara Garson in her excellent book about "routine work," *All The Livelong Day.* "The Sex Object," she writes, "is just another word for The Scapegoat."

Now wait a moment. Before you start feeling too paranoid, be assured that there's no *deliberate* male conspiracy afoot. It's just the Male Mystique. Men are supposed to dominate their environment—which, in a working environment, is not easy. In most working environments, it is impossible. This means they can only dominate certain *elements* of that environment. And that, too often, leaves only you. In order to justify their need to dominate, men perpetuate the myths regarding your inferiority as a working colleague. To name just a few:

Women only work until they have children.

Women change their jobs as often as they change hair styles.

Women are too emotional to handle responsibility—especially during their period.

Women get sick more often than men.

Even when they stay single, women have a shorter work life than men.

An Open Prejudice

I scarcely see in the hands of a woman an employment that ought to be in the hands of a man, but I constantly see in the hands of a man employment which might be more beneficially and economically in the hands of a woman.

—WILLIAM GLADSTONE, 1871

However, the Labor Department calculates that of the 31 million females in the work force, 40 percent are mothers. (And of these working mothers, 36 percent have children under the age of six.) Available figures on labor turnover cite that net differences between men and women are so small as to be insignificant. A recent Public Health Survey of work time lost due to illness or injury revealed that women lost on the average 6.6 days as compared to 5.3 days for men. (And this includes time lost for pregnancy and childbirth.) And HEW estimates that the average woman worker, single *or* married, has a work-life expectancy well within the work-life range of the average man worker.

But just because the statistics prove you're his equal doesn't mean he'll accept you as one. As we've seen, he can't—at least until today's legal guarantees of equality are further reinforced by the social changes that, fortunately, seem to be taking place.

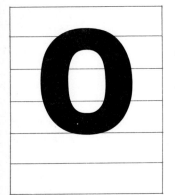ffice affairs

Men and women working together often means men and women sleeping together. Company sex can often be charted as pragmatically as company profits. Flirtation, seduction, recrimination, abdication—all can be patterns of behavior related to the position each participant has in the work structure.

"Power is the greatest of all aphrodisiacs." Of course, this remark is meant to be a somewhat smug observation of the effects of high position on females. In truth, however, the aphrodisiacal effects of power seem to act more on the powerful one than on any innocent or not so innocent bystander who happens to get within range. There is something about a title, and the power that comes with it.

It's been previously discussed how impotence in sex may be directly related to impotence in work. But consider the reverse: The more potent a man's job, the more potent his sexual feelings. Of course, this potency is often illusionary. By the time most men climb to the top, they're middle-aged, exhausted, and somewhat less than at their sexual best. Which may be why many powerful businessmen who by virtue of their position could go after the typical objects of male sex fantasies—actresses, models, stewardesses—choose instead

to go hunting within their own private domain. In the outside world, who he is is not always as important as what he can do with it; in the office world, the reverse is true. In the office his sex appeal may be not so much physical as it is psychological.

Lord and maid, lady and footman

Except when genuine love appears, male executives very seldom get romantically involved with female executives. It's too dangerous. No, the vast majority of powerhouse executives prefer the typing pool or the clerical staff. Here the women are young, pretty, accessible, disposable, and best of all, easily impressed.

When a woman is the boss, a working man's world turns topsy-turvy. Anne Jardim, co-author of *The Managerial Woman*, writes: "In the occupations that give meaning to a man's life, his sense of mastery is being upset...If you've got someone to look down on, it makes you look better in your own eyes. In a three-year-old boy's head, he is better than a three-year-old girl. What happens when he grows up, goes to work, and finds he is reporting to that little girl?"

What happens is that he has a real problem accepting her

A secretary is not a toy.

—FRANK LOESSER,
"How to Succeed in Business
Without Really Trying"

The hell she isn't.

—A SECRETARY

as more powerful than he. Instead, he relates to her as a mother, a buddy, a surrogate wife—or a lover.

In an article commissioned by *Esquire* magazine, Marilyn Bender describes how men often feel a sexual attraction to a female boss, even when—or even because—that boss is considerably older.

But, as Bender discovered, this is mostly male day-dreaming. All the woman executives she interviewed stressed the fact that "it would be an absolute mistake to let sex intrude in business." Even so, real or not, the tendency men have to become physically enamored of the women they work for is a pretty strong indication of what office sex is really about. One man she talked to summed it up: "When they get angry, they revert to thinking that the only way a man can control a woman is in bed. They also think that only in bed can they take from her the source of that power."

You might think that an office relationship involving two people with similar jobs would put that relationship on a more equal basis. Not so. "In office affairs," writes Michael Korda in his book *Success!*, "women are always in the wrong." If the affair gets out of hand, if it begins to interfere with work, or even if it becomes merely inconvenient, the odds are it will be the woman who is fired.

Sex as a weapon

Naturally, a woman can use sex to get ahead, too. "The working world is where the men are!" exults *The Cosmo Girl's Guide to the New Etiquette.* But despite the image of career woman as sexpot, it's more often the career man who will try to use sex as a weapon. (Actually, he doesn't even have to bother with the real thing. Encouraging gossip about himself and a female colleague will reduce her image in the office and enhance his.) And even when a man is honestly attracted to a woman co-worker, he may find that he has, reluctantly or not, the edge.

Only in religion is it not a sin to love one's enemy.

—JULES FEIFFER

> *I met Susan when we were assigned to the same project. We worked together on it for months, spent a lot of time with each other, got to know each other, learned to care for each other. Finally the day came for us to make the presentation. I had pre-viously met most of the guys at the conference, but Susan was new and feeling nervous and…I don't*

know. I suddenly felt really protective toward her. So I put my arm around her shoulders, and introduced her by saying, "Gentlemen, this is Susan, and I want you all to understand that this project is mostly hers."

Well, what happened, of course, was that everybody there immediately assumed the project was mine. Susan was upset. More than upset. She accused me of deliberately setting her up, and so on. So I lost a really close friend. And the hell of it is, maybe I did—subconsciously at least—set her up.

"Sometimes," said (a probably exhausted) Freud, "a cigar is just a cigar." And sometimes office sex is just sex that happens to have been generated in an office. But good sex requires equality, and there's still precious little equality between working men and working women.

Sexless office marriages

Is it just sex he wants from his underling? Sometimes on the surface that's all it seems to be. In an adult-education course entitled "How to Choose a Job," the businessman/instructor advises his class that "a careful applicant will always insist on meeting his prospective secretary. If she isn't relatively young, attractive, and competent"—and please note the ranking of these qualifications—"he should not accept the position."

In *Success!*, Michael Korda includes secretaries (after, however, office furniture) in a chapter naming the most important success symbols.

And in a government study, executives asked to list the most important requirements necessary to their jobs consistently placed "suitable secretary" at the top. (When polled privately, it was learned that their idea of "suitable" was women helpers who regarded them with nothing short of hero worship—but that's another story.)

But it's not just sex. The man and his secretary form one of those classic duos—like the Lone Ranger and Tonto—in which the hero is absolutely dependent on his faithful guide and companion. A good secretary makes the boss his coffee (and often every other male worker's coffee as well), buys his ties, selects his gifts, listens to his problems, advises him on his

Success Symbol

If a man has an office with a desk on which there is a buzzer, and if he can press that buzzer and have a little lady come dashing in response—then that man is a bonafide success.

—ELMER FRANK ANDREWS, 1938

love life (unless she happens to *be* his love life, in which case the boss will probably turn to another secretary for counsel), lies for him, reinforces his ego, stoically bears his complaints about her performance, and comforts him when others complain about *his* performance.

Since work is central to most men's lives, it stands to reason that their working associates form many of their central relationships. No matter how sympathetic their "real" wives, men are seldom able to fully articulate the tangled web of pressure and tension, victories and defeats, cause and effect, that shapes their work lives. They will often turn to their female secretaries—the women they're closest to at the office—for comprehensive sympathy. Sometimes a working man and his secretary grow so mutually dependent that they're unable to function successfully without the other and a curious symbiosis is formed. It resembles a marriage—in fact, it *is* a marriage, although a limited nine-to-five one.

> *My wife just can't comprehend the nature of my job. Oh, she knows what I do, of course, but there's no way she's able to react to it. When I want praise for work well done, or comfort for a screw-up, or just a sympathetic ear, that's when I turn to my secretary. She's out there on the line with me, day by day, and she knows—well—everything worth knowing. I sometimes think she understands me a hell of a lot better than my wife.*

In boss-secretary "marriages" there is rarely any sex. Why not?

> *Why should there be? If I started sleeping with my secretary I'd louse up our entire relationship. We've got us a great thing. Sex would just confuse it.*

The office "wife" may very well represent the beleaguered and self-doubting working man's ideal solution to his own problems: a relationship that is essentially one-sided, a relationship that offers him comfort, support, loyalty, and dedication to the furtherance of *his* career. (Though it is true that the office "wife" can expect to be taken with her boss on his rise to the top, she merely becomes a better-paid secretary.) Also, the relationship is without the complications of sex, emotional demands, or responsibilities of any kind.

inal stronghold

Nothing simple about the Male Mystique. It demands much, but promises much in return. As the bastions of traditional male beliefs crumble on every side, the working place still holds fast to the old, out-of-date party line. Not that cracks aren't beginning to appear, but the working man is working hard to maintain domination of his stronghold.

And, really, is it any wonder? You've invaded their private clubs, you've insisted they share the household duties, you've challenged their most cherished concepts of not only their world but also the place you occupy in it. Not very surprising, then, that they're so determined to hold onto what may very well be the Male Mystique's last stronghold. (The obvious irony here, of course, is that men are fighting to maintain the very system that has failed them so grievously.) Women's Liberation has defined the underlying cause of this struggle as "sexist." But that's not it. Nor is it "economic expediency" or "social conditioning" or "biological necessity." No, men's denial of equal opportunity to women is finally a matter of the prisoners imprisoning their fellow prisoners.

But the prison walls are about to fall down. Not only have you come a long way, but it's been an incredibly fast trip. You may feel, and rightly so, that there's still much distance to be covered, but at least the roughest part of the journey is over. And although many men continue to resist this advance, your ultimate—and certain—triumph will also be their triumph.

It's not important that the old-fashioned definitions regarding masculinity and femininity no longer reflect the way in which we all live—if indeed they ever did. It's not even important whether or not most of us still believe in those definitions. What is important, however, is that as long as men and women do live by such stereotypes, they will be captive within them. If you insist on breaking free of stereotyped roles, and you are doing just that, then you'll eventually force men to do the same with their stereotypes. By liberating yourselves, you'll help liberate men as well.

Willie Sutton, who's broken out of more prisons than anyone else in history, was once asked what motivated his escapes. Fame? Fortune? Psychological need? "Hell, no," Willie replied. "It's freedom. Freedom's what it's all about, ain't it?" Ain't it?

FRIENDS

FRIENDS

ale friendship: the ideal, the real

Men grow up with an idealized picture of friendship. A man expects camaraderie to be strong, competition to be friendly. He expects schoolmates and army buddies to be loyal, mentors to be kind, and a best friend to stand behind him to the bitter end. Paul Newman and Robert Redford as Butch Cassidy and the Sundance Kid portray the ideal: two equally strong men linked together against the world.

In the ideal, a man will do anything for his best friend. He'll lend him money in large and small amounts (to save a failing business, finance a date, buy a case of beer); he'll give him a place to stay, for months if he asks (and even if he doesn't ask but just looks desperate); he'll drive hundreds of miles to bail him out of trouble; he'll even risk his life for him. In the ideal, a best friend can be counted on, too—to listen to a man's deepest worries, to stand beside him when he's down and out, or just depressed. But however a man would like to believe in the ideal, he also knows that business and friendship don't mix; that you can't trust anyone with your wife or your girlfriend—not even your best friend; that every man has a price.

And of course the ideal rarely, if ever, materializes. Although he may want and need the closeness of other men very much, a man's relationships with other men are not likely to be very intimate. Conversations do not often go beyond the "safe" topics. A man wants other men to see him as confident, successful, sexually assured. He may know he's not, but he won't admit it to other men, if to anyone.

The fact is that men do not trust each other. A man is unwilling to disclose vulnerabilities when he thinks the information could be used against him. He fears that if he tells someone that he's insecure about the kind of work he's doing, the guy will try for his job; that if he tells a friend he's worried his woman doesn't love him any more, his friend will start stalking her. And worse, he senses that if he admits he's scared, depressed, lonely, or sexually unsure, he'll lose face, be considered less manly. As indeed he would be. Men are harsh judges of one another. They are unsettled when a man doesn't "cut it." Weakness in one man hints that *any* man may be weak.

A man who does break down in front of another man creates a painful scene. The man who witnesses the emotional upset is going to feel less sympathy than desire to get the hell out of the situation immediately. And the man who broke down will feel ashamed of himself for a long time. Being raised to "tough it out" and hide their feelings has cheated men of the close, intimate friendships that almost all women share. There is pain and loneliness in the way men react to one another, but the fact remains that they just cannot turn honestly to one another for help.

So male friendships don't live up to the ideal, and men can't or don't trust one another. This is something men accept rather philosophically. The world, a man knows, is not perfect. "Boys will be boys," and "All's fair in love and war," he tells himself. And sometimes he's pleasantly surprised. Every now and then, just when a man thinks he's alone in the world, a friend will come through. That's at least some consolation against all the other times when it's *every* man for himself.

Early impressions

From childhood it was clear that men and boys did more important things than women and girls. Men had jobs and made money. Women, even if they worked, were responsible for the more mundane things, like housekeeping. Men were airline pilots, women were stewardesses. Men were doctors, women were nurses. Though attempts in the last decade have made some headway toward altering this perception of sex differences, it still prevails—and any adult male today grew up when the role divisions were clearly defined. There was something special about anything he did with Dad. It was with his father that he had his initial male experiences; it was with his father that he got to go to baseball games and auto races; it was with his father that he went camping and fishing.

When friends or family came to visit, he witnessed the segregation into sexes. He went with the men into the living room to watch sports on television, or out to the workshop to discuss men's things. He learned that men who are friends drink, talk, relax, and do things together. He learned that men sometimes get drunk and sometimes make passes at women, or get into fights with other men. Women, he learned, don't do these things. The men do everything centerstage.

Men's work was exciting and exotic. Father used power tools and he had special, magical skills. He built things, fixed things, and understood how cars, toasters, TV sets, and light fixtures worked. In his workshop there was no amiable chatter or giggling. Work was serious business. Horsing around or acting rowdy led to accidents, he was told; he or his friends could get hurt. Worst of all, however, he could be thrown out and have to leave the cherished manly hemisphere. And where would he go? Women used soap and mops and did boring things. He learned how to listen, to keep his mouth shut, to get the job done right. If he did well, he would get praise. But the men's world was special enough that just being allowed to participate made him glow.

But a good friend is hard to find

Loneliness is something every man feels—and probably denies, even to himself. A man sometimes socializes with people in the effort to prove—to himself, to women, to other men—that he is not alone or lonely. After breaking up with a woman who has reached the deepest part of him, a man is sometimes shocked to discover that he has no close friends to fall back on.

After my divorce I realized that I had allowed all of my friendships to drop, and I had no one to talk to.

It was pretty lonely. I began sleeping around a lot just to be with someone. And I started hanging around this one bar on nights I didn't have a date. I'd always be with people, but I never got what I wanted. It was like a sieve—the loneliness was a bottomless pit.

The masculine cult of toughness and independence demands that a man not need anybody. This keeps men apart. When a man's feeling down he can't call up another man and say, "Hey, I'm lonely. Will you come over and keep me company?" He can play tennis or go looking for women when he wants to be with someone, but he can't speak honestly about being lonely. That's too uncomfortable, and he's concerned that if he admits that "weakness" he'll lose the other man's respect.

Men are caught in a bind. On one hand they are reluctant to reveal themselves to their men friends, and on the other hand they long for male companionship. Afraid to be intimate, and lonely when they aren't, men alternate between keeping distance and seeking closeness. Most men secretly feel that they don't have any real friends. Even if he has a wife

or girlfriend who's close to him, a man often feels that no one really understands him.

Even when the friendships men create among themselves are warm and loving, they shy away from intimacy. Built on external foundations—doing things, playing or watching sports, drinking—men's friendships stop short of talking about the threats to closeness that are posed by the masculine ego. The dynamics of competition, the fear of failure, the constant comparing and one-upmanship that goes on—all make it impossible for men to really relax with one another.

When you meet another man the big question is always, "Is he better than me?" Even as you are shaking hands, you are measuring the strength and sureness of his grip as compared to yours.

Limited contact with other men is accepted as normal. And even with his closest friend a man will avoid conversations that touch on intimate or deeply felt subjects. No man presses another about how his relationship with his girlfriend is going. And work problems can be embarrassing enough to cause a man to end a friendship rather than endure the pain of talking about a failure. According to writer Tom Powers,

We speak, when we speak at all, of neutral things and take a long time to be at ease with each other, and let years go by without meeting just as if we had five lifetimes in which to be friends, and could afford to squander this one.

On another, perhaps unconscious level, men look to other men for a deeper kind of communication which is fleetingly, if ever, realized. Men seek the company of other men with a need deeper than companionship. It is a need that runs as deep as childhood feelings, as deep as the pain, frustration, anger, and hurt of their unrealized friendship with their fathers.

Medieval stories of knights and dragons have a moral for today's men, for within each man there is a dark castle with a fierce dragon to guard the gate. The castle contains a lonely self, a self most men have suppressed, a self they are afraid to show. Instead they present an armored knight—no one is invited inside the castle. The dragon symbolizes the fears and fantasies of masculinity, the leftover stuff of childhood. The

"If You Want A Friend..."

"One only understands the things that one tames," said the fox. "Men have no more time to understand anything. They buy things all ready made at the shops. But there is no shop anywhere where one can buy friendship, and so men have no friends any more. If you want a friend, tame me."

—ANTOINE DE SAINT EXUPÉRY.
The Little Prince

dragon is fearsome. To face it may mean being devoured by it.

Afraid, however, of being cut off, challenged, judged, men keep up their masculine defenses. In their armor they joust on the field while their inner self watches in lonely and frightened isolation.

Most men will acknowledge (perhaps uncomfortably) that imagery such as this strikes a familiar chord. A man knows that it's difficult, perhaps impossible, to confront the dragon of masculinity at the gate. He is afraid of it, uncertain of what it represents (his father? his own idea of what it means to be a man?). Whatever, he knows he would feel unbearably vulnerable without it. The dragon seems to protect his inner self from rejection by other males, from failure, from the universal void. The territory within is only vaguely intuited, an unexplored and terrifying realm. And it feels safer to keep up his defenses—a man can never know for sure if those strange inner feelings are shared by other men, or whether he is simply "too sensitive."

Men may claim they are satisfied with their friendships when, in fact, they are not. What they are saying is that they are glad for the friends they do have, even though the friendships are not always as deep or warm as they would like them to be.

Who his friends are

When a man talks about "a friend" he may be talking about a co-worker, a neighbor, a weekly tennis partner, a drinking buddy, or an acquaintance. He could also mean one or both members of a married couple, a former lover-turned-friend, an old roommate, a close woman friend, a cousin, or even a bartender. And he relates differently to different kinds of friends. A tennis partner may also be a close friend, a former lover may be a confidant, a business associate may also be a drinking buddy. A man is probably aware of the different levels of different friendships, and he knows the potential as well as the limitations of each. He may talk to a tennis partner about how tough his job is, but he won't tell him about the fight he had with his boss. He may tell his drinking buddy about the fight, but not that he felt humiliated by it. To a good friend he might admit that the argument led to his being fired. But probably he'll tell no one that he's humiliated by being fired and terrified that he won't find another job.

What Happens To Friendships In Old Age?

To find out, two Iowa State University professors interviewed 234 men and women aged 70 or older. They learned that:

About one-third of their close friends were relatives, more than half were about the same age, and only one-tenth were members of the opposite sex.

Older men keep in touch with a larger number of people than women, but their contact is basically limited to wives, casual friends, and children.

Women are more likely to have an intimate friend. Almost half the men said they don't have—and never did have—a close friend. Many said jokingly that their only friends were their wives.

Male friendships are often slow to evolve, and many men may have hesitations about developing intimate ties with other men. During his teens, twenties, and early thirties a man works hard to prove his sexuality, establish his career, start a family. Because of this, a man may find himself in his mid-thirties and realize that he has no solid, intimate friendships with other men. Then he slows down and begins to look at what he wants from life. His marriage, family, and career take shape, and his emotional and physical security grows. As self-understanding and personal growth begin to reduce the need to prove "masculinity," a man is more open to two-way friendships with other men that will have real value to him.

As circumstances in a man's life change, friendships change. High school and college buddies may drift away when a man gets married. Later, after family and careers are stabilized, two old companions may renew their relationship. And sometimes a crisis, like a career change, death in the family, or divorce, may draw the two men closer as one calls for, or the other offers, support.

I had a close friend I stopped seeing because he had an argument with my wife. I had no contact with him for three years. When she and I separated, he heard about it and called to tell me I could stay at his apartment. He never said anything about her; he never asked me what happened.

Men who fail to develop strong long-term friendships often find themselves isolated when they grow older. It's hard to begin making friends when children first leave home, or when he retires—by then he's out of practice, and out of touch with friends from the past. Older men in America are very dependent on the women in their lives, usually their spouses, for companionship and caring. In fact, the death rate of single or widowed old men is twice that of women in a similar situation—indicating that loneliness weighs heavily on them.

In the last few years, men have begun to change. They have begun to share child care and housework, to enjoy friendships with women, children, older people, and one another. The man who has begun to redefine his roles becomes less fiercely competitive, more sensitive, and more able to share his feelings, and to be, on the whole, a better candidate for a solid friendship.

roups—men together

"Male bonding" is a phrase often used to describe the behavior of men in groups. Supposedly a holdover from the time when men survived by banding together to hunt, it is now considered the motivating force behind men's clubs, bars, poker games. The "good old boys" system shows up in football, politics, the corporate structure.

A man is drawn to other men for numerous reasons: their strength of character, their style, the way they talk, swear, fight, bounce a basketball, get angry, wear their clothes, or drink their beer. He may emulate a successful man, befriend him, try to learn from him. He will also establish other relationships which give him a chance to share information and skills.

In groups and on teams he learns to value himself as an equal, as he learns to follow orders, rules, and codes. When he first joins a group or team, he may be greeted by indifference, and perhaps he is subjected to some sort of trial. But the first rude comments may signal acceptance, not rejection. Later, he may assume leadership himself.

In business, men don't always follow the rules, and once a man has been taken advantage of, he learns to discriminate between friendship and business. When he leaves a job he is sometimes surprised and hurt to discover that he has lost some friendships as well.

The comradeship that's often present when men get together gives a man a feeling of self-affirmation as well as a connection to other men. Even in situations that are clearly unequal—between a boss and an employee, between a father and son, between rivals—there is still a sense of common ground which, though it may be fought over, is defined as male turf. Men share a common perception of the world simply because they are all men. This felt reality binds them closely.

A loyalty code was further reinforced when he either joined the military team or, during the '60s, stayed away, as part of a movement, from the military. Again when he joined the team at the office or factory. But friendship has its limits, and these are most obvious in competitive situations where team choices, and advances, are made on the basis of ability, not friendship. At all costs, the team has to remain united and strong, even if some members leave the team or are replaced.

Having favorites, he learns, can lead to emotional rather than rational choices at critical moments: choosing a friend, or starting him on a team when another player is clearly superior in the position; saving a buddy's life at the risk of losing control of a strategic military position; supporting a friend by advising he be kept on even though performing poorly in his job.

Team sports give a man a sense of himself as part of a group. He learned to be competitive at the same time he learned to mesh his individuality into the group. The activity and excitement of competition is an important factor to men.

For example, an office baseball team. Baseball is the all-American sport, and the men have been playing the game since childhood. They enjoy the opportunity to see if they can hit the ball, catch it, throw it, work together as a team. While individual ability and performance are important, the men know that equally important to victory is how well they work together. Personal likes and dislikes will be shelved. The shortstop may not like the third baseman because he encroaches on his defensive territory, but that won't prevent him from rooting for him in his turn at bat, or from appreciating a fine defensive play, even at his own expense. After the game the team will gather at a local hangout, often in the company of the opponents. Rivalries are clearly seen for what they are: conventions for the purpose of generating competitive spirit and excitement. Everyone enjoys a good, hard-fought game—and the socializing afterward. Competitive play is hard work, most players feel, and socializing and drinking after the game are viewed as an earned reward.

Why I Returned to Football Coaching

I've been in politics and I've been in business. And I don't mean to knock them, but the emotional aspects of the game are stronger than anywhere else. The feelings you had toward shipmates in World War II, those are the feelings you have in athletics.

—BUD WILKINSON

If the group is special or in some way esoteric—an exclusive club, for example—then mutual respect for privacy may be an important element. A man may belong to an athletic club, where he goes for a workout and a game of squash three times a week. Most of the other men will be regulars also, each involved in his own carefully worked-out program of exercises and conditioning. There will be practically no contact between the men. The athletic rigors are a personal challenge. One man may ask another for advice on how to operate a machine; one man may watch another man doing yoga for a while before asking for information on doing certain exercises; two men may briefly discuss their goals or regimen. But conversation is almost nonexistent, the religious silence broken only by an occasional grunt accompanied by a nod toward a familiar face. The atmosphere is self-contained and strained, intense in its self-absorption. The club membership consists of a select group training for a noble rite of masculinity.

Men's groups affirm old values. They assure familiarity; they are relaxing, inspirational, distracting, often seemingly mindless. They can give a man a feeling of confidence about his value as a man and an opportunity to gauge himself in relation to other men in a positive setting.

> At the plant the boss is always on me. But out on the baseball field I shine. When I came here this team wasn't worth much. I got them going. Last year we were league champs. We'll probably do it again this year. Everybody in the whole plant knows who I am because of it. And I got their respect. Next year I'm running for union rep, and I'll probably get it, too.

Men view competing and hanging out with each other as equals relating to equals. A man seeks approval from a woman, but he may consider the admiration of another man an even higher reward.

> If I told my wife I shot 986 in skeet, she would say, "That's terrific." She supports what I do, what I enjoy. But she really doesn't know what it means to shoot that high. Another man knows and appreciates what I'm talking about in a way a woman can't, at least one who doesn't shoot skeet. Harry, on the

other hand, is a top shot, the team captain. When he heard what I shot he came right over and congratulated me. He told me I could make the team if I kept it up. I don't know if I can keep it up, but I'm sure going to try. I was flying for a week after he told me that.

Boys' night out

The sight of men together may well make you feel like a tourist in a strange country inhabited by an exotic tribe. Accustomed to the way women interact, to the way men act with you or other women, even to the way men perform in business or sports, you may well wonder what tribe this is that, left to itself, is so quick to posture, overreact, drink excessively, act foolishly, shout, jab, and grunt without seeming to communicate on any recognizable level.

What is really going on out in the garage when a man and his friends gather around the opened hood of a car like a team of surgeons about to perform open-heart surgery, debating heatedly about spark plugs and needle valves? From the outside, all you see is a steady stream of beer bottles moving out of the refrigerator and through the back door. While the gathering starts out innocently enough, it slowly becomes cacophonous. Less and less work seems to be getting done. Eventually, all pretense of work ends and the group piles in to "test" the car. You don't see him until late that night. What, you may well ask, is this strange ritualistic behavior all about?

The "boys' night out," as concept if not as cliché, is an American institution. Depending on the man, it may mean Wednesday-night bowling or basketball, a poker game or a chess game, weekend softball leagues or camping trips, fishing or hunting expeditions, butterfly collecting or drag racing. It may include some plain old carousing. It could mean occasional drinking, or nightly gatherings at the watering hole. Regardless of the specific activity, however, most men are likely to reserve (or wish for) some time to spend strictly in the company of other men.

What men talk about

Men talk about cars, sports, women, work, hobbies, daily events, and politics. Everyone knows that. They keep distance

Going Down The Mine Elevator

The miners talked, as men in such quarters will, of women, fishing, hunting, the biggest tomato they ever grew, and women.

—*The New York Times*

Overheard In McSorley's Ale House In New York, When It Was Forced By Law To Open Its Doors To Women For The First Time, 1970

You know, they have a stereotype of women in this place that isn't true. They think there aren't any women who like onions and limburger cheese. Why, I know a lot of women who like onions and limburger cheese.

this way, they relax, they can be with each other while the heaviest issue of the day is whether the bantamweight boxing class is lighter or heavier than the featherweight boxing class.

"Is that really all that's going on?" you ask. The answer is, "Yes and no." The talk is merely words; on another level it allows men to be together without "doing" anything. Words are familiar code sounds. And then, of course, there is the humor, an important part of being together "talking about nothing." It allows for safe discharge of tensions and anxieties, competition and hostility, feelings of anger and insecurity. And when one man greets another with a string of four-letter words, it is the tone of voice that signals that he likes his friend and is glad to see him.

Men's sounds, while they may seem to you discordant, belligerent, and gruff, have a curious harmony. Language and the sound of words are used to show masculinity, toughness, competitiveness, club membership, heterosexuality. Any regular gathering of men, whether in a bar across from a plant, a college faculty club, or an American Legion, will have a special language, a coded noise-making that communicates as much, if not more, to the other members of the group as do dress, body language, or facial expressions. A steelworker may exclaim loudly that his boss should "blow it out his ass," while a college professor will circumspectly and quietly declare that his chairman is a "retromingent onager," but the men gathered around each will understand that their friend is letting out anger, asking for a vote of approval and agreement. Men not only communicate with words, but with presence, style, gesture, manner, and intonation. And other men in the group know instinctively how to read what is being said in this peculiarly male language.

Surprisingly, television has helped men talk about painful subjects. Television is a fixture of every tavern, from exclusive clubs to rowdy bars. And the dramas of television, frequent barroom fare, provide events close enough to the drama of men's lives to spur them to comment on their own. A family drama in which a wife leaves her husband will lead a man to comment to the man next to him, "I know what they're talking about; it happened to me." TV police arresting a teenage offender may lead a man to talk about his own troubles with his children. The television, by showing a painful situation, makes it OK: It can happen to any man.

Talkers and listeners

For many men, barbers are a race of ears, with the power to cut hair, shave a beard, and *listen*. As a barber silently, rhythmically clips, a man may spill out his worries or his triumphs. A man may know his barber as well as a woman knows her hairdresser.

Bartenders are another breed of professional friends who make great listeners. Some bars are like an extended family; longtime regulars, old friends, business associates, company men, meet and greet each other through the years of ups and downs. The bartender, in a bar of this kind, is a friendly, familiar fixture who provides a sense of stability that holds the group together. Knowing that "good old Gus" can be counted on to be behind the bar makes the place a refuge for many men.

> *David was a bartender at Caffrey's who had a knack for names. If you came in once he would remember your name for years, and probably what you drink too. He had a reputation for running a lively bar because he knew how to introduce people to each other. He'd get a barful of strangers engaged in incredible conversations. David would never participate, except to get things started and keep the glasses full. He was everybody's friend. On his nights off, the place was like a tomb.*

A good bartender talks little and listens lots. He is attentive and interested, he helps give perspective, he asks the right questions. The talk between bartender and customer can be beneficial, and the confession can run deep.

> *A drinking man alone is usually looking for some-one to talk to, especially if he's a regular, I can tell. If his friends aren't around, I find out what's on his mind. It's good business and he does most of the talking. When I'm busy, I'll try to get him into a conversation with someone else, which usually isn't too difficult. Most people are pretty social, and they are not here to be alone. I've heard men talk about their deepest troubles—women, business, wives, gambling, you name it—sitting right here at this bar. Usually, all a guy is looking for is someone who'll hear him out.*

Men In Bars

There's a bunch, you know, who'll say before the bar opens that Vietnam was a disaster, but a couple of hours later they're giving you all the old war stories, seven-eighths of which aren't true anyway.

—an American pilot,
at a reunion of Vietnam veterans

mportant connections

Whether it's a next-door neighbor he chats with over the hedge on Saturday mornings or a buddy he trusts more than anyone else, there are many people in any man's life who connect with him in important ways. These people may include any or all of the following: a close friend, first friend, a brother or sister, a milestone friend, a doing-things friend, a mentor friend, a convenience friend.

Close friend

Men love to talk, to have an audience, to know the answers or hold forth on any topic, even when they don't know the answers or what they are talking about. Competition and struggle for dominance in conversation is a kind of game for men, especially in groups. Any bar on a Friday night is a chaos of arguments. In mixed groups of men and women, men will compete with each other to get the women's attention. But in a close friendship, a man can get past big talk and small talk both. Less competitive, less defensive, aware of how they feel about each other, close friends are there for each other in times of need.

Even with a close friend, a man may resist talking about problems, hurts, or uncertainties. Good friends know each other well enough to spot the dodging. But on some subjects, like women or family trouble, it goes against the male code to push a man to talk when he's uncomfortable. Joking ("It only hurts when I laugh"), keeping a stiff upper lip, gritting teeth, are peculiarly masculine communications which say, "It's tough, but I'm man enough to take it."

The show of physical affection between men is forbidden. In situations where a man and a woman would dance, hold hands, or hug, two men are limited to slaps on the back, a friendly punch or two to the shoulder, and an embarrassed laugh. The scene of two drunken friends holding each other up singing barroom songs is a familiar one. If they weren't drunk, they wouldn't be able to keep touching each other without feeling uncomfortable or on the spot.

Men like to be close to other men—which is part of why they get together in groups. But men are mysterious to each other as well as to women. Maybe this is because a boy was turned off his father's knee at such an early age. Girls get to hold hands, touch each other, and curl up on Mommy's lap for

years while boys must confine touching to handshakes, contact sports like football and wrestling, and the backslapping and punches that become the trademarks of masculine interaction. Getting drunk is a way to make contact—to touch each other and be close if not necessarily affectionate.

Most men do not want to be perceived as gay, but that is not the main reason that they do not openly express affection with other men. What they fear is being considered unmasculine, which is something quite different. Men are not as horrified by homosexuality as you might imagine; many men in this country have had some homosexual experience, and still consider themselves heterosexual—as indeed they are. They regard their homosexual experience as a normal and healthy part of growing up—and as something that "doesn't show." Masculinity, however, is an *image,* not a form of behavior such as homosexuality. Most men—even many gay ones—feel they have no alternative but to maintain that image, to act the way they think men are supposed to act.

Verbal expression of affection is not easy either, even for close friends. Men will do things for each other, buy each other drinks, make insulting or cutting remarks intended as flattery or affection. Men will feel more comfortable paying a compliment or communicating appreciation, affection, or love for a close friend to someone else, another man, even to a group, rather than to the friend himself.

> *I knew Steve liked me, but I found out how much one night at a scouting group we were leading together. The kids were sitting around the fire having a discussion about what love is. Steve was encouraging the boys to come up with images of different kinds of love. He was giving examples of how he loved his wife, his son, his mother, and then pointing at me, he said, "And I love Hank, too." I felt really good. We've never talked about it, but for sure we love each other.*

A man may express love for another man in dramatic ways—by saying, for example, that he'd "do anything" for a specific friend or he'd "put his life on the line" for him. Most likely his heroic loyalty will never be tested. But a man likes to believe that he would come through. And letting another man down can give him a painful sense of failure.

I do with my friends as I do with my books. I would have them where I could find them, but I seldom use them.

—RALPH WALDO EMERSON.
Friendship

When we were 16, my friend Jerry and I and several other friends were hanging out on the corner. We got into a shouting match with a couple of other guys. They came over and accused Jerry of calling them names. I had actually been the name caller.

But I was afraid to speak up. They were rough and I was afraid they would beat me up. All my friends were there. We watched the confrontation between Jerry and this one guy. The guy provoked a fight, which Jerry lost. He wasn't hurt, but it was humiliating for Jerry. And for the rest of us, because there were ten of us and only two of them, yet we all stood around and watched him get knocked around. I took no responsibility for my part in it. But I felt awful and ashamed for years. I still do.

Men tend to keep the same friends for many years. A friend made in high school, a college buddy, the guy he met the first day on the job—surprisingly, this man may still be a best friend 20 years later. Even when new friendships evolve, a man will continue to hang onto old friends. He may recategorize them but he will tell himself that he still has them. Close friendships, cut off by marriage, a job change, or simply separate interests, have a way of renewing themselves years later. Friendships between women often follow a similar pattern. But with men there is an unconscious provision, an assumption almost, that when close friends part they will meet again. Men believe friendships, like love affairs, will last forever. Romantic as this notion is, there is truth in it. Men will tell stories of friendships that were renewed after a lapse of 20 or 30 years and that proved deeper than ever.

First friend

A man's earliest remembered friend will probably have been another male.

"Big boys don't cry," I was told when I cried in kindergarten. I wasn't going to do it again when I entered first grade. But I did. I was embarrassed, but I saw the kid sitting next to me looking at me as if he was interested. He looked relieved. Later I found out he had flunked first grade. He probably felt as scared and self-conscious as I did. With him it

---

"Misfortune is the Test of True Friendship"

Two men were traveling in company through a forest, when, all at once, a huge bear crashed out of the brush near them.

One of the men, thinking of his own safety, climbed a tree.

The other, unable to fight the savage beast alone, threw himself on the ground and lay still, as if he were dead. He had heard that a bear will not touch a dead body.

It must have been true, for the bear snuffed at the man's head a while, and then, seeming to be satisfied that he was dead, walked away.

The man in the tree climbed down.

"It looked as if that bear whispered something in your ear," he said. "What did he tell you?"

"He said," answered the other, "that it was not at all wise to keep company with a fellow who would desert his friend in a moment of danger."

—Aesop's Fables

was OK that I cried because he understood how I felt. He turned out to be my best friend for eight years.

A first friend connects a man to a self he scarcely remembers when he's an adult. A first friend knew him when he couldn't even write his name, when he threw popcorn in the movies, when he got beaten up by a girl. Childhood feelings run deep. Scenes from a first friendship may appear with a clearness a man can scarcely summon for the events of last week. Sleeping over at each other's houses, a special hiding place, peeing off the roof, playing doctor with the girl next door—the events and contexts of a childhood friendship can make it more intense than any other friendship he'll ever have.

Less idyllic, because far more self-conscious and even guilt-producing, is the intense friendship that may develop between adolescent boys, especially in all-male settings such as prep schools. In early adolescence, a boy—like a girl—has a great deal to think about and talk about, and he badly needs a friend of his own age, whether or not of his own sex. Such friendships are not homosexual in motivation, yet inevitably they become charged with sexuality as the two friends share their thoughts and become emotionally dependent on each other. The one thing they cannot talk about, of course—except in adolescent friendships that do lead to sex—is that they have come to love each other, and that the love is partly physical. Consequently, a man may feel embarrassed in later life to remember that he had such a friendship—yet he is apt to recognize that the friendship was good for him and helped him to grow up, and he is likely to think of this as his first *real* friend.

Brothers and sisters

Sometimes, of course, they don't even like each other. But even so, because they are branches from the same tree, a man will feel a sense of oneness with his brothers and sisters. A man is likely to be loyal to brothers and sisters with a fierceness that is unequaled in any of his other relationships, including his relationship with his wife. That there is a blood tie may be reason enough for a man to offer help (a place to sleep, money, job-hunting assistance); empathy (a willing ear to a tale of woes); tolerance (defense for a brother or sister, even when he or she has behaved badly). Perhaps sharing a common past—even an unhappy common past—is part of the reason for this special tie.

A brother is a friend given by nature.

—GABRIEL MARIE LEGOUVE

Bob and I are several years apart. We weren't particularly close as kids, but there is a special feeling I get when we are together. We each learn about ourselves when we talk about things, different views of our parents, how we felt growing up. Being with my brother is like taking a look at my childhood through new eyes.

Because she's female, a sister is likely to get her brother's protection whether she needs it or not. Even if he has tormented her all through childhood, he'll spring to her defense with a vengeance.

Even if my sister were really whoring around or something, if I heard anybody say something dirty about her I'd go into a rage. I'd probably try to kill the guy. Why? She's my sister, that's why.

And sometimes a sister is the person he goes to for help:
I am often mystified by behavior of women I'm in love with. My sister has really helped me understand what's going on with women, both socially and sexually. She's done a lot to help me understand my own behavior, too.

You can choose your friends but you can't choose your relatives.

—CHARLIE BROWN

Many men feel a duty-bound sense of reverence for family. It's important for him to know that there's a place where he'll always be accepted, people who he can trust, and who can trust him. Brothers and sisters, like parents, are related to him in an unalterable way.

Milestone friends

Friends from the past are important to a man because they shared crucial times in his life: the kid from North Carolina who went through basic training with him, the guy he met in Copenhagen and traveled around Europe with for six months, the college roommate who shared the ups and downs of his first love affair, the guy he lived with when he was trying to get his career going. With a milestone friend a man can talk about old times as if they were yesterday—and the feelings of those days are probably still very much alive. Even if they have gone separate ways and have little in common any more, they may still write each other once a year or so.

> *John let me live with him after I got fired—it was almost four months before I got another job. I've never told him how black it looked then, but he knew. If it wasn't for him I might have wound up working in the family business—pure misery. But he kept at me to keep plugging. One morning he literally poured water on me to get me out of bed for an interview. I only see him every couple of years now, but I'll always feel close to him.*

It may seem that men endow milestone friendships with an overly romantic glow, but the reason for this is that the friend connects him with who he once was—and that is an important component of who he is now.

Doing-things friends

Sharing mutual interests or activities is enough to bring men together. Not all friendships need be deep, nor need they involve family or work. Into this group will fall the weekly tennis partner, the guys on the company hockey team, the members of the service lodge, the guy he designs and builds model airplanes with. The key word in all these relationships is *doing*.

> *This guy Jack and I are squash nuts. We're evenly matched. And so twice a week we get a chance to really unwind. After we play, all we talk about is squash. It never goes any further than that.*

When men are really only interested in playing the game they may skip post-game socializing altogether.

> *I play chess once a week with another man, and we don't even have a drink afterward. The game is almost businesslike. The competition is fierce and we both love it. It forces us to concentrate and gets our minds off other things.*

When women get together to do things, it is often an excuse to share on other levels. But for men, the activity itself is a sufficient reason to get together. They don't want to talk about anything. They want to forget it all.

For most men, jobs are very demanding and emotionally draining. Family life, too, requires an enormous commitment of energy and time. It's relaxing for a man to do things that free him from having to talk or think about other areas of his life. Frustrations, anger, tensions all disappear as he involves himself in an activity which is clear-cut in its demands, rules, and direction.

> *All you have to do in a tennis game is get the ball over the net. And if you don't it's not such a big deal. You can work on it. It's strictly between you and the ball.*

Mentor friends

His father was the first man he looked up to, respected, imitated. He learned from him how to fish, play ball, cut wood with a power saw, mix and drink a martini. Later, he met men who filled some of the roles his father did—mentors. A mentor provides a man with an image of who he wants to be.

> *He taught me a lot about writing, about the ins and outs of publishers, agents, and magazine writing. Our friendship had a lot of other sides to it as well.*

*We went out on double dates, began an organiza-
tion and worked on the newsletter together, played
sports together. But writing was the foundation.
Later, after I got a few contracts, we lost touch. I
still respect him as a writer. But our relationship is
more distant, more equal now. We have a different
kind of friendship. I'm as likely to give him advice as
he is me now. But we've lost that intimacy we once
shared.*

Friendship with an older man is important to a man when
he seeks to map his future. The unknown can be terrifying.
Knowing someone who has been where he wants to go, who
has accomplished things he seeks for himself, diffuses that
fear.

Convenience friends

Many of the men he is friendly with are not so much
friends as they are men he exchanges favors with. At work he
may have someone who covers for him when he's late or
takes a three-hour lunch. The guys in the car pool or the guy
who picks him up when his car is in the shop are also
friendships of convenience. At home he can borrow a lawn
roller from Sam down the block, hedge trimmers from Al next
door, and a bottle of Scotch from Jack across the street. In
return, he makes available his outboard motor, his engine
timer, and his whiskey sour glasses.

These friends will take Timmy and keep an eye on him
when he can't make it to the Boy Scout meeting, will take care
of his car and water the plants while he is on vacation, and will
help him clean up the back lot so they can plant a vegetable
garden.

Convenience friendships are not only convenient, they
provide many things afforded by the small communities of the
past, the extended families and villages of our ancestors.

Convenience friends may know little about each other—
there is no need for them to. Seldom do convenience
friendships extend beyond the problems of the neighborhood
or the office. It's unlikely a close friendship, even a couples
friendship, will develop. Friendships of convenience are
valuable just as they are, and generally he will find little reason
to try to expand them.

Friendships with women

A man's closest woman friend is almost always the woman he lives with and/or is sexually involved with. Sexuality and intimacy blend into a deep fulfilling closeness. As you know, there are some things lovers and spouses talk about that are unique and shared with no one else. Much of the communication will be a nonverbal, intuitive sensitivity to one another's inner workings.

A man may have an intimate friendship with a woman in a nonsexual relationship, too. The absence of sex can give room for illuminating insights that sexual involvement might blur. Free from the tensions that come from sexual involvement, and free from the restrictions that surround friendships with men, a platonic friendship with a woman allows a man a balanced, honest exchange of feelings. A man will expect something different from a relationship with a woman friend than he will from a man friend. He may not call and ask her to help dig his car out of a ditch at three in the morning, but he will call her when he feels helpless and alone. Instead of confining his talk to surface things as he may with men friends, he'll want a woman friend to dig deeper into his feelings. With women, a man will be more willing to let down barriers, show his weak side, reveal his silliness, make mistakes, let out half-baked ideas and outrageous fantasies. A woman friend can give him insights into the woman he *is* sexually or romantically involved with, and he may be able to ask his woman friend questions that seem too threatening to ask his woman lover directly.

Since in many ways a friendship with a woman is less threatening than a friendship with a man or a relationship with a lover, a man may talk to her about feelings and motivations that he's uncomfortable revealing elsewhere. The ability to do this may be a kind of psychological muscle-flexing ("See, I *am* open and in touch with my own feelings"), and it makes a man feel good about himself.

> I feel comfortable talking with my woman friend
> Jess, about anything—work, family, sex, my day-to-
> day problems, my ideas and insights. She has a way
> of asking the right questions that get me to thinking.
> She never makes me feel like I'm on the spot. If I
> feel stuck or depressed or just confused, she seems
> to know what to do. She talks to me about the men

*in her life, her problems at work, and I try to help
her. Sometimes that means telling her my experiences about the business world. Other times it'll be
how men think and why they act the way they do.
As I talk to her I am often surprised at how much I
know in ways I wasn't aware of before.*

**Can Men and Women Be
Friends?**

Redbook magazine posed
this question to celebrities,
and got these answers:

Tom Jones: *I've never seen
it happen. Well, maybe you
can if there's something sexually wrong with you.*

Mick Jagger: *Some of my
best friends are women. Men
and women have been close
friends for thousands of
years.*

Joe Namath: *I personally
have several—all around the
country.*

Andy Warhol: *No. Men get
tired of women too easily.
Men are simply better than
women. My best friend is my
dog.*

Friendships with women are not always easy to initiate or
to sustain. Any teenager who seems more interested in being
friends with a girl will be ridiculed as a "sissy." In high school
and college, the focus is on dating. Sexuality, if it's not
centerstage, is always lurking in the wings.

And, of course, sexuality is always a part of any
relationship between a man and a woman. The feelings may
be light or intense, in the unspoken background, or always
cropping up to the surface, but it's there. And sometimes sex
can destroy a potentially satisfying friendship. This can
happen when a man and woman try to fit a potential
friendship into bed and it doesn't belong there.

Friendships sometimes survive a misguided fall into bed.
And while lovers do not necessarily make the best friends,
friendships often develop out of a relationship that began in
the bedroom.

*Lucy and I went together for a year. We broke up in
anger and didn't see each other for over a year.
One day she called and said she thought we'd
missed something by not staying friends. And since
we began seeing each other as friends, it's great.
Because we have been on intimate terms we can
talk about things I can't discuss with anyone else—
men or my girlfriend.*

Whether a man chooses an older woman, a gay woman,
an ex-lover, an ex-wife, a sister, a co-worker, or a classmate to
be his close friend, and whether they go hiking, play tennis, eat
out, go to movies, or just sit and talk, the aspects of the
friendship he values most will be feeling able to be open,
relaxed, and understood in a direct, honest way.

COUPLES

hat does a man want?

These days no woman would try to mold herself to fit any man's dream, would she? Since the Women's Movement, women no longer depend on male approval in order to feel good about themselves, do they?

Maybe not consciously. But you'd still like to know what turns men on. And whoever you are, and however much you may love yourself, you probably think you're missing a few crucial parts. If you're waiflike, you think you should be a *femme fatale*. If you have small breasts, you think he really wants a woman who's a 36D. If you're less than beautiful, you're sure that if you looked like Catherine Deneuve your troubles would be over. If you're knock-down gorgeous with a shape like Raquel Welch, you worry that he's only after you for your body. Who is the woman of his dreams, anyway?

There's good news. When 40,000 men were asked (in a 1978 *Redbook* survey) to describe the most important traits in the ideal woman, the winning quality turned out to be: *love.* More than 81 percent of the men listed "her love for me" as the most essential characteristic of their ideal partner.

Tell me who you long for in your secret dreams.
Go on and tell me who you wish I was instead of me.
I'm not necessarily the girl you think you see.
Whoever you want is exactly who I'm more than willing to be.

— Carly Simon and Jacob Brackman

Okay, you may say, but what else? For sure, the next most important quality has got to be a pretty face or a beautiful body, right? Wrong. Listed before (way before) "beautiful body" or "pretty face" were:

> intelligence
> sense of humor
> a career of your own
> self-confidence

What about breasts? Legs? A perfect nose? And all the other things you've been hating yourself for not having all these years? Those things are nice if you've got them, but not essential to being the woman of his dreams. (About breasts: It seems that some men prefer small-breasted women just as some prefer large-breasted women.)

But wait. Why do men stare, ogle, point, jab each other in the ribs, pant off down the street after a woman who looks like a *Playboy* centerfold? What about all those ads that show the proud grin of a guy who has a busty beautiful blonde in a fuzzy sweater hanging onto his arm and batting big, adoring eyes up at him? Isn't that the woman who really turns him on? Isn't she the one he fantasizes about?

> *Sure, a big busty dame is a curiosity—guys like to*
> *stare. And though I may want to take a woman like*
> *that to a party, she's not really the woman I want to*
> *be with. The woman that really turns me on is*
> *softer, more real.*

It will come as no surprise to you to hear that men like to impress each other. More often than not, all the snickering and drooling that men do over a *Playboy* bunny-type woman is done to show off. Which is not to say that he doesn't get aroused when he thumbs through girly magazines, that he'll mind if you are beautiful as well as being warm, loving, and self-assured, or that if Sophia Loren called and asked him out he'd turn her down. It's just that beauty, however nice it is if you've got it, can't serve as a substitute when the more essential things are missing. In fact, when a man is around a totally beautiful, glamorous, brilliant, sought-after woman, he'll likely be so awed that he'll feel like a stuttering clod. And though it may do something for his ego to be seen in public with such a woman (he imagines people thinking, "Wow, that guy must be something special to get *her*"), if she isn't warm, and sensitive to him, the ego high only lasts as long as he's with her in public. Men like women who make them feel good, confident, alive, not ones who leave them paralyzed with fear and insecurity. A beautiful woman may need extra amounts of warmth, affection, and sincerity for a man to feel comfortable enough with her to fall in love. Knockout good looks may make for excitement, but scare love off.

What really turns a man on?

Warmth.

A woman who has the quality of intimacy...in the sense that she gives me the feeling she knows me, and appreciates who I am.

A woman who's natural. A woman who can talk to me, who looks into my eyes and really sees me.

A woman with smarts. Not necessarily educated, or up on foreign affairs, but a woman who's with it, alive, on top of things.

A woman who can make me laugh.

What turns a man off?

A woman who just sits there. I don't care how pretty she is, if she's not alive, who needs her?

Heavy makeup.

Perfume so strong it could knock you down.

A woman who always worries about her hair. She won't go swimming, because it'll wreck her hair.

Women who are helpless. Who depend on me to decide everything.

Sexy, it seems, doesn't have so much to do with how you look as with how you act and how you feel about yourself. Self-confidence is sexy. Being able to take care of yourself is sexy. The happier, more confident, and more in control of your life you are, the more a man will want to be around you.

It's not that a man doesn't want you to need him. He does. But in the sense that he wants to be essential to your feeling of well-being, not in the sense that he wants to be depended on for survival—financial or emotional.

The clinging-vine routine is a notorious turnoff. Which figures. If you are happy and in tune with yourself and still need him, that's a compliment. That makes him feel good, important. If you are a little girl lost, helpless, afraid, desperate, clingy, the fact that you need him doesn't do much for his ego. If you're desperate it probably looks as though just about any guy would do.

The woman who's willing to mold herself to be "what he wants" is caught in a cruel irony, since any man with a strong sense of his own identity wants a woman who's real. Solid. Unless he's wishy-washy himself, wishy-washy will most likely turn him off. Which is probably something you've already discovered if you've ever tried desperately to hang onto a man by changing in order to please him.

Reasons men ask women out

What makes a man want to ask you out in the first place? From the way they talk about women, it often sounds as though men are out to "get something." And although "Get much?" is a question men supposedly don't ask one another after high school, there are still times when you may feel very much like a sexual quarry. Is he out to "score"? If you have been giving him signals that sex is something you're after, that may be what he has in mind. And though the possibility of sex is always in the back of his mind (just as it's in the back of yours), it's not always the reason (or even an expectation) behind his asking you out.

Does he want to show off to his friends? If you are very beautiful, successful, famous, or otherwise have some clout in the circles you move in, this could be true.

The reason a man asks you out isn't always your beauty, your sexy body, or your star quality. He may just want the same thing from you that you want from him: warmth. Someone to talk to. Someone to have fun with, to make him feel good, and if things go exceptionally well, someone who'll understand him.

He's afraid you'll turn him down

The thing you may not realize is that by the time a man gets himself together enough to ask you out, he has created a mental picture of what you'll be like. Even if his total exposure to you consists of a glimpse across a crowded room, he will have put together some expectations. He feels he knows you. So what you've got on the other end of the phone is a man with a positive mental picture of you who has decided he wants to spend some time with you. However unrealistic or ridiculous this may be, the fact is that you are talking to a man who cares about you. And this makes him vulnerable to hurt if you turn him down. Few women realize the extent to which a man fears being rejected.

Sometimes, if a man is really attracted to you, his fear of

The meeting of two personalities is like the contact of two chemical substances: if there is any reaction, both are transformed.

—CARL JUNG,
Modern Man in Search of a Soul

being turned down is so great that he'll *never even ask you out.* Which is why the man you noticed staring wistfully at you at a party never called. And why a lot of beautiful, talented women sit home alone on Saturday night.

You might think that the fear of getting turned down is something a man outgrows, but it isn't. Nor does he outgrow some of the other awkward, uncomfortable fumblings that take place on a first date. It may be hard for you to believe that this terrific-looking, adult male person who has just charmed you over dinner could be standing there on your doormat wondering, "Should I ask myself in? Will it turn her off if I kiss her?" But he may very well be doing just that. There is a little bit of Woody Allen lurking behind *every* man's exterior—no matter how cool and in control he acts.

The appeal of a hard-to-get woman

If a man's so worried about being rejected, why does he like a hard-to-get woman? There's a difference between hard to get and impossible to get. A hard-to-get woman is a challenge. An impossible-to-get woman is a rejection. If he has the feeling that with you there's no way, he's not likely to hang around for long. But if underneath your "no" there's a "yes" struggling to get out, he may find that a big turn-on. Breaking down your resistance can give him a sense of power and importance. It feels good to know he's irresistible.

But however much a man wants to know that he counts, he doesn't want to count so much that he becomes responsible for you. Being hard to get not only gives him the feeling that you're worth something, it also gives him the feeling that you can take care of yourself. And that's important. If you can take care of yourself, he won't have to worry about getting "stuck." He can get involved with you, change his mind, and get the hell out without feeling he's leaving you bloodied by the side of the road. Most men do not want to hurt you. Most men, in fact, are so worried about hurting a woman that they go to great lengths to avoid doing so. Which is why if you appear helpless and vulnerable you're likely to find men staying away in droves.

What does all this mean to you? If you really like a man—zonko!—on first sight, should you hide your feelings? Hide, no. Keep in check, yes. And if this sounds like game-playing, it is. But it's a game everyone plays. Even you. If a man is crazy about you right off the bat, fawning and pawing and pouring on compliments when you haven't done a thing to deserve any adulation, you probably think there's something wrong with him. You feel much more comfortable about him and about yourself when you see him being won over by your wonderfulness in slower, more realistic degrees. A man feels more confident with this too.

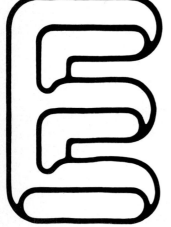lusive men

Why did the guy who met and adored you at a cocktail party never call for a date? Why does a guy take you out, pour his guts out to you, make love to you, leave you with the feeling that this could be the start of something big, and then wander off, never to be heard from again? Why does a man go out with you twice a week for a month or more and then stop calling with no explanation?

The bastard! What does he want? What is he doing? He doesn't know himself. And one thing is sure: There is a lot of conflict and confusion going on for a man at the beginning of a relationship. Sometimes he's afraid of getting into something too heavy too soon. Sometimes, if he's afraid of getting hurt (he thinks he likes you more than you like him; or you are so open and direct that you slice in too close to the marrow), he may suddenly pull away. Every man walks a tightrope between a side of him that hungers for the warm security of intimacy, and a cynical and cautious side of him that fears getting hurt or sucked into something that looks tempting today but may turn him off tomorrow. The desire for adventure, freedom, and variety is always at war with the need for love, security, and closeness to one woman. Add to this the fear that love will make him soft, "demasculinized," and you have enough confusion to make anyone act peculiar.

For years, male conditioning has been telling him to stand on his own two feet. To depend on no one but himself. To stay cool, aloof, in control. But falling in love always means giving up some control. Loving you puts him very much in your power, and this scares him. He doesn't want to be dependent on anyone. If he's been stung by love before (and who hasn't?) you can add that to his arsenal of reasons to keep you at a distance.

He needs to feel in control

He may feel that the only way he can love and stay safe is to retain a lot of power. And this translates into power over *you.* Consciously or not, he may be attempting to protect himself from you when:

He insists on being the boss. You may notice that he gets jumpy when you take any initiative in the relationship, even if it's just suggesting that you go see a certain movie a week from Tuesday. (If he makes all the decisions, he retains the power.)

He plays the gallant. With great, sweeping gestures he takes over your life. He knows what's best for you. You can depend on him. (You're vulnerable, he is not.)

He gets possessive. He has to know where you go and what you do every minute you're away from him (You're *his.*)

He criticizes you a lot. Why do you wear your skirts so short and your hair so long? Why did you put so much garlic in the sauce? Whatever you do, he knows how you could do it better. (He's the teacher, you're the student.)

He keeps reminding you how much he needs his freedom. Don't ask him where he'll be next year, next month, or even tomorrow night. Do not have expectations about the future. (He is the master of his own fate.)

He refuses to deal with feelings. He hides his upsets. Refuses to fight about anything. Starts clowning or making jokes when you start to get what he calls "heavy." (If feelings are kept at a distance they can't threaten to take over.)

Everyone needs some bushes to go hide in when he feels vulnerable. And naturally the shakier a man's sense of identity and masculinity, the thicker the underbrush. Some men can handle loving and being loved better than others. The extremes run from a man who's capable of total openness, total honesty, deep intimacy, to a man who's always dodging out of relationships that threaten to get serious. An extremely gun-shy man may feel threatened if he doesn't have at least two relationships going at the same time. He feels he needs two women, each to protect him from the other.

A man who keeps himself just beyond your reach can be irresistible—especially if you have commitment or intimacy fears of your own. But this is the stuff that makes for endless games, and a lot of pain—however thrilling the high drama may be. Can you get a man to come out from behind his defenses? Sometimes yes, sometimes no. But one thing is sure—you'll feel a lot better about dealing with the whole thing if you are able to recognize a defense for what it is, and not see it as a put-down or a rejection of you. It takes a fair amount of courage and confidence to recognize that the tougher he acts, the more vulnerable he feels. But if you can see what's really going on behind his defenses, you'll be getting closer to the truth about who he is.

omantic men

A romantic man is not necessarily the guy who arrives at your door with a handful of daisies. A romantic man is the one who believes that Love Will Conquer All. He convinces himself that all he needs is to find the Right Girl, and then things will turn out. When he has the Right Girl, he thinks, games will stop, barriers will crumble, conversation will flow, love, loyalty, and trust will be assured, and he'll never be lonely again.

A romantic man needs the good, safe feeling that he has found his ideal woman, and he will go to great lengths to protect his ideal picture of the relationship, and of you. He pushes away problems by assuring you (and himself) that they will "work out," (whatever's wrong, love will solve it). He also expects love to transform you both into totally giving people. If he really doesn't want to pick your mother up at the airport, or to go out in the rain to buy aspirin for your headache, he won't admit it, even to himself. Nor will he notice that even though you say it's OK, you really do mind watching three hours of football on TV with him, or entertaining a group of his very drunk, very boring college buddies. "You're so good, so understanding," he says, and if there are times when you're not, he refuses to notice.

Fighting is *out*. A romantic man would rather give in than get into an argument. In his mind, perfect couples do not fight, they *compromise*. Couples who do fight, or who are always "working on" their relationship, are, in his judgment, weak. A relationship that was "meant to be" doesn't have to be "worked on."

He needs to think you're perfect

All of this may be fine with you—for a while. But eventually you're bound to feel the pressure build. He thinks you're perfect. You know you're not. And if you secretly hate his mother, his cat, or the liver-and-onion "treat" he cooks on Sunday nights, you keep your feelings to yourself, figuring that if he knew the truth about you, he couldn't possibly love you. If there are times when you'd love a good fight to clear the air, you repress the urge, wondering, with some guilt, where all your hostility is coming from. But the fact that it's not OK for you to be sloppy, selfish, or lazy sometimes will weigh heavily on you. You may feel that there's a yawning gulf between you, but that to try to cross it is to confront his implicit message: Don't rock the boat. For sure you have the feeling that you can't destroy his illusions without destroying the relationship.

Dealing with feelings is scary

Why does he keep his head in the sand? Why does a romantic man have such a hard time dealing with reality in a relationship with a woman? Men have been conditioned to think, and to act. But when it comes to dealing with feelings, a man is grossly unprepared. Feelings are a mystery to him. He may consider feelings and emotions "girl stuff," something he'll never understand. Blindly expecting love to make things "work out" is his way of pulling the romantic wool down over his eyes so that he won't have to deal with what he doesn't understand. He's most comfortable thinking that love has a magic power to fix things and that emotions cannot and should not be examined up close. "If you've got a good thing going, don't question it," he says.

The fear of dealing with feelings is so great in some romantic men that they would rather give up the Right Girl than face uncomfortable emotions. One way he might reason away the loss is by telling himself that she just wasn't the Right Girl after all.

Getting stuck in the past

Another way a romantic man may deal with the "one that got away" is to idealize or immortalize her. If his Right Girl didn't love him back, married his best friend, died, or took off for parts unknown, he may become obsessed by her memory in such a way that it becomes a block to his ever really loving again. With her he had a perfect relationship and nothing else can ever measure up to it. He may make it into a compelling story and tell it over and over again to anyone who'll listen—fancying himself Gatsby longing for his Daisy, or Poe for his Lost Lenore. Moaning over the one that got away is easier than building a new relationship—he can remember his lost love any way he wants to remember her; she can't disappoint him, and she can't talk back, either. Of course, obsessions aren't really love. And a romantic man who won't let go of the past may be more interested in wallowing in the delicious tragedy of the loss than in finding a replacement.

If you are a romantic man's Right Girl, the biggest danger for you is in believing that his ideal image of you is what you should be. If who-you-really-are becomes the enemy as you struggle to live up to his perfect image of you, you lock yourself in a deadly battle that you can only lose. If either of you has to deny who you really are to have your relationship work, you're sitting down squarely on a time bomb.

It may be that some romantic men are hopelessly stuck with the need to dream an impossible dream. But other romantic men may come around to seeing that feelings and reality, once faced, are really not all that scary. If you are willing to wrestle long enough and hard enough with him, he may finally realize that you can fight without destroying each other or the love between you; that being real (if sometimes less than beautiful) can actually make your relationship stronger; that dealing with problems is, in the long run, safer than pretending that the problems aren't even there.

Unfortunate Coincidence

*By the time you swear
  you're his,
Shivering and sighing,
And he vows his passion is
Infinite, undying—
Lady, make a note of this:
One of you is lying.*

—DOROTHY PARKER

ependence

Does the man need you or not? The way he acts when he loves you—coming close one day, pulling away the next—can be confusing. There are times (he doesn't call, or suffers silently through a problem) when it seems he doesn't need you at all. Other times (he sleeps with his arms tightly around you all night long or he cries, literally, on your shoulder about a hurt he's carried around for years) you're convinced that the man can't survive without you. Is he strong and tough, weak and dependent, a little of both, or what? Does he really need you or are there just times when he wants a mother and you happen to be handy? And if men need women as much as women need men, why can't they show it?

The man who loves you not only needs you, he is, in many ways, dependent on you. This is a fact that he doesn't like to admit, and will work hard to deny, even to himself. (He has, after all, always been taught that the man should be the strong one—that it's OK for you to be dependent on him but not vice versa.) But the degree to which a man needs the warmth, understanding, and affection of a loving woman cannot be overestimated. In a world where to be "a man" he's got to constantly prove he's brave, strong, and smart, you may provide him with the only relationship in which he can let down his guard and be himself. The temptation to put his head in your lap and let you mother him will be overwhelming at times, whether he gives in to the temptation or not. Does this need to be mothered mean that he's weak? He may think it does. He may think it's childish for a man to need another person so much. And since he may not know that other men feel this way (no one admits it), he may find the whole needing bit embarrassing. But longing for close, intimate contact with a person he can depend on isn't weak or childish. It's a basic human need. What honest, close involvement can give him—a sense of okayness about himself as he really is—is in fact vital for complete emotional health.

Men deny dependence on women

It takes a lot of courage for a man to admit to having deep dependency needs for a woman. And many men don't have the strength or maturity to let that need show. Instead, quite unconsciously, a man may build up a wall around himself, hide his dependency under one of a number of male

The Abdication Speech of Edward VIII, 1936

You must believe me when I tell you that I have found it impossible to carry the heavy burden of responsibility and to discharge my duties as King as I would wish to do without the help of the woman I love.

fictions like bravado, toughness, or stalwart independence.

For example, a man's insistence that he can separate sex from love may in part express his fear of becoming dependent on just one woman. "For me, sex doesn't have to include love," he claims. "Guys can detach." And, of course, sometimes they can, just as sometimes women can. Walking away from a sexual encounter that didn't involve him emotionally can make him feel powerful. It seems to say for him, "I control women, women don't control me." It can be unsettling, even devastating for him to discover that he depends on one woman and one woman alone for sexual satisfaction.

> *I knew I was in love with Maggie, and I wasn't too happy about the fact. She was still dating other guys. One night when she was out with someone else I met a really exciting, good-looking woman at a party. She dug me. I went home with her. We got into bed, and nothing. My penis just didn't want to play. My penis was hung up on Maggie, for God's sake. I was humiliated in front of this dynamite woman, and I was furious with myself. I can accept that sex is better with love, but I don't want to accept that sex is impossible without it.*

When he can't separate sex from love, he feels powerless. If he needs you to have sex, it puts him under your control. The disturbing aspects of this become compounded when he realizes that if you want to have sex without love you don't have to depend on an erection to do it. Theoretically, since all you have to do is "lie there" you have the power to cheat on him and he doesn't have the power to cheat on you. Terrifying.

Extreme reactions to dependency

Some men go on fighting their need for a woman, endlessly coming close and pulling back, making your relationship a constant taffy pull between closeness and denial. Other men go to the other extreme. Glad to be out of what felt like an emotional wasteland and to have someone he can really relate to, such a man may drop all outside contacts and concentrate on you. Once he knows that he can trust you—that you are his ally—and you penetrate the defenses around his vulnerability, he may become profoundly and

---

Sex Without Love

Guys detach, and it has nothing to do with liking, loving. You put guys on a desert island and they'll do it to mud. Mud! So if you caught your husband with mud: "EEEEEEEK! Don't talk to me! Go with your mud, have fun. Get your mud to make dinner for you!"

—LENNY BRUCE

totally attached to you. You've always had women friends to talk to about feelings, and after you fall in love, those friends are still there. If he doesn't have other close relationships to fall back on, then losing you would be a life-shattering experience for him. And in that sense, his dependence on you is greater than yours is on him. An uncomfortable position for a man to be in.

He may react to this by trying to bind you to him as tightly as possible, becoming jealous and possessive, wanting to be with you every minute (and maybe driving you up a wall). He might try to make you into his mother, giving you total charge over him. (This is different from looking for mothering from you. Needing mothering—tenderness—is fine. Asking you to play out the role of Mommy is not fine.) When you become his mother, he becomes the naughty little boy, and the whole relationship is likely to go into a lopsided skid where neither leaned-on nor leaner does the other much good.

Most men don't have such extreme reactions. Often, the fear of dependency is so deeply buried a man isn't even aware that it's there until the relationship gets into trouble and he faces the possibility of a breakup. Then he may be shocked into recognizing that he'd feel completely at sea without this particular woman.

The more comfortable a man is with a sense of his identity, the less likely he'll be to insist on smothering you or on holding you off at a "safe" distance. But however strong his identity, finding a balance between himself as an individual and as part of a pair may take years, even a lifetime, to achieve.

MARRIAGE &

SEPARATIONS

MARRIAGE & SEPARATIONS

**arriage—is it bad for men?**

In a *New Yorker* cartoon, a young man stands, hat in hand, in front of an older man seated in a wing chair. The older man is saying, "No, you can't marry my daughter. But would you consider taking my wife off my hands?"

"Take my wife," says comedian Henny Youngman. "Please."

If you listen to the way men talk about marriage, you may get the impression that they don't like it much. They talk as though they consider marriage to be a trap that will destroy them. But for all the jokes men make about it, studies show that marriage does make them happy. According to the statistics, marriage is good for men, physically, socially, and psychologically—it is, in fact, a lot better for men than it is for women. A married man tends to be healthier, more successful, and less likely to commit crimes than a single man. And at the rate divorced and widowed men remarry, it would appear that men like marriage so much that they are in a rush, once out of it, to get back in.

Why then do they complain so much? Why do men denigrate the institution of marriage? In *The Future of*

Marriage, a book that concludes that marriage is a pretty good deal for men and a pretty bad deal for women, sociologist Jesse Bernard suggests that "the verbal assaults on marriage indulged in by men are a kind of compensatory reaction to their dependence on it."

Is this true? Is the old bear growling because he loves you too much, and hates himself for being such a mushy, dependent old sop?

Look, if I tell the guys I don't want to go drinking with them, I'm not going to say it's because I want to go home and be with my wife.

If he's aware of needing you, he doesn't want to admit it to other men. To do that would be to face possible ridicule and the (perhaps silent) accusation that he's weak and dependent, not a "real man." He'll say, "I gotta go home, she needs me." But never, "I gotta go home, I need her."

At some level, everyone is an emotional sop. Everyone's hungry for love. Men and women expect marriage to provide them with a revisitation of the total loving they received in infancy. He expects you to take care of him emotionally just as you (admit it) expect him to take care of you. One of the temptations of marriage for both of you is the idea that it will provide a soft, quiet place where you can sink back with a sigh and be totally loved. And though wanting that may feel OK to you as a woman, a man isn't comfortable with so much emotional yearning. Becoming dependent on you scares him to death. It makes him feel weak and unmanly. He's going to deny emotional needs that make him feel weak, even to himself.

Why does a man marry?

For companionship. And steady sex. To have a home. And to build, if not a family, a sense of something solid—an expansion of himself. And when he makes the decision to get married, he feels pretty good about it. He's taking on a responsibility—an adult responsibility. Marriage is a challenge that he accepts, "like a man." And this gives him a sense of pride. When he stands there at the altar, any fear he feels is more likely to be about things like "Is my tie straight? Will I flub my lines? Who are all these people?" than it is about having fallen into a trap.

Marriage is an evil most men welcome.

—MONISTIKOI

A House, Not A Home

Women marry men without giving the serious chasm between their essential natures a thought. They think that a man wants a home. Well, he does, in a vague sort of way. Not so much a home, however, as a house. He likes to be able to say where he lives when he goes to vote, and things like that.

—JAMES THURBER and
E. B. WHITE, *Is Sex Necessary?*

Having accepted the challenge of marriage, he expects some things in return. To feel like an adult. To be viewed by others as more stable, more powerful. He's crossed an important threshold, dammit, and the act of becoming a married person is supposed to have its built-in rewards. But marriage is not a little box you crawl into with another person and wait for things to *turn out*. Marriage doesn't make him (or you) into an adult. It is no guarantee of good sex, or of emotional support, or of love. All it is, in reality, is a promise to work toward those things with another person. Few people realize this, least of all men.

I didn't think about it much, I guess. I figured I'd be a good husband, which to me meant I could be depended on, would be a good provider, a good lover, and someday a good father. I didn't realize how complicated it would be. Hell, I loved her. She loved me. I figured the rest of it would just work out.

His intellect, like yours, may know perfectly well that a successful marriage requires a lot of hard work, but his gut knows no such thing. It's not just love that blinds him—the culture he grew up in did a lot to sell him the idea that if he finds the "right girl" having a happy marriage will be as easy as falling off a log.

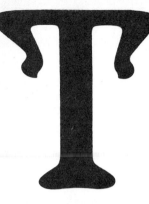

The myth of a good husband

The myths and the fairy tales about marriage that he grew up with set him up for a shock. The pictures he created of the kind of person he would become when he got married became indelibly etched in his mind. In spite of the fact that everyone now knows that a man is tender and vulnerable and as much in need of an occasional "good cry" as a woman, certain things are still expected of him—by society, by women, by himself. A man, when he becomes a husband, is supposed to be:

A good provider.   Preferably, a terrific provider. He'll be happy with the work he does, and dedicated to his job, but not so dedicated that he neglects his home life. He'll climb whatever ladder he has set out for himself to climb at a steady rate, earn more and more money each year, and feel more and more powerful and confident with each promotion.

Smarter than his wife.   He'll be the one to handle the money, figure out the income taxes, decide what kind of insurance to buy. He'll understand politics and foreign affairs and be able to explain them to you when you don't.

Sexually confident.   He'll always want to make love, of course, but will be sensitive to you when you're not in the mood. He won't have any sexual problems, but if you do he'll know just how to help you get over them.

Braver than his wife.   If someone in the family dies, he'll hold you up so you can cry. If there are strange noises in the basement in the middle of the night, he'll be the one to go and investigate. If another man (or dog) attacks him (or you) on the street, he'll know how to take care of it, and will. He'll argue with the TV repairman, the garage mechanic, and the angry neighbor who complains that your stereo is too loud.

Endowed with social graces.   You may get nervous when company is coming to dinner, but he won't. He'll know how to break the conversational ice, mix the drinks, carve the roast. In a restaurant he will read the menu in French, order the wine, and know all about the proper way to sniff and sip when the wine steward brings it to the table.

 Stronger than his wife.   He'll be the one to carry the heaviest suitcase, get the car out of a ditch, put up the storm windows, haul out the lawnmower.

In exchange, you, as his wife are expected to bow down to his authority, at least when push comes to shove. You are supposed to recognize that in matters of importance his word is the last word, and that his job comes before yours. (If his promotion takes him to Houston, then no matter how much you have invested in your life in Chicago, Houston it is.) You are also expected to be in charge of the Relationship, which is to say you're responsible for keeping the emotional fires burning and if anything goes awry to set things back on course.

Does all that sound ridiculous? Perhaps. But these are the kinds of expectations that operate for both of you, even if you've vowed not to be drawn in by them. You may allow that you are as strong and as capable as he is, and that he is as emotional as you are. You may totally agree at the outset to see one another as people, not as role players. But once you're married, you may find your conditioning runs deep. You, who as a single woman were in charge of your own life, may as a wife find yourself buying the Dodge instead of the Chevy simply because he says it's better. And he, who as a bachelor had no qualms about calling the super in to fix a leaky faucet, may feel that as a husband it's his duty to single-handedly install all new copper pipes in the downstairs bathroom. You, who may have felt perfectly confident that you love him for the tender, vulnerable man he is inside, may come unglued when he starts to cry, or mortified when guests come over and he doesn't know how to make a Martini or carve a roast. The idea that your husband must be stronger, smarter, braver, and tougher than you may strike you as absurd, but when the car has a flat on the thruway in the pouring rain, the idea has appeal. And when your Uncle Louie comes around peddling life insurance, you may find yourself retreating to the kitchen, glad that this is a subject "men know all about."

eeping the myths alive

Suppose he doesn't know any more about life insurance than you do? What if heavy suitcases hurt his back? If he's scared of dogs and night prowlers? Or doesn't know a capon from a prime rib, much less how to carve one of them? What if he has twice as many sexual insecurities as you? Can you take knowing those things? Would you still love him? He feels that you wouldn't.

If you appear to love him because he's big and strong and wise, your flattery makes him feel good—for a while. But he's not big and strong and wise all the time, and he knows it. If he has the feeling that he's being loved for something he's not, he'll feel a little edgy. And if he can't admit at least to himself and to you that he's *not* Mr. Superior, then he's got to fake it. To lie. And then, if he's successful at pulling off the lie, the best he can get is admiration for being something he's not. And that's not as good as being loved for the person he really is, whatever way you slice it.

No matter how liberated either of you are, no matter how realistic, or how sensitive to one another, you're bound to discover that the male mystique just doesn't seem to die. Why do the myths about men stay so firmly in place? Because you both want to believe them.

You want to look up to him

He wants to be big and strong. He will probably always want that.

Sure, the idea that I have to keep up the image of Mr. Success wears me down sometimes. There is pressure in it. But I want to handle it.

The Perfect Husband

*He tells you when you've got on too much lipstick.
And helps you with your girdle when your hips stick.*

—OGDEN NASH

And you like it too. It's nice to think you can count on his bravery when you hear a burglar in the basement, and on his know-how when the TV blows a tube or when the waiter brings the wine to be tasted. But accepting the myths about men as real has some dangerous repercussions—for both of you. When he does the deciding (what movie you'll see, which wine to order, when to make love, whether to have a baby), he gets set up. He's not only got to make the decisions, he's got to make the right decisions. If not, then when the movie stinks, the wine tastes funny, or you find you had the baby a few years too soon, he feels he's to blame. This, by the way, is the

The Modern Triangle: Husband, Wife, and Television

Record companies, wondering how their customers spend their time, found out that married people watch twice as much television as singles.

Hours watching TV in an average week:
  Single: 11   Married: 20

Listening to the radio:
  Single: 16   Married: 19

Reading:
  Single: 12   Married: 10

Listening to records:
  Single: 10   Married: 9

Concerts attended in last year:
  Single: 4   Married: 2

original setup that created the nagging wife and the hen-pecked husband. He makes the decisions and you sit back and judge those decisions. Henpecked husbands are supposed to be a thing of the past, but they're not, and this is why. It's a pattern that springs from an imbalance of power that's rooted in the persistent need to believe that the husband is boss. And it's a pattern that always backfires in resentment.

But if he wants to be boss and you want him to be boss, what's so bad? It's not just that the tougher-smarter-wiser myth about men is a lie. If believing lies would make them work, then the me-Tarzan/you-Jane setup might work. But the problem goes deeper than that. The you-be-boss-and-I'll-pretend-not-to-notice-when-you-screw-up game makes real contact impossible. It puts a man in isolation. If he has to pretend everything is fine, then he has no one to talk honestly to when everything isn't fine. In order for him to feel close to you he needs to be able to let you look beneath his exterior and see his frailties, vulnerabilities. For him to feel that marriage supports him in a solid, emotional sense, he has to know he can show you those imperfections and still be loved. If, on the other hand, he feels he has to smother his weaknesses and fulfill a "husband image," it'll only be a matter of time before marriage makes him feel stifled.

He won't let down his defenses

It's not easy for him to let down his defenses. He feels he needs those defenses. He fears that if he exposes the needs and the vulnerability under his armor, he'll be weakened, and coping in this dog-eat-dog world will become even tougher than it already is. Actually the reverse of this is true. Becoming conscious of the emotions that operate behind his behavior makes him better able to control them, not less so. Most men can't see it this way, but times are changing.

It's hard for me to admit I haven't got all my stuff together. It's hard enough to admit it to myself. My wife helped me see that pretending everything was cool all the time was making me distant—unreal. She didn't like that, and neither did I. Once I saw that she wasn't counting on me to hold it together, that she wouldn't crumble when I felt depressed or helpless, I began to feel better about letting her see my feelings.

These days it's more likely for a man to be able to see that he doesn't need to hide behind his defenses all the time. And a man who realizes that self-awareness makes him stronger begins to relax and accept that his weaknesses mean he's human—not unmasculine. A man with a high degree of self-awareness realizes that looking under his armor and accepting what's there doesn't mean he has to drop the armor or stop acting assertive. He knows that there are times when armor is perfectly appropriate—and necessary. He knows a show of confidence is a good idea when he's closing a business deal, and that if he feels like crying when his best customer cancels an account, it's a good idea to wait until he gets home from work. But this kind of man *can* let it down when he gets home from work—*can* discuss what his anxieties are. Marriage works best for any man when it gives him the confidence to take his armor off at home.

etting rid of the myths

Some men can't take their armor off, ever. Why is this harder for a man than for a woman? The feminine ideal allows you to be weak, emotional, dependent, so recognizing those feelings isn't terribly threatening. But the masculine ideal doesn't allow him those feelings. And he's uncomfortable with those aspects of himself that don't measure up to the ideal. Any person who looks inward with any amount of honesty is going to have to admit that there are weaknesses there. But a man's definition of himself often rests on the stronger-braver-wiser myths. If he has built his marriage on those myths, then he can't have any honesty about his feelings without shaking up his world a good bit.

A man who thinks his armor is *him* isn't even aware that there's anything going on beneath the surface. When he's feeling tough and angry, he doesn't realize that the feelings are self-protective.

For example: He's driving home from work. Something happened during the day that's bugging him, and he needs to hear your opinion about it. He's smiling to himself, thinking about how helpful your perspective can be. He thinks ahead, visualizing getting home, sitting in front of the fire with you, having drinks and talking while dinner simmers. He feels good, drives a little faster. When he gets home he finds the

*Unhappiness in marriage is
the difference between what
you want and what you get.*

*—Facts of Love and Marriage
For Young People*

house empty, dark, cold. He remembers now that you told him you might have to work late, but he still feels alone, deserted. He knows those feelings are ridiculous, and shoves them aside as he slumps down in a chair. He knows it makes sense to go in and start dinner, but he can't get himself to move. He starts getting angry. By the time you get home he's convinced himself that you have failed in your duty to him as his wife. That you are never there when he needs you. That your job is more important to you than he is. As you step into the living room, you're likely to hear one or all of the following accusing questions: "What took you so long?" "Why can't a man come home to a decent meal once in a while?" "Why aren't you ever here when I need you?" "Why can't you be like other wives?" And if you respond to what he's saying, you may shout, "Don't start with me, I've had a hard day too. Would it have killed you to make dinner for a change?" The war is on. And the void between you becomes deeper.

His feelings play tricks on you both

What's happening here is that he's not telling the truth about what he's feeling. And you can't see that what he's saying to you in anger is a way of protecting himself from the

hurt and vulnerability he feels. If he were to tell you the truth he'd say that he'd worked himself into an angry rage because he was lonely when he got home and needed mothering. And needing but not getting made him feel helpless. He blamed you so he wouldn't have to look at his own sense of helplessness. If he could see all that and admit it, it would be so simple. No fight. No sulky distance between you. You could see what he needs and give it to him. But he's not likely to come up with that kind of truth. To him, it's not OK to feel lonely and helpless. He's much more comfortable lashing out at you—feeling tough, angry, wronged.

Men are changing, however slowly. Since blacks, women, and the young have rebelled about being locked into roles, it has become easier for men to see that they have been as much repressed by their roles as anyone else. But still, coming to terms with the fact that he has dependency needs isn't easy for a man who's been conditioned all his life to "tough it out" and "act like a man." And there are some areas where the conditioning has settled in like cement. When you begin to cut through some of the myths together, you're bound to hit upon some rock-hard areas. Particularly when it comes to money, work, housework, fighting, sex.

1. GO TO BANK!

2. ASK ANGELA TO DINNER FRIDAY NITE

3. APOLOGIZE TO SALLY

4. IRON SHIRTS   UGH!

5. FINISH **REPORT** FOR THE BOSS!

HOW HE FEELS ABOUT...

How he feels about...

Money. He feels he's responsible for it. No matter what kind of money you make, he'll undoubtedly consider himself the primary wage earner in the family (as does society, and as, probably, do you). He feels he knows best how to spend the money, too. Money is power. Power, traditionally, belongs with the man.

You may think this is ridiculous—you may insist that pulling the weight together makes you a stronger pair. But however right you may be, the fact is that he was raised to believe that as the man of the family, he'd be the one in charge. It won't be easy for him to change this belief, or to share some of the burden of responsibility with you. To him, sharing power feels the same as giving up power, and he'll feel that if he's not the boss at home, he's not a real man. And if you should start to earn more money than he does, he'll need a strong ego. However glad he is to see more money coming in, it will hurt him not to be the bigger wage earner. He has been taught to compete, and that makes it inevitable that he'll measure his strengths and successes against yours.

Work. He considers his work more important than yours. This can make you pretty angry, especially if you're dedicated to what you do, proud of your accomplishments, and just as dependent on success for your self-esteem as he is. But the myths about men make it important for him to believe that his work is more essential. If he believes that his work defines him (and most men do), then it's crucial that it take the front seat to your work—which he probably perceives as a terrific extra: "Not only is she a great wife, she brings in an income too." Because of this deeply ingrained point of view, he's likely to balk when your job requires that he give something up. If his boss is coming to dinner and your job sends you out of town, he'll feel deserted. If you've got to work on some reports until midnight and he feels like making love, he'll grumble a lot. And even if he hates his job with a passion, it's a rare man who'd give it up so you can accept a promotion requiring a move to another city. Any time your work has him saying, "But what about me?" you'll run into conflicts.

These days a man is less likely than he used to be to feel the need to prove his masculinity by having you dependent on him. Even so, if you are dedicated to your job, and if there are times when it requires a lot of your attention, you're bound to hear complaints that you care more about your work than about the marriage. It takes a while for a man to see that you can find identity and self-esteem in your job and still need him very much.

Housework.   He considers this your job. Unfair? Of course. But who plays fair when it comes to getting out of the dirty work? (You're not so crazy about handling the life-insurance policies either.) If you think you can get philosophical agreement from him that it should be a shared responsibility, or shame him into doing housework by playing on his guilt, forget it. He doesn't have any guilt about it. Somewhere in his heart he knows that it's his dust just as much as yours, but that awareness isn't going to send him running for the furniture polish.

But he knows your guilt is there, and that when you see him fumbling with the iron, or choking the washing machine with too much detergent, you'll probably bail him out. He's not above playing dumb to get out of housework. The fact is, anything he does around the house he considers helping you, and if this offends your sense of fairness, it still won't bother him a bit. But of course the quickest way to get him to learn how the washing machine works is to let him run out of underwear, and you can, perhaps, console yourself with the knowledge that if the car makes a funny noise or the storm windows need to come down, you probably expect him to take over.

Fights.   Some men love a good battle, even seem to thrive on tossing out barbs and picking out things to bicker about, and other men refuse anything that even remotely resembles a fight. What matters is not whether you fight or not, but whether you are dealing with the unresolved feelings, hurts, and misunderstandings that are usually the basis for a row. To have a healthy, workable marriage, you've got to be confronting those things. Confronting doesn't have to mean fighting, and fighting doesn't necessarily mean you are confronting. It's a tricky business, which is why you are so often advised that it's important to learn how to fight right.

He grew up being told that guys don't hit girls. And if he's a man to whom all fighting seems like hitting, he may just sit there doing a slow, quiet burn while you flail away trying to get a rise out of him, and never, to your dying day, succeeding. If he's a man who's very threatened by anything that seems like female manipulation, he may lash out with irrational shouting whenever he feels you have crossed the line.

Good fighting doesn't involve stony silence or all-out bloodshed. Good fighting is truth-telling in a positive, nonaccusing way. This doesn't rule out aggression, but doesn't require it either. In a relationship where you are committed to telling the truth about yourselves, conflicts are inevitable and good. If he's being honest about himself, confrontations are less likely to be battles, more likely to be clarifying. A good fight is a kind of communication that leaves each of you more fully aware of the other. It helps if you realize that the alternative—burying what's wrong—will just cause problems to mushroom and be more difficult to deal with later on.

Sex. For some married men, sex gets better and better over the years. For others, married sex gets boring. Why? If it's true that good communication and being fully known is the best guarantee of an expanding, perpetually satisfying sexual relationship, then the reason is pretty clear: A man who doesn't have honest, free communication in his marriage won't have exciting sex in his marriage. It follows that if he's living out the husband-is-braver-stronger-wiser myth, the ability for true intimacy will be beyond his grasp. And if there isn't open communication between you about your fears, fantasies, and satisfactions, sexual and otherwise, there will be distinct limits to your married sexuality.

He may not be as secure about his sexuality as you think. He may worry that you expect him to want to make love all the time, just as he did before you were married. Men are "supposed to" want more sex than women. And when he's married and living with you and lovemaking is an everyday possibility, he may feel he has to live up to, among other things, his own sexual past with you. This kind of pressure is something most men don't like to deal with. And on days when he's too tired, too preoccupied, too depressed to feel in the least bit sexy, his reaction may be to peck you on the

---

An Old Wives' Tale Debunked

There is an old folk theory that if you put a bean in a jar every time you make love in the first year of your marriage, and take a bean *out* of the jar every time you make love after the first year, there will still be beans left in the jar when you die.

Dr. David Martin of Washington State University didn't actually count the times newlyweds made love, but figured out with a computer that, mathematically, the theory is "highly unlikely." Even if you made love three times a night the entire first year and only once a week afterward, you would still run out of beans in 21 years.

cheek, roll over, and go to sleep, leaving you to lie there wondering why he's gotten bored with you. And this is a shame. If he could talk to you about the pressure he's feeling and if you could in turn recognize that his self-doubts and occasionally low libido have nothing whatever to do with you, you could both relax, and some nights just hold each other peacefully instead of making love.

He may worry that his sexual insecurities will turn you off. Men are "supposed to" know what women want, and to do what women want them to do without being asked. Will too much talk kill romance? Is his penis too small? Too big? Is he too rough? Too gentle? Do you really like oral sex? Do you wish he'd use his hands more? Less? What do you think about when he's inside you? If he doesn't feel he can ask you, he has to wing it—hoping for the best and probably not daring to explore very much. He's likely to opt for the safer, tried and supposedly true lovemaking patterns that *do*, after a while, become boring for you both.

If you can't talk to each other about sex, you can't build trust, you can't become more fully known, and you can't be truly intimate. If, on the other hand, you do muster the courage to be honest and open about what feels good and what doesn't, about what scares you and what excites you, you can begin to reassure each other that it's OK to feel awkward and unsure—that your insecurities make you more lovable, not less so. And then, as you both become freer, you'll be more willing to take sexual risks, to make mistakes, to relax and have fun at it.

> —*My husband is dead.*
>
> —*I'll bet he's just using that as an excuse.*
>
> —GROUCHO MARX

hy a man may fear intimacy

He may think that intimacy will make him weak, dependent on you. Sexual intimacy and total involvement with and need for a woman can feel very threatening to a man. There's even a term for it: "pussy-whipped." When he acknowledges that he is dependent on you and you alone for emotional and sexual satisfaction, he's out on a limb. He needs you and he could somehow lose you. He is under your power, and for a man this is a forbidden emotional state.

Men build impenetrable defenses against intimacy without even realizing that they're doing it. It feels safer to keep you at a distance, to keep his feelings to himself. In order to be totally open about his feelings a man must be willing to feel powerless, to risk rejection, to make a high investment of self. It takes a kind of courage and ego strength that's rare.

The fear of being swallowed up, made helpless by an overwhelming need for one woman, is often influencing a married man when he looks for affairs outside of marriage. Giving his all to one relationship may make him feel unbearably vulnerable. One way to avoid that feeling of vulnerability is to have more than one relationship at a time.

Of course, there are other reasons men have affairs. Usually the same kinds of reasons that women have affairs—to prove that he is sexually exciting (if communication is closed off at home, he can't prove that there); to increase his sense of power ("Look how many people I can bring to their *knees*"); to get revenge ("If you don't love me, I'll find somebody who will"). But affairs are not about sex. Sex is the vehicle used in the attempt to get what's missing at home. The real causes are likely buried beneath an enormous web of contradictions and defenses. And, like it or not, the only way through that web is to develop the ability for honest communication and confrontation with the truth about yourselves. If things aren't working and you two aren't talking, at some point you have to decide whether you want to get all the way in or all the way out of your marriage.

Splitting up

The end of a marriage, as of most living-together relationships, means more than just a parting of ways. For most men it is the end of a home or a stability they've at least thought was central to their lives. They feel it is a public announcement of failure. No matter how little of himself a man may seem to have invested in making the relationship work, he probably believed in it. He needed it. And it hurts when an imagined closeness becomes a real separation.

Splitting up is not very pleasant for anyone. Most separations begin in bitterness or self-doubt. "Where did we go wrong?"—or worse, "Where did I go wrong?" It's a prelude that becomes an endless refrain.

Which spouse feels worse when a relationship ends? This question is as old as divorce itself. Men usually say that they feel worse, and women usually say women do. Dissatisfied with this neat solution, sociologists Morton and Bernice Hunt questioned more than 1,000 separated people for their book, *The Divorce Experience.* Their answer, not unexpectedly, is that the spouse who was taken by surprise is usually the one who gets hurt the most.

They came up with other conclusions, too, confirming some popular assumptions and exploding others:

Marriages and Divorces in the United States, 1877–1977

	Marriages	Divorces
1877	411,000	16,000
1887	513,000	28,000
1897	635,000	45,000
1907	937,000	77,000
1917	1,144,000	122,000
1927	1,201,000	196,000
1937	1,451,000	249,000
1947	1,992,000	483,000
1957	1,518,000	381,000
1967	1,927,000	523,000
1977	2,176,000	1,097,000

Women feel more liberated by separation than do men.

About the same number of men as women feel absolutely shattered right after splitting up.

Ending a marriage is just as painful for the young as for the middle-aged and old, and just as awkward for those with short-lived marriages as for those married many years.

At least in the early stages, couples with children deal with divorce more easily than those without, and the spouse who gets custody of the children copes best of all.

The one who initiates the breakup doesn't get off emotionally scot-free.

Breaking up isn't something one learns to do well by experience; it doesn't feel any better the second time around.

Many men can ignore most marital problems because they don't think there should be any. Therefore, there aren't any. It's simple. All they have to do is say the magic words, "I love you," and problems vanish. Love is the answer. "All you need is love." Why not? All their lives they've been hearing these lyrics.

What hurts him most? That depends on what he was getting out of marriage. If it was having his cooking, cleaning, and social life taken care of, then what could be most painful is having to look after himself. If it was having someone to show off socially, then what may hurt most is standing alone with only a drink to hold. If it was just having another warm body around, he may not be hurting so badly.

But if he was really in love, if it was an emotionally fulfilling relationship, then at first it's worst at night. Alone. Reliving every moment, wondering what went wrong and, especially, what could possibly be left for him now. Crackups come when he can't confine those nightmares to the night-time.

They're real to him. He feels attacked, on the defensive. That job you think he can fall back on? Most likely he now sees it as drudgery he only put up with for the sake of others. For many men, the thought that work is all that's left is more horrifying than the breakup itself. "If all I can do is make more money for someone else, then there's something wrong," he may be thinking. Indeed, what *is* the point in getting up each morning at seven, dragging a razor over his chin, and facing the day with half-open eyes? No longer is there a home to bring the bacon to, or a family to win the bread for.

Why go on? What's next?

When a man can't answer these questions for himself, it often shows up at his workplace. Divorce counselors report that men are more and more often referred to them by employers. Why? Because many men depend so completely on marriage for emotional support that when the marriage ends there's often nothing left but a job.

What answers to these questions do men eventually find? That depends on the man. Many men remarry quickly. Government statistics indicate that men are 20 percent more likely than women to remarry within the first six months after divorce. Others find relief by giving more time to their work, or at least convincing themselves that they can maximize the work situation. But most men eventually put their troubles in the background and go on living. Time and revisionist memories are the real healers.

Each marriage and breakup is unique. Yet to hear men talk you might think that most separations are similar. You will seldom hear a man say that "No one could have suffered as much as I did," but after a while most men's stories take on the air of consistent tragedy. No one teaches him how to react—no schools offer Coping with Divorce 101—but nearly every man has similar feelings though the intensity and persistence of the feelings may vary.

Common denominators

The blow to his self-image when he realizes his marriage is ending. Whether he makes the decision himself, makes it together with his wife, or returns one night to an empty house, the moment comes as a shock. His conception of his life is challenged. He must rethink it entirely.

The struggle to cope with life on his own. This is a time of intense soul-searching and self-doubt. A few men feel exhilarated right after breaking up, but most withdraw into loneliness. The task he faces, and that a friend or counselor can help with, is to make his life meaningful again.

The justification of his actions when a man tries to deal intellectually with what happened. He may blame her, he may blame himself, or he may blame both at the same time, but he'll always try to satisfy his need for a reasonable explanation—especially one that doesn't hurt too much.

The return to normalcy, when a man feels "over the hump." A moment comes when he realizes the world isn't ending. But that's only the start of the rebuilding process.

When the other shoe is dropped

Breakups are predictable. Many happen in January, because few people want to ruin the holiday season. They happen on Mondays, too. One Hollywood divorce lawyer claims celebrity clients call him after rainy weekends—having spent two or three days cooped up together. And as Lenny Bruce pointed out, anyone who breaks up more than once or twice learns to do it in the daytime. Who wants to get kicked out in the middle of the night?

Actually, breakups do occur at every conceivable time and in every conceivable place. A man can get the final word from a note on the kitchen table. Or he can discover that he's involved in the end of a relationship at night as he stares at the ceiling and realizes there's no place left to go. It can be lipstick on his collar, or another man's name whispered instead of his. It can be a complete surprise or a welcome relief. It can be his idea, her idea, or both of theirs.

Researchers report that more women than men initiate divorces. No one has any hard data, but that's the consensus. Yet emotionally, the man may already have pulled out of the marriage. By the time she calls his bluff, he's just going

It's best to break up on your day off, in the afternoon. You get out and you go to the movies. Otherwise you're standing on the lawn at three o'clock in the morning with a pillowcase full of clothing and the door locked behind you.

—LENNY BRUCE

through the motions. It doesn't matter if he's sleeping with someone else or not. That's more often a symptom than a cause of divorce. When a couple stops communicating and loving, the split starts to feed on itself.

The death of a marriage can be a slow and tedious process, with enough ups and downs so that you're never really certain it's dead. The final days can be like a poker game. Who will call whose bluff? Who isn't bluffing? Each wants to be able to say, "The divorce was my idea, but it wasn't my fault." And the man particularly doesn't want to end up looking and feeling like a patsy. If he calls it quits too early, then he didn't do all he could to save it. If he waits too long, he loses the edge. And nothing humiliates a man more than getting kicked out of what he considers his own home.

Does it offend you that he's worrying about his ego when he should be worrying about important things, like his wife and marriage? It happens because men often live their marriages in their heads, not with real wives.

Walking out on his own two feet means he's still the "man" in the marriage. Closing the door gently behind himself—instead of having it slammed in his face—means he's kept control. This is how most men would prefer it to end: standing at the helm of a sinking ship, even if he has to go down with it.

The thought of what he'll be able to say to his friends can be as big a factor behind his actions as saving the marriage. "My marriage failed, but I'm still a man." Sound silly? Sure it is, but a man feels he must retain his pride. After all, he'll have to tell his friends himself. It's not proper that his Uncle Charlie, or an old college buddy he hasn't seen in ten years, should hear the news from somebody else. He wants the edge in the divorce, so he'll be able to say, "I did my best. She had some problems!"

This is when the rituals begin—dividing up friends to call. He calls his friends and she calls hers, and if she calls any of his friends it means war. Some men even sit down and make lists of who calls whom—like guest lists at their wedding—just to make sure there are no mistakes. The false niceness begins now, too. Voices aren't raised, until they get home, so friends don't find out prematurely. And the lawyers become shields. "You have a terrible lawyer and he's causing my lawyer to be terrible, but it's the lawyers, not us."

This is how fantasy dies. His fantasies were real to him—perhaps they were all that was real to him. It's hard—and painful—for him to let go of them. His world starts to teeter and fall. And what often hurts most is the feeling that he's lost control over his whole life. Even if he ended the marriage himself he feels helpless. "Where does she come off ruining my life? I'm the only one allowed to do that."

After we split up I used to eat lunch at the same bar every day. It was when "Send in the Clowns" was a big hit. It was the perfect about-to-be-divorced man's song, and I would go up there and play it twice on the juke box. But the song kept playing over and over and over through lunch, and I realized there were two other guys at the bar punching up that same song. I was surrounded by it. The bartender said yes, they were getting divorced, too. There we were, three of us, burying each other with the same beat-up-your-brain music.

Send in the Clowns

Isn't it rich?
Are we a pair?
Me here at last on the
*   ground,*
You in mid-air...

—STEPHEN SONDHEIM,
©1973 Rilting Music, Inc. and
Revelation Music Publishing Corp.

How does it feel to be free?

Many men, after a divorce, grow beards. Or buy a motorcycle. Or do crazy things they'd never dream of doing while they were married. Things like skydiving and mountain climbing. Men who were terrified of airplanes suddenly take flying lessons. The risk itself becomes important, and it doesn't have to be a big one. Even picking up a woman in a bar has a risk. Or going to a massage parlor.

This is a time of experimentation. A man may try on personalities like hats at a haberdasher's, or try out all the latest therapies and gurus. Many men are surprised by what they do during this period, and by any unanticipated pleasures. "I'm not supposed to feel good—I'm alone!" Yet it happens to almost every one, and it's a healthy sign.

But it would be a mistake to confuse these feelings with having a good time. He isn't. This drive to enjoy himself is more of a compulsion, something he has to do no matter how little he gets out of it. He's scared that if he stops moving the despair will catch up.

Many things seem strange to him. He is no longer certain of much that he's always taken for granted. This isn't all just in his head, because there are real changes taking place. His wife is becoming his ex-wife. His in-laws, ex-in-laws. Many friends, ex-friends. His secretary (who suddenly looks much prettier) becomes in his mind a potential lover. The near-stranger at the next desk becomes an after-hours confidant. His daily routines change overnight.

Signals

One of the hardest things for a divorced man to do is relearn the signals, the unspoken hints that men and women give each other. A man who has been out of the game for a long time (that is, focused on one woman) may find himself making incorrect assumptions. His first tentative sexual encounters will tend to be disappointing—especially because at first he's probably more interested in restoring his sense of masculinity by toting up "scores" than in making any solid connections with the opposite sex.

Restoring a sexual balance will occupy much of his time. He has a lot to learn, such as that there are a lot of other people out there who are just as interested in contact as he is. He may rediscover sexual powers he'd forgotten he had. He may run through a lot of women before realizing that he is interested in more than sex. Some men, of course, never realize this and attempt to live out a playboy fantasy for years. But most divorced men liked being married, miss it, and eventually remarry.

Fantasy plays a major role in his life. Surprisingly, a divorced man's fantasies usually center around warm relationships as much as around sex. Many men fantasize easy love and happily-ever-after romances. Just what their marriages were not. In their real-life relationships, though, they're more often extremely careful to *relate*—to avoid making the same mistakes over again. In fact, so eager are they to demonstrate to a woman what they've learned that they can become crashing bores.

The ups and downs

Many men lose weight. It's not just the unstructured life they live that takes off the pounds. It's their sense of time. Many men are hardly aware of the passing of the hours and minutes. Familiar routines are gone, and often they simply forget to eat.

I ran into a friend a month after we split up. I looked like a beanpole. The very first thing he asked

---

We held each other close. She shivered a little. Then there was a certain amount of struggling, and the next thing she was laying on the cold bench with her dress climbed way up on her and crying and breathing heavy and strangling me and saying 1 minute "Hank! Hank! Yes!" and the next minute "No! No!" and I said "For the love of Pete which is it, yes or no?"

—MARK HARRIS,
The Southpaw

*me was how much weight had I lost. "Eighteen
pounds," I said. "That's nothing," he told me. "The
first time I got divorced, I lost twenty-seven."*

If that gets your maternal juices flowing, quell them. He
probably wants this to happen, and he'll even encourage the
feelings. He may not be eating but if he's a drinker he'll start
drinking more than ever. The same with marijuana smokers,
or even moviegoers. Whatever his escape, he'll retreat deeper
into it.

Death, too, is on his mind. Everyone thinks about death
at some time or another, but divorcing men dwell on it more
than ever. Not necessarily as an escape—the ultimate
escape—but just that it's really going to come.

Sound dramatic? It is, and that's part of why men do it.
Many immerse themselves in depression—acting as tragic
heroes. They may write death notes that they'd be embarrassed to acknowledge should they be discovered years later.
Death becomes real, and life becomes heightened by the
awareness that it will end.

At other times everything seems lucid. His whole life
spreads out before him like a rainbow. Even the air tastes

sweeter. It can be sparked by the tiniest things—a smile perhaps, or a compliment. These are the times a man is happy with his new life. But it seldom lasts long, and few men mistake it for the freedom it appears to be from the outside.

Ups and downs are his only constant. Most men realize, because they've already tasted it, that their greatest freedom will come from building a strong relationship with another woman; they know it will free them from the obsessions and haunting emotions they've dredged up during the separating.

We just grew apart.

Part of recovering is to stop feeling guilty. Blaming himself and blaming her are two sides of the same coin: that he's uncomfortable with the series of events that led to the breakup. Only when he stops fretting about who was right or wrong can he get on with the business of living.

The hardest thing for some men to do after a divorce is explain it. Not just to you or some other person, but to himself, too. It can take a long time for a man to accept what happened: that he's earned a share of the blame himself, or, for some guilt-ridden men, that it wasn't *all* his fault. And in the process of coming to terms with his guilt, he can think up some real whoppers, ludicrous, self-serving explanations of why the relationship failed. How often have you heard men say things like "Her father turned her against me?" Did you believe him? Or were you really wondering about the things he *wasn't* saying?

Think of a man's rationalizations as a knock-down, drag-out divorce trial—all in his own head. Because in a way a man puts himself on trial after a divorce, before a judge and jury of one: himself. His lame excuses may not resemble what really happened, but he needs something he can tell the judge. His conscience won't accept any hemming and hawing. In order to deal with his own sense of failure, a man has to fit a complex relationship into pigeonholes every bit as narrow as divorce laws. But these excuses serve an equally worthwhile cause—his peace of mind.

Does he really believe them? Maybe, if he's the easygoing type. But allow a man at least this one self-delusion. No matter how honest he is with himself, it takes time to come to grips with a truth that hurts. That he is a failure? No, of course not, although it may appear that way to him. It's just that life is

When a woman marries again, it is because she detested her first husband. When a man marries again, it is because he adored his first wife.

—OSCAR WILDE

not so simple as he thought, and he'd been wrong to think that it was.

Eventually, he'll probably settle on a simpler explanation, one he can hand out for public consumption. Ask him what went wrong and he'll be glad to tell you—in one or two sentences. Like "We just grew apart," or "I caught her sleeping with my best friend" (or the other way around). Neither deals very well with the contradictions and subtleties of a relationship. But forgetting is a necessary step in starting to live in the present again.

Still, most men never completely forget. A marriage never really ends—it just gets a new name: "divorce." Even if there aren't any children, there is property to split up and maybe alimony to pay. And meetings with lawyers, and occasional bump-ins on the street. And Christmas cards from ex-in-laws. And, of course, there are memories.

But after a while, all this doesn't matter so much. The pain ends, as—deep inside—most men really knew all along it would. No matter how dramatic they were, they knew that they'd survive, that one day they'd be able to look back and not cry. And they were keeping half an eye out for that day, too. That's what kept them from doing something *really* stupid. Like jumping when they were fooling around on that cliff, trying to scare you. Or mailing that letter they wrote late at night to their ex. Or pushing that new motorcycle to its limit. They want to survive, and they will. At least, they've made it this far.

FATHERING

Samuel was decorated by the duke himself.

Josephine was always different.

Fannie always liked the men.

Aunt Anna scrimped and saved.

Pappy Joe ate molasses on his eggs.

Aunt Penelope sang in public for money.

Hercule: the French hanged him.

Marie married a pirate to punish her mama.

Liana Carol won a fortune at Blackjack.

Uncle David never did a lick of work.

Victor: They had to take him away.

Uncle Mort lost all his chickens in '88.

Auntie Bess sneezed for three weeks straight.

Uncle Simon never thought of anybody but himself.

Aunt Trudy always liked nice things.

Albert kept jawbreakers in his pockets for the kids.

Sarah took a trip to Chicago once.

Morris didn't have the sense God gave geese.

Lois had the first Victrola in Des Moines.

Irene could dance all night.

Charles couldn't touch sugar or salt.

Brian and Debbie don't want children.

Old Hiram fell off the ship coming over. Mammy Rose lost her grip.

Charlotte drank Gin and liked it.

R.C. had his Daddy's eyes.

Eula was clever with her hands.

Cousin Jack: too much schooling scrambled his brains.

Young Hiram never could remember the punchline

Maude married beneath her.

Nelson was big for his age.

Matthew joined the army and was never heard from again.

Cousin Pearl saw Bernhardt on the stage in person.

Poor Ethel bore up as well as could be expected.

Uncle Harry disappeared occasionally.

Clara drove too fast.

Clifton was in the right place at the right time.

Susan frittered her youth away.

Uncle James lost his will to live after the scandal.

Cousin Sandra was quite mad.

Eugene had a dirty mind.

FATHERING

reely chosen, freely enjoyed

Today, more than ever, fathering is a matter of choice. Rarely in this age of contraception do men—and women—have to have children. Even more rarely do men and women have to get married because an unwanted baby is on its way.

No one questions any more that parenting is less popular than it used to be. The average number of children per family has halved in the last two decades, until it is now less than two. As more and more women work outside the home, bearing children is seen as a chore or burden. And most fathers are not yet ready to reverse roles and stay home with the kids, nor has day care taken up the slack.

But somehow, the *intensity* of fatherhood seems to be growing. There is no objective way to measure this, but a feeling is emerging that fathering can be the greatest fulfillment of all. Not too long ago, of course, this hardly needed to be said out loud. But over the ages men really *have* lost some touch with their feelings, and this includes the joys of fathering. Now that these can be freely chosen, they can be freely enjoyed as well. The biological imperative is given new meaning.

bortion

Long ago, "chivalry" meant a man risking his life to protect a woman's honor. Today it more often means paying for her abortion. Unpleasant as it may be, abortion has become a fact of life.

The man's side has been overlooked in the abortion debate. The emotions aroused have been women's—and rightly so. After all, it is your body that is directly affected. But whenever there is a relationship that will continue afterward, the man is involved, too. And as the number of abortions continues to grow—there is now one abortion for every three live births in the United States—it is a problem more and more men face.

Few men remain unaffected by the decision not to bear what would otherwise have become their child. The strain of abortion often lingers long after the actual operation. Linda Bird Francke, in *The Ambivalence of Abortion*, writes that many men keep their feelings locked up inside: "Men see their roles under these circumstances as being totally supportive of the woman and her needs, and tend to discount or suppress their own....In many cases, this adds to his unexpressed guilt and anger and can fester in him for months afterwards."

What are these feelings men aren't expressing? This depends largely on his age. When it comes time for a man to deal with his wife's or lover's abortion, the generation gap becomes a yawning chasm. Men's attitudes toward abortion are changing—and fast. A younger man simply isn't as troubled by abortion as his father would have been.

There is an exception to this. The men *most* troubled by abortions are the very youngest who face them. This is not a matter of generations but of life experience. Teenagers simply aren't prepared to deal with questions of life and death. The idea of fatherhood may never have crossed a teenager's mind until his girlfriend's unexpected pregnancy.

At any age, what can disturb a man most is finding himself acting against his own beliefs. An ardent opponent of abortion may find himself having to give his wife emotional support—or risk losing his marriage—after the decision was taken out of his hands. Likewise, a man who favors abortion can be puzzled by his mixed feelings while he sits in the waiting room. It can be a revelation for a man to discover these hitherto unknown feelings.

Live Births and Legal Abortions in the United States

	Live Births	Legal Abortions
1972	3,258,000	587,000*
1973	3,137,000	745,000*
1974	3,160,000	1,034,000
1975	3,144,000	1,115,000
1976	3,168,000	1,180,000

*Abortions were not legal in all states for the entire year

Teenagers

Teenage pregnancies are largely caused by ignorance. Interviews with teenage boys in abortion-clinic waiting rooms indicate that for most of them, it was their first or second sexual encounter. Their girlfriends are rarely more experienced than they are. Even when they weren't completely ignorant of birth control methods, they didn't use them. Either they were too nervous to bring it up ("I didn't want to blow my chance") or too eager to bother.

> My brother told me to dump her. He said she only got pregnant to make me marry her. He's two years older than me and I usually follow his advice, but this time he's wrong. We just never thought this could happen. I hate to put her through all this abortion stuff, but there's no way we could get married now. If our parents found out it would be all over.

Teenagers are often more scared of their parents finding out about the abortion than of anything else. They're more likely to talk it over with a brother, sister, or friendly teacher than with their parents or even friends. The most important thing in their lives can become just keeping it secret.

Adolescence, after all, is a time when a whole new world of adulthood is opening up. Physically, but not emotionally, mature, teenagers are often denied the privileges of grown-ups that their bodies tell them they are ready for. Their love affairs are often dismissed as childish even though they are physically able to consummate them, with the resultant possibility of pregnancy. Yet an abortion can sometimes strengthen a teenage relationship. Few teenage couples have faced such a serious decision before. If they survive this ordeal, they'll have added a measure of substance to what was probably not a very complex relationship.

At the same time, teenage boys are more likely than older men to feel guilty. Their morality is still guided by their parents more than it will be, later, when they're older and on their own. The feeling they may be doing something wrong, and will be punished for it, worries them. Then, too, a vague feeling that it would be *nice* to have a baby may be welling up inside them. These are feelings few teenagers understand, and even less often bring themselves to share with others.

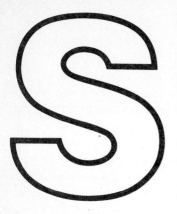ingle men

Young, single men often take abortion for granted. It's one of the pitfalls of sexuality—the dark side of the new sexual ethic. He does his best to avoid it, but faces up to it when the time comes.

Many single men expect their lovers to have an abortion as a matter of course. In their view, both sides knew the score when the game began. If you lose, whether it was by relaxed vigilance or plain bad luck, you've got to pay the penalty. He'll probably help pay the cost, but expect—or insist—that you go through with it.

This doesn't mean he's using abortion as a method of birth control. Only as a last resort. No matter how willing he was to share the responsibilities of birth control, he knew that the ultimate responsibility was yours. That wasn't his decision, but nature's. And no matter how willing he is to share the blame for your pregnancy, there's no way he can share the burden. That's yours, too, and all he can do is make it as easy as he can for you.

Many men find themselves caught in a bind. They know you need their emotional support, but at the same time need support themselves. Their biggest concern, after your health, is probably the future of the relationship. Most men sense it will be difficult for the relationship to pick up where it left off before the abortion. From the moment you discovered you were pregnant, something changed. At the very least, you and he were forced to answer questions like "Should we get married?" and "Should we have a baby?" right away.

Besides, he knows you're going through a period of re-evaluation. He doesn't want to push his luck; if there's any residue of resentment against him for "causing" the abortion, he wants to let it die down. He also wants to know that he isn't left out of your future. And most of all he wants to be reassured that the warmth you once shared is still alive.

Even if a man wants to deal with these new feelings, he can be scared to bring them up. He believes—whether or not it's true—that you're judging him by the amount of support he's giving. The "strong silent type" is still a popular ideal; he has been conditioned to think that a "real man's" job is to help the weaker sex through its emotional frailties. Any of his own needs he expresses will only detract from his performance.

Who Are "The Men Who Wait?"

More than half the men surveyed while sitting in a New York clinic's waiting room were in their 20's and single:

Age 17-19	6%
Age 20-24	29%
Age 25-29	26%
Age 30-34	21%
Age 35-39	13%
Age 40-49	4%
Age 50 and over	1%
Single	60%
Married	35%
Separated	4%
Widowed	1%

His insecurity isn't helped any by post-abortion abstinence. Most clinics recommend two weeks without sex afterward, and many women feel turned off anyway. Yet sex can be the only way left for him to ask for emotional reassurance. For inarticulate men, used to giving and receiving their affection in the form of sex, this can be frustrating emotionally as well as sexually.

Not surprisingly, the closer a man is to a woman, the more anxious he is about an abortion. Interviewers of single men at a Detroit clinic found that the better the man felt about the relationship, the worse he felt at the time of the abortion. The more involved a man stayed with her, and the more emotional support he gave her, the less confident he felt about himself.

Single men who don't want an abortion

When an unwanted pregnancy occurs, single men— especially younger single men—are likely to want it aborted. When asked, most say they were the ones who first suggested the abortion—although they invariably add that their women friends share their view. A typical comment is, "Once I explained to her that this was the wrong reason for marriage, she agreed that abortion was the only alternative."

But there are exceptions. In 1977, a 23-year-old New Jersey man offered to marry his girlfriend rather than let her abort her pregnancy. When she refused, he got a state supreme court order barring the operation on the grounds that it would violate his right to "future fatherhood." The girlfriend had the abortion done in another state, before the papers were actually served on her.

Other men have other reasons for not wanting abortions. Some, naturally, oppose them on the religious grounds that the fetus is a human being. But more often it's the sense of loss of a potential child. Often a single man is unaware of the strength of his fathering instinct until actually confronted with a pregnancy. Such a man may punish himself with guilt long after the abortion is over.

Even the men who favor abortion do so as the lesser of evils. The alternatives—marriage, an out-of-wedlock child, or giving up the baby for adoption—seem crueler. "Why should she lose nine months of her life for a baby someone else will bring up?"

Single men who run away

Other men vote with their feet. These are the ones who never make it to the waiting rooms, the ones who force an abortion by running away—or ending the relationship—when their lovers get pregnant. Why? What makes an until-then supportive man turn about face and hightail it for the county line? What makes a man suddenly turn off his emotions and become stone cold?

It's not as rare as you think. The temptation to bolt out of the relationship crosses nearly every man's mind at a time like this. It's not too late to call it off, he thinks. He never meant to get in this deeply. He's scared. And he still hasn't signed in blood. There's nothing keeping him in if he wants out, and he knows it.

If a man has been having any second thoughts about a relationship, this is when they'll rise to the surface. This is when he'll feel he has to make a decision about the relationship. In or out. And if it's "out," he may not let you know in the usual manner. Instead of running away, he may withdraw. What's really going on is he's fighting a war within himself, and *you're* on the losing side.

Most men eventually vote "in." The temptation to flee subsides. Men who mistake their fear for a need for freedom may heed its call. But if he cares for you and can answer the questions he's asking himself, he will be there when you need him.

arried men

Often, the men in the waiting rooms are husbands. Abortion has become an increasingly acceptable alternative for married couples. Newlyweds may want to delay their first child, while older couples often feel like calling it quits with childbearing. But whatever the reason, married men and women no longer feel compelled to carry an unwanted pregnancy to the end.

We married too young. She got pregnant, and the only other choice back then was to put the baby up for adoption. So we got married, and wham, three babies in as many years. Five years later we're still trying to catch up with our debts, and then this happened. But now we can get a safe abortion. If we'd been able to do this the first time around, we'd never have gotten stuck in this hole in the first place.

Legal Abortions by *Married* Women in the United States

1972	174,000
1973	204,000
1974	246,000
1975	270,000
1976	306,000

When a husband suggests an abortion, it's usually for practical reasons. Like money. Or time, or health, or just plain convenience. There's usually less of the wrenching self-examination that an unmarried man can face. Since he's already married, he doesn't have to decide whether he wants to marry.

Married men are more likely to have discussed the abortion with their wives, and less likely to regret the decision later. Eileen Milling, interviewing men waiting in a New York clinic, found that three-fourths of the married men arrived at the decision jointly with their wives. The rest said *they* were the ones who'd insisted on it. But any survey in a waiting room naturally leaves out most of the men who didn't want the abortion. Men who oppose their wives' decision rarely accompany them to the clinic.

Some men continue to harbor resentment long afterward. A woman doesn't need her husband's permission for an abortion, and legally the decision is hers. But "legally" isn't always enough. Few marriages can easily weather the trauma of an abortion that half the marriage didn't want. Even a man who suppresses his opposition, for the sake of his wife's needs, can carry the unspoken resentment inside. This can express itself in sexual problems, like temporary impotence. More than one husband has found himself unable to make love with his wife for a while after she got an abortion he didn't want.

hat your doctor thinks

There's another man whose attitude toward abortion can affect you: the doctor who performs it. If you've ever had an abortion, you don't need statisticians to tell you that most abortions are performed by male doctors. Roughly 95 percent. And for most doctors, abortion is a routine operation they do over and over again for the simple reason that the law says only doctors can perform it.

Most doctors don't let their misgivings, if they have them, interfere with their work. Their professional responsibility, ultimately, is to the physical and mental health of their patients. Sometimes, though, you get a clinker. A doctor who keeps referring to a fetus as "the baby" can thoroughly demoralize a woman whose feelings are already mixed. Linda Francke tells of a Brooklyn doctor who baptized every fetus he aborted with sterilized water. Even the battle-hardened nurses couldn't take it.

But the times, as they say, are a-changin'. A recent survey of 20,000 health professionals found that medical students, the next generation of doctors, felt more positively toward abortion than any other segment of the medical field. More in favor of it than doctors, nurses, or medical-school faculty members.

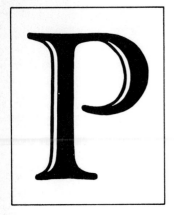

Parenthood

Biologically, parenthood began in the remote past as an alternative to simple cell division. Genetically, parenthood starts when a sperm penetrates an ovum. Culturally, parenthood may start well before puberty in role-playing games and solitary fantasy—for boys as well as for girls. But for you and for him, parenthood starts when you say, "I'm pregnant." Life will never be the same again for either of you.

You may not be able to express all the feelings you have about your pregnancy to him or to anyone. One feeling may be a terrible loneliness, as if you had just been told that you had a deadly disease—a fearful awareness that something is growing in *your* body. Another may be a fierce resentment—inexplicable, perhaps, yet still there—of the man who is responsible, who has merely projected part of himself into you and is free to walk away, his body uninvaded. Another may be doubt and distrust: You'll do your part, but will he do his? Does he really want a baby? Will he be a good father?

The father of your unborn child may be rich, respectable to a fault, deeply in love with you, and married to you. Still—foolishly, you know—you wonder. You want to be able to rely on this man, both in the short run during your pregnancy and in the long run after the child is born.

There are legal ways of forcing a man to admit paternity, and legal ways of forcing him to take responsibility for his children. Though there are also many ways he can get out of it, the law is almost always in your favor. But let's assume that you're not going to have to call down the law—he's said he wants to be a daddy. Is that all there is to it—he's willing, even eager, so you have no more worries? You know that your own feelings are very complicated, contradictory, variable. What really worries you is that you don't know what his feelings are. Well, what are his feelings?

She is pregnant

It's only in the movies that his face lights up. Perhaps that's what makes us cry—men too—at such scenes. If only life were like that—if only he were Jimmy Stewart...

She's getting a little cranky now...fourth month. I'm looking forward to it, but Christ, I hope she's not going to act like this the rest of her life. We had a helluva blowout the night she told me she was preg-

Insanity is hereditary. You get it from your children.

—sign in a
pediatrician's office

*nant. I guess I just didn't seem that happy. Not that
it caught me by surprise—I knew she had something
to tell me, and I knew what it was. Hell, we'd been
trying long enough—you know, off and on, sometimes with and sometimes without, like Russian rou-
lette. But when she said it, my face froze just for a
minute. I guess I was scared.*

He knows that you need a lot from him now—and he
knows that maybe he won't be able to provide it. Even if you
and he have no practical worries about money, you have
become a different person: a woman carrying his child. This
person acts differently and has different needs. He doesn't
know if he can meet them, you don't know if he can meet
them. It's not just taking care of the child that's the problem—
more immediately, it's taking care of you. When you and he
settled down together, he thought one of the painful delights
of single life was behind him: "She loves me, she loves me
not..." Now he's not so sure what he's feeling—but he knows,
and you know, that one of the feelings is fear.

Of course he wants it, but...

You both know that not all of the changes a baby will
bring are going to be good ones. No matter how strong your
urge to have a child, or his, for most American couples of
ordinary means a child is a great intrusion on their way of life.
Fortunately, perhaps, they have no way of knowing how great
it will be when they are expecting their first child, and by the
second pregnancy they are aware of the rewards. But they do
have some premonitions.

*She's been wanting to have a child, wanting to have
a child. And so have I... I'll be 30 next year. Time
for it. In fact I kind of pressed her about it. When
her boss had a stroke she thought she'd get his job,
and she probably would have, except she was pregnant. I didn't want her to get an abortion. We'd had
this little celebration when we got the confirmation
from the doctor, but she hadn't told anyone at
work. When her boss got sick we just kind of eyed
each other for a few days and didn't talk about
whether she'd go on working or not. Anyway, suddenly I got very hearty and jolly about telling people*

we were having a baby—pretty much made the deci-
sion without her—so there we are. We both agree
that it would be too hard on her to keep this job
and *have a baby. But how are we going to get along*
without her salary?

It isn't really all that expensive to have a baby, if one of
you has group health insurance to pick up the hospital and
obstetrical costs. Babies don't have expensive tastes in food,
and the standard baby gear—crib, changing table, and so
on—is cheap enough, or available from relatives. What really
hurts, if you work, is the loss of income. And he worries about
that—perhaps a lot more than you do, for impending motherhood is a state of mind in itself, and can block out more
humdrum worries.

Neither of you knows yet what it's like to live in a
household that includes a child. But you probably do think of
what the homes of your friends with children look and feel
like—noise, disorder, distraction. You have wondered how
people can live this way. And so has he.

When we bought the house we had children in
mind. We'd thought the finished room in the attic
would be great for a kid—lots of space and privacy.
But we never got around to putting heat up there,
and anyway she wants the baby right next door
where we can hear it if it cries. There goes my study.

You know that your pregnancy is going to cost you in
many ways. It may terminate, and will certainly interrupt, your
career. It will end a self-sufficient independence that you
enjoyed. Being a mother takes strength and requires sacri-
fices physically and emotionally. It will cost him too, and he
knows it. But most men also suspect that they will be well
repaid by the joys of being a father.

I'm going to be a father

If his face froze when you told him you were pregnant,
probably one of the things that made it freeze was joy. The
desire for a child is very strong in men. There are very few men
who do not want to be fathers—eventually, anyway. They have
had fantasies—probably as many as you have—about being a
parent. They were sons; they expect sometime to be fathers.

Imminent fatherhood is many things to the father-to-be, and one of them is membership in an enormous yet exclusive club in which all fathers are brothers. His initiation comes as a surprise—for the club is secret even when it is most open; the nonmember is bored by its rituals and oblivious to their significance. When he discovers that his male friends, his male subordinates and superiors at work, and his most casual male acquaintances are without exception happy for him and somehow proud of him, he becomes a father on another level: a proud father. He may have received the congratulations of his family and in-laws with pleasure—and these may be the individuals most important to him emotionally—but the new status he has in the male world at large is broader, deeper, and different.

He has proved his masculinity, of course—always a good thing to prove. He is a father, or at least a father-to-be; his sperm are capable of reproducing. But he is not proud just of that, any more than your pride as a mother-to-be is simply in pride in your fertility. He is proud because he is going to be a *father.*

He is not sure what a father is, what it will be like to be one, whether he will be a good one. He doesn't know just what kind of father he *wants* to be. His own father wasn't that great—or maybe was too great; he'll never measure up. But he's going to be a father.

We're going to have a baby

For most couples there is a certain point in early pregnancy when the reality is accepted: You're going to have a baby. It may be a happy moment and yet a rather solemn one, as you look ahead to times that may be difficult and pressures that will have to be borne, but you feel all at once a certain relaxation in the fact that you are allied and are going to have the baby together. Or it may not be that way.

Some men are unable to cope with the reality of pregnancy. Your pregnant body may seem unclean. The swelling, blue-veined abdomen, the flutter of kicks in later pregnancy, and the mere thought of the breaking of the waters may disgust him.

Contemptible! But if the father of your child seems to be reacting this way, try not to hate him for it. As your pregnancy has advanced, you probably have been developing a new and

Undisputed Masculinity

The world's greatest father, according to the *Guinness Book of World Records,* was the Emperor Moulay Ismail of Morocco (1672–1727), who reputedly fathered 548 sons and 340 daughters. His nickname was "The Bloodthirsty."

rather callous consciousness of your own body, with its objective changes that the obstetrician or gynecologist checks out periodically. It's almost like the surprising willingness you develop to stick your finger in your eye when you get contact lenses. Culture, your glands, and necessity combine to sensitize you in some ways and desensitize you in others. He may remain just as squeamish as ever.

Most men who have this feeling of revulsion will get over it or at least manage to conceal it. But even those who don't can turn out to be good fathers. He can ignore the unpleasant physical aspects of reproduction. You can't.

And an extreme negative male reaction to the physical aspects of pregnancy is rather rare. Many men find pregnant women extremely sensual and sexually exciting. And a man may be fascinated by the daily changes in your body. As the baby grows within you he may want to monitor every change, put his hand on your abdomen every time the baby kicks, put his ear against you to listen for the tiny heartbeat. A reaction that will naturally make you glow with pride and warmth.

et's have it together

"Natural childbirth" is becoming increasingly popular in the United States and other Western countries. It isn't "natural" in many ways—it takes place in a hospital, the child is delivered by an obstetrician, and the mother is trained beforehand in sophisticated methods of controlling her own sensations—but the birth usually takes place with little or no anesthesia, which is the way it was done in the old days. In addition to the numerous benefits of natural childbirth for both mother and child, there are the pluses for the father. "Natural childbirth" programs invite the active participation of the father—from mid-pregnancy to delivery, and this participation is gratifying for a man who'd otherwise be a sideliner.

In the past, the father has always been left out. Males have always been denied even standing room at the labor bed. Childbirth has been part of the Female Mystique, and if men have historically been happy to have it closed off to them, women have historically been willing to keep this mystery to themselves and the medical professionals. Objections to the various "natural childbirth" programs probably are as apt to be voiced by women as by men.

*She didn't want any part of it. She had this thing
going with her mother all the time—whispering and
whatnot. Just like with the first baby—I'm like an
enemy, or least a neutral party or something. I don't
really mind being shut out. What's important is that
she's comfortable about it.*

Maybe you're the one who wants to do it together, get him
involved, and he's the one who is holding back.

*Well, we went to the first class. Lots of couples all
over a gymnasium floor, with the husbands squat-
ting over their wives like a lifesaving class or something. The nurse made us husbands say why we had
come. I said because I was used to doing what I
was told. I guess I sounded pretty stupid. But the
class is OK. What bothers me is the exercises at
home. Lying there on the end of the bed with a
stopwatch and listening to her pant and blow. I
don't know, it embarrasses me.*

The "natural childbirth" programs certainly don't work
for everyone. Separation of men from childbirth is an ancient
cultural tradition, and having him there may seem unnatural
to one or both of you. But those who experience it claim
there's nothing comparable.

*When we were in the labor room, she was doing
pretty well, not panting yet, you know... well, there
was a couple across the hall in another labor room.
He was just settling her down there—he was going
to have to leave. She was kind of hysterical and
chewing him out. He kept muttering to her, trying to
calm her, and she'd scream, "I'm having labor pains!
Can't you see that? Call the nurse! Get the doctor!"
She sounded young. I was rubbing Mary's back.
She turned over and looked at me and we smiled at
each other. I guess we felt superior. All through it...
you know that screaming they do in the movies,
and the husband beats his head against the wall?
Mary never screamed. She lost control for a minute
toward the end, and I wanted her to have a cau-
dal—the doctor was right there with the needle—but
she said no, and she took it right on through.*

When the child is born, there is going to be an inevitable separation between you and the father. He is going to be on the outside, you on the inside—with the baby. You will be a patient, he will be a visitor. This will be hard for him, perhaps, but less hard if he has helped you bear your child and been present at the birth.

I guess the big moment was just when the baby came out, all blue, and the nurse put her on a table and splashed her eyes with something. Then the baby lay there bubbling through her nose and moving her arms and legs a little bit. Not crying. I was afraid she would roll off the table. I should know a baby that age can't roll off a table. I was watching the episiotomy too. The doctor kept getting more sutures from the nurse, but it didn't seem to bother Mary. I was holding her hand and she didn't wince. So now I've got three, girls, but she's the first one I saw being born. Mary was crying. Hell, I was crying too.

Fathers and mothers

He's a father, you're a mother. That makes you both parents, and as parents a man and a woman have at least as many concerns in common as they have individually. Whatever motivations each of you had for having the child in the first place, now you're parents.

You have changed and he has changed, and the child, as well as being the cause of the change, becomes a connection through which to communicate the change. When you touch the child, you are touching each other.

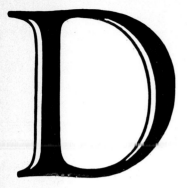

id he really want a son?

Probably he did really want a son, unless he already has one. Maybe you wanted a son too. There may be no way of expressing the disappointment, even to yourself. But a child—at least a first child—catches you by surprise. You didn't know what you would feel, and now you feel it. It is the same for a man. You need not fear that because he wanted an imagined son he will not love his real daughter.

Yeah, I am glad we had her. For one thing I finally feel grown up. Grown-up problems ahead, all right. But it's not just that. It's the baby herself. You know, it used to be when we came to your house I could take about a minute of having your kid pawing my glasses and then I wanted to get away. Well, I've been giving her her two-o'clock feeding. Half the time after she's finished the bottle and gone to sleep I don't put her back in the crib for a while. I just sit there with her, and I don't want to read or smoke or anything.

He may not feel the same about a daughter as he would about a son. He may be relieved to have a daughter rather than a son—he may have been afraid of the peculiar competition that develops between father and son, and afraid that he wouldn't be able to improve on the relationship he had with his own father. Or he may just like girl babies.

Fathers and sons

Whatever a man's state of liberation from the Male Mystique, he is likely to imitate at least some of the behavior of his own father and his father's contemporaries. He is, after all, a child of his culture, and bound to some degree by its conventions. He will want his son to be a little man—and he will both push his son to be a better man than he is and dread the day he succeeds.

In infancy, a child is not much of a threat—though he, or she, is certainly a burden and an inconvenience. As he grows older, a male child does begin to become both a threat to the father and an extension of him. Always in the back of his mind is the awareness that a cycle has been repeated, and that his son may hate and fear him as much as he hated and feared his own father.

A Poet-Father

We practice peaceful poetic coexistence. I'm proud of course that he's fulfilling his nature, that he's successful, and has fame and fortune. A father's natural pleasure of seeing him soar high. But in the end it's sort of complementing—he sees things, I see things a different way, according to our inner compulsions and inner natures.

—LOUIS GINSBERG

My old man believed in spanking, and I remember a period when I got whaled every night as soon as he came home, but he was basically a gentle guy. I always got along with him, and in the last few years we've really gotten very close. He's good with the kids, for one thing. But I remember one time when I was about five, going off to kindergarten, I spit my scrambled egg back onto my plate. He lost his temper and said, "If you ever do that again I'll make you eat it." He didn't mean it, but I thought he did. I used to have nightmares about having to eat huge plates of food.

In some ways, he may consciously treat his own son differently from the way he was treated. If he was forced to clean up his plate, he may insist that his son be allowed to eat whatever he wants whenever he wants—perhaps conflicting with your own ideas of how a child should eat. But in other ways, both consciously and unconsciously, he may treat his son as he was treated. Although he may be very affectionate with his son, he is apt to be rough about it—tickling and teasing rather than caressing. Especially when angry, he is apt to be sarcastic with a son, beating him down verbally and proving that he is wittier and wiser.

Eventually his son will rebel, as once he rebelled. The child may do it by running to you and complaining about him, or by making a smart crack that leaves him speechless and warns him that his little son is not without a critical eye and verbal weapons, any more than he once was. This is a touchy moment, for both son and father. Both may have to back off.

The other day I blew at Christopher for no reason. Or rather, the reason was that I'd been up all night working on a report, and he wanted to play games about putting on his shoes...you know. He was still sobbing when he got on the school bus. When I got home that night he didn't seem to hold any grudge, but I'd been brooding about it all day. I picked him up and sat him on my lap and apologized to him— told him daddies weren't perfect either. He was very nice about it, in that distracted way kids that age have. He was more interested in telling me about some spark plug he'd found on the street. But then later that night I bawled him out about something—ripping up the newspaper, I guess. I kissed him a few minutes later, and he said, "Tell me you're sorry, Daddy." I did tell him I was sorry I'd gotten mad, but that he shouldn't have done it. He got almost hysterical. I wanted to tell him it wasn't his fault, the way I'd done before. But it was his fault. How the hell do you teach kids right from wrong?

A Poet-Son

When I read my father's poetry very often there is a tremendous melancholy awareness of how much he is aware, an almost tearful realization that I should have been kinder when we were around together.

—ALLEN GINSBERG

Somehow, father and son must try to work it out. There will be victories and defeats for both of them, and victory is often defeat too, because they love each other. And there is no way you can stay out of the battle. Just remember one thing: The battle is immensely important to them, yet they cherish temporary truces and long for a permanent armistice.

Fathers and daughters

You probably know a good deal about this relationship already, because you had a father of your own. You may also have suspected that one reason that your relationship with your father was so warm and cozy was that he did not really expect very much of you.

Attitudes toward girl children change as attitudes of adult men and women change. But nevertheless it is likely that a father will perceive a little boy as like himself, and a little girl as unlike himself. She *is* unlike himself.

He is culturally conditioned to show a daughter tenderness and to encourage her femininity. He doesn't feel obliged to live his life out through his daughter. He expects to misunderstand her and to be misunderstood. So his relationship with a daughter is likely to be relatively relaxed, at least for the first few years.

His acceptance of his daughter as a person as real as himself will depend greatly on his acceptance of you as a person. If he perceives you (and most women) as a lovable, sexy, but essentially trivial housekeeper—and if you have allowed him to perceive you that way—he will probably be a kindly but rather wishy-washy daddy who doesn't expect very much from a child who's "just a girl." If he respects you—and women in general—he will insist that his daughter show the virtues and capacities he knows women can have, and will be as active a parent with his daughter as he would be with a son.

Strangely, perhaps, few men are ever reminded of their mothers when they look at their daughters in the way that they are reminded of their fathers when they look at their sons. They are not apt to replay with their daughters the conflicts they had with their mothers. A man's relationship with his daughter is closer to the present—and in some ways closer to the bone. It is you he sees when he looks at his daughter, and just as his relationship with you seems unique to him, his relationship to his daughter seems unique. He is freer to design his own relationship with her, or at least as free as he was to design his relationship with you.

Not that mothers are unimportant to men. A man is apt to feel his mother's shadow behind him all his life. He's apt to feel his father's shadow behind his son—and your shadow behind his daughter.

djusting to parenthood

In spite of advances in the social rights and privileges of women and in spite of an increasing public willingness of men to reexamine and qualify their attitudes toward work and family, a man is still apt to feel at some level that raising children is a woman's job. And you probably cannot escape the same feeling.

Once men could leave it all up to you. They still can, and many do, but they no longer feel comfortable about it. As in any period of social change, there are conflicting principles at work. You both feel the conflict, and it intensifies every situation. The soiled child is repeatedly the occasion for a grudge match: Which of you will get disgusted or guilty first and change the diaper?

He is as unhappy about this kind of silent squabble as you are. And it isn't always so silent. Just when you have a sleeping baby to consider, you have more reason to scream at each other than ever before.

You may or may not have to bear an unequal share of the burdens of your parenthood, but you will probably suffer equally from disruption of your marriage when there's a newborn child in the house. If anything, he may suffer as much as you do. You are absorbed with baby care details; his functions are likely to be more indirect and supplementary. Your sex life may be infrequent, tense, or otherwise disturbed, and he doesn't know how long that will go on—or even if he cares; he's pretty tired these days himself, and you're not the same person you were when you conceived the child.

Failure

Marriages that don't end in divorce are still slightly more numerous than those that do, so somewhere along the line most parents work out a method of coping.

In the early years of fatherhood, every man is intensely aware of his failures as both husband and father. Every man is a failure some of the time and in some respects—nobody's perfect. You're bound to feel like a failure too—but it's likely that there is no escape from motherhood for you; there is no one to take your place, so you must persist. You do, and you find you can fail now and again, but forgive yourself and persevere. A man, however, *can* escape. There are still no strong social conventions that oblige a man to be an active parent or that prevent him from seeking sympathy because he feels his home life is so awful.

> *Every minute it's something. As soon as I get home I'm supposed to give everybody a big hello and get down on the floor and play with Timmy. Then the kid runs wild all over the house while I'm trying to watch the news. I yell at him and the wife yells at me. Hell, when I was a kid I was smacked down pretty quick if I bothered the old man. But she spoils him.*

You can't complain to strangers like that—you can share your feelings with women friends, perhaps, but if you whined about the difficulties of motherhood in public, especially at the corner bar, you'd get not sympathy but contempt. It seems unjust, and it is.

Since he can escape, he's likely to do it occasionally, and he may make a habit of it. It's a hard habit to break. He feels he is failing, and that he is giving up opportunities to be close to the child he probably wanted as much as you did. He doesn't want to fail as a father, but he can't stand the little incidents of failure, the times when his actions and attitudes shame him. So he drifts away. He escapes from day-to-day problems by conceding defeat and considering himself an all-round failure.

Fathers Under Siege

Fathers are getting it from all sides today. The sociologists remind us of our multifaceted inadequacies. Closer to home, a husband often becomes the target of chronic hostility from his wife as she becomes aware of the gross inequalities in the marriage. The media add their bit with the Dagwood Bumstead Syndrome. It isn't easy to be an open, loving, giving father when you feel under siege.

—HOWARD CLINEBELL

That sounds rather childish, you say. It is indeed. When the child comes on the scene, the father wants you to love him as much as you love the child—or more. He wants you to forgive him when he misbehaves, and he'll be glad to give you the opportunity by misbehaving. You have your hands full, all right—a little child and a big one.

Sometimes you're just not up to it, or his demands are impossible. You go separate ways, within the marriage or out of it, while your child observes and grows.

uccess

When a man becomes a father he is under many new pressures and may feel helpless. But he is not, in fact, a child, and he is not helpless. Fatherhood, after all, is not the first responsibility he has faced. All his life he has been under pressure to achieve success of one kind or another—academic, athletic, social—and to act like a man. He has not won every battle, perhaps never really excelled in any way, but he has done well enough, become enough of a man, so that you found him acceptable as a mate. No matter how great he is, he has been defeated often, probably more often and in more different ways than you, but has learned to put defeat behind him; he has not been crushed by it. He is usually physically stronger than you are, and it is quite likely that the world has made him tougher in other ways as well—more able to conceal emotion, to force himself into unpleasant or frightening situations, and even to accept the dependence of others.

He wants you to reassure him, he wants you to tell him everything will be the same as before, he wants to believe that there will be no hardship ahead. But he is used to stifling the cries of the child within him—he has made the cruel but necessary choice of becoming a man—and he is able to offer support rather than ask for it, at least aloud.

So he isn't helpless in the face of fatherhood. In addition, the birth of his first child is most likely an exhilarating and energizing experience for him—he is happy about it, a fact that cannot be stressed too much in this chapter devoted mostly to warnings about the dark side of fatherhood. You may have had a great surge of energy and vigor in the last few weeks of pregnancy, as many women do. Something like that happens to him too, as the completely new emotion of fatherhood floods him and he feels himself expand enormously as a person.

He has defeats and humiliations. At first the diapers make him gag. You snap at him when he tries clumsily to help with a nursing problem. He may snap back.

He has successes. You're afraid to give the baby its first bath at home, and he does it—the baby can't smile yet, but looks as if it's trying to. He cups the baby like a football, skull in palm, and walks downstairs with it, long before you've dared the same maneuver—and you know he won't slip, and he knows you know it.

Of course, a good start doesn't always mean a good finish. The euphoria of new fatherhood is soon gone, and a man may begin to feel himself slipping into the ranks of losers at any time in the decades ahead. To keep being a good father, he must keep trying to be a good father.

And he does want to be a good father. He values the rewards—the child's love, and yours. He does need support from you, just as you need support from him; he needs to know that you respect his efforts and are both aware of his successes and forgiving of his failures. It can all add up to success.

"Don't Forget" Memos for Father's Day

Talk to David about empty wine bottles in his room.

Find out who hid grass in Mom's jewelry box.

Have Alice Cooper poster framed that Ellen gave me for Father's Day, and hang it in den (at least until she goes back to school).

Tell children at dinner tonight what a wonderful Father's Day I had, and how proud I am of each and every one of them.

—ART BUCHWALD

SELECTED BIBLIOGRAPHY

THE GENETIC MAN

Bronowski, Jacob. *The Ascent of Man.* Boston: Little, Brown, 1973.

Colligan, Douglas. "Tipping the Balance of the Sexes," *New York:* Nov. 7, 1977.

De Coursey, Russell M. *The Human Organism.* New York: McGraw-Hill, 1974.

Documenta Geigy. *Scientific Tables.* Ardsley, N.Y.: Geigy Pharmaceuticals, 1962.

Hanaway, Thomas P. and Gordon M. Burghardt. "Girls, Boys and Books," *Psychology Today:* Aug., 1976.

Kimura, Doreen. "The Asymmetry of the Human Brain," *Scientific American:* Vol. 228, no. 3 (March, 1973).

Langman, Jan. *Medical Embryology.* Baltimore: Williams & Wilkins, 1975.

Levine, Seymour. "Sex Differences in the Brain," *Scientific American:* Vol. 214, no. 4 (April, 1966).

Maccoby, Eleanor E. and Carol N. Jacklin. *The Psychology of Sex Differences.* Stanford, Ca.: Stanford University Press, 1974.

Mead, Margaret. *Male and Female: A Study of the Sexes in a Changing World.* New York: William Morrow, 1975.

——. *Sex and Temperament in Three Primitive Societies.* New York: William Morrow, 1973.

Money, John and Anke A. Ehrhardt. *Man and Woman, Boy and Girl.* New York: Mentor Books, 1974.

Money, John and Patricia Tucker. *Sexual Signatures: On Being a Man or a Woman.* Boston: Little, Brown, 1976.

Pfeiffer, John. *The Cell.* New York: Time-Life Books, 1969.

Rorvick, David M. *Your Baby's Sex: Now You Can Choose.* New York: Bantam Books, 1971.

Tanner, James M. "Growing Up," *Scientific American:* Vol. 229, no. 3 (Sept., 1973).

Tavris, Carol and Carole Offir. *The Longest War.* New York: Harcourt Brace Jovanovich, 1977.

Weisz, Paul B. *The Science of Biology.* New York: McGraw-Hill, 1971.

Witelson, Sandra F. "Sex and the Single Hemisphere," *Science:* Vol. 193, no. 4251 (Jan., 1977).

IMAGES

Agee, James and Walker Evans. *Let Us Now Praise Famous Men.* Boston: Houghton Mifflin, 1940.

Anant, Victor. "A *Woman's Own* World," *New Society:* Jan. 1, 1976.

Anast, Philip. "Differential Movie Appeals as Correlates of Attendance," *Journalism Quarterly:* Vol. 44, no. 1 (1967).

"Anything Goes: Taboos in Twilight," *Indian Journal of Social Research:* Vol. 11, no. 2 (Aug., 1968).

Aramoni, Aniceto. "Machismo," *Psychology Today:* Jan., 1972.

Binderman, Murray B., et al. "A Portrait of 'The Life'," *Urban Life:* Vol. 4, no. 2 (July, 1975).

Cameron, Paul. "Social Stereotypes," *Psychology Today:* July, 1974.

Campbell, Colin. "Our Many Versions of the Self," *Psychology Today:* Feb., 1976.

Carpenter, Edmund. *Oh, What a Blow That Phantom Gave Me!* New York: Holt, Rinehart & Winston, 1973.

Chambers, Marcia. "Rape and guile separated as a suspect is acquitted," *New York Times:* May 2, 1975.

Ciardi, John. *In Fact.* New Brunswick, N.J.: Rutgers University Press, 1962.

DeMott, Benjamin. "After the Sexual Revolution," *Atlantic:* Nov., 1976.

DuMaurier, Daphne. *Myself When Young.* Garden City, N.Y.: Doubleday, 1977.

Eiseley, Loren. *All the Strange Hours.* New York: Charles Scribner's Sons, 1975.

Fisher, Seymour. *Body Experience in Fantasy and Behavior.* New York: Appleton-Century-Crofts, 1970.

Frankl, Viktor R. *Man's Search For Meaning.* New York: Pocket Books, 1963.

Gould, Roger. "Adult Life Stages," *Psychology Today:* Feb., 1975.

Gross, Leonard H. "Short, Dark, and Almost Handsome," *Ms.:* June, 1975.

Hardin, Garrett. *Stalking the Wild Taboo.* Los Altos, Ca.: William Kaufmann, 1977.

Iversen, William. *Venus USA.* New York: Pocket Books, 1970.

Jacobson, Edith. *Depression.* New York: International Universities Press, 1971.

Johnson, Ronald W. and Joan MacDonnell. "The Relationship Between Conformity and Male and Female Attitudes Toward Women," *Journal of Social Psychology:* Vol. 94 (1974).

Kornheiser, Tony. "That Damn Yankee," *New York Times Magazine:* April 9, 1978.

La Barre, Weston. *The Human Animal.* Chicago: University of Chicago Press, 1954.

LeMasters, E.E. *Blue-Collar Aristocrats.* Madison, Wisc.: University of Wisconsin Press, 1975.

Levinson, Daniel J., "Growing Up With The Dream," *Psychology Today:* Jan., 1978.

Levinson, Daniel J. et al. "Periods in the Adult Development of Men: Ages 18 to 45," *Counseling Psychologist:* Vol. 6, no. 1 (1976).

McLaughlin, Mignon. *The Second Neurotic's Notebook.* Indianapolis: Bobbs-Merrill, 1966.

Maitland, Leslie. "The verdict on women as jurors," *New York Times:* April 10, 1978.

Maslin, Janet. "He was obsessed with James Dean," *New York Times:* April 5, 1978.

Packard, Vance. *The People Shapers.* Boston: Little, Brown, 1977.

Popplestone, John A. "The Horseless Cowboys," *Trans-action:* May–June, 1973.

Rensberger, Boyce. "Outlook of boys is found shaped before 10th grade," *New York Times:* March 29, 1978.

Rosen, Marjorie. "Popcorn Venus, or, How the Movies Have Made Women Smaller Than Life," *Ms.:* April, 1974.

Rubin, Jerry. *Growing (Up) At 37.* New York: Pocket Books, 1976.

Seltzer, Shirley. "Quo Vadis, Baby?: Changing Adolescent Values as Reflected in the Lyrics of Popular Music," *Adolescence:* Vol. 11, no. 43 (Fall, 1976).

Severo, Richard. "The tragedy of Joanne: from a small Ohio town to despair in New York," *New York Times:* Oct. 15, 1976.

Shannon, Thomas W. *Personal Help for Men.* Marrieta, Ohio: Mullikin, 1918.

Sheed, Wilfrid. "Now That Men Can Cry," *New York Times Magazine:* Oct. 30, 1977.

Stix, Harriet. "Study reveals you are what you were," *Los Angeles Times:* Nov. 21, 1975.

Stokes, Geoffrey. "The Things That Frighten Men," *Mademoiselle,* Jan., 1978.

Tresemer, David. "Assumptions Made About Gender Roles," in Marcia Millman and Rosabeth Kanter, eds., *Another Voice.* Garden City, N.Y.: Doubleday, 1975.

U. S. Department of Commerce, Bureau of the Census. *Recent Social and Economic Trends.* Washington, D.C.: U.S. Government Printing Office, 1976.

Van Horne, Harriet. "Missing: big stars, old magic," *New York Post:* April 5, 1978.

Wolff, Michael. "The Making of a Vassar Man," *Ms.:* Sept., 1974.

Yarian, Sharon. "The Comic Book Hero, A Cultural Fantasy," Ph.D. Dissertation, Adelphi University, 1974.

A MAN'S BODY

Biology: An Appreciation of Life. Del Mar, Ca.: CRM Books, 1973.

Diagram Group, The. *Man's Body.* New York: Paddington Press, 1976.

Ekman, Paul. "Face Muscles Talk Every Language," *Psychology Today:* Sept., 1975.

Farb, Peter. *Humankind.* Boston: Houghton Mifflin, 1978.

Freud, Sigmund. *A Popular Introduction to Psychoanalysis.* New York: Simon & Schuster, 1969.

Gasner, Douglas. "The Face-Builders: Medical Master Craftsmen," *Medical Dimensions:* July–Aug., 1976.

Gordon, Suzanne. "Pain is good for you," *New York Times:* Dec. 13, 1977.

Katchadourian, Herant. *The Biology of Adolescence.* San Francisco: W. H. Freeman, 1977.

Leonard, George, ed. "The Rediscovery of the Body," *New York:* Dec. 27, 1976–Jan. 3, 1977.

Maccoby, Eleanor E. and Carol N. Jacklin. "What We Know and Don't Know About Sex Differences," *Psychology Today:* Dec., 1974.

Montagna, William and Richard J. Harrison. *Man.* New York: Appleton-Century-Crofts, 1974.

Morris, Desmond. *Manwatching: A Field Guide to Human Behavior.* New York: Harry N. Abrams, 1977.

Nourse, Alan E. *The Body.* New York: Time-Life Books, 1970.

Root, Harmon Knox. *The People's Medical Lighthouse.* New York: published by the author, 1854.

Rubin, Leonard R. "The Anatomy of a Smile," *Journal of Prosthetic Dentistry:* Vol. 53, no. 4 (April, 1974).

Sears, Robert R. and Shirley Feldman, eds. *The Seven Ages of Man.* Los Altos, Ca.: William Kaufmann, 1974.

Sheldon, William. *Atlas of Men: A Guide for Somatotyping the Adult Male of All Ages.* New York: Hafner Press, 1970.

Sullivan, Walter. "Boys and girls are now maturing earlier," *New York Times:* Jan. 24, 1971.

Tanner, James M. "Earlier Maturation in Man," *Scientific American:* Vol. 218, no. 1 (Jan., 1968).

Tanner, James M. and Gordon R. Taylor. *Growth.* New York: Time-Life Books, 1965.

Tavris, Carol and Carole Offir. *The Longest War.* New York: Harcourt Brace Jovanovich, 1977.

THOUGHT, STRESS, & SLEEP

Asimov, Isaac. *The Human Brain.* New York: Mentor Books, 1965.

Baker, Paul. "The Right Brain is the Dreamer," *Psychology Today:* Nov., 1976.

Buzan, Tony. *Use Both Sides of Your Brain.* New York: E. P. Dutton, 1976.

Calder, Nigel. *The Mind of Man.* New York: Penguin Books, 1973.

Dement, William C. *Some Must Watch While Others Must Sleep.* Stanford, Ca.: Stanford Alumni Association, 1972.

Engel, George. "Can Your Emotions Kill You?" *Reader's Digest:* April, 1978.

Ferguson, Marilyn. *The Brain Revolution.* New York: Taplinger, 1973.

Colligan, Douglas. *Insomnia.* New York: David McKay, 1978.

—— "The Sleep-Starvation Cure," *New York:* Dec. 5, 1977.

Fischhoff, Baruch. "The Silly Certainty of Hindsight," *Psychology Today:* April, 1975.

Friedman, Meyer and Ray Roseman. *Type A Behavior and Your Heart.* New York: Fawcett World Library, 1975.

Gazzaniga, Michael S. *Fundamentals of Psychology: An Introduction.* New York: Academic Press, 1973.

Giambra, Leonard M. "Daydreams: The Backburner of the Mind," *Psychology Today:* Dec., 1974.

Glass, David C. "Stress, Competition and Heart Attacks," *Psychology Today:* Dec., 1976.

Goleman, Daniel. "Split-Brain Psychology: Fad of the Year," *Psychology Today:* Oct., 1977.

——. "Why the Brain Blocks Daytime Dreams," *Psychology Today:* March, 1976.

Goleman, Daniel and Jerome Engel, Jr. "A Feeling of Falling," *Psychology Today:* Nov., 1976.

Goodman, David A. "Learning from Lobotomy," *Human Behavior:* Jan., 1978.

Hart, Leslie A. *How the Brain Works*. New York: Basic Books, 1975.

Hobson, J. Allan and Robert McCarley. "The Brain as a Dream State Generator: An Activation-Synthesis Hypothesis of the Dream Process," *American Journal of Psychiatry*: Vol. 134, no. 12 (Dec., 1977).

Holmes, T.H. and R.H. Rahe. "The Social Readjustment Rating Scale," *Journal of Psychosomatic Research*: Vol. 11, no. 2 (1967).

Jung, Carl G. *Psychology and Alchemy*. Princeton, N.J.: Princeton University Press, 1968.

Lamott, Kenneth. "Why Men and Women Think Differently," *Horizon*: May, 1977.

Linde, Shirley Motter and Louis M. Savary. *The Sleep Book*. New York: Harper & Row, 1974.

Mitler, Merrill M., et al. "Sleeplessness, Sleep Attacks, and Things That Go Wrong in the Night," *Psychology Today*: Dec., 1975.

Ornstein, Robert. "Right and Left Thinking," *Psychology Today*: May, 1973.

Piaget, Jean. *The Development of Thought*. New York: Viking, 1977.

Richardson, Frank C. and Donald L. Tasto. "Development and Factor Analysis of a Social Anxiety Inventory," *Behavior Therapy*: Vol. 7 (1976).

Rose, Steven. *The Conscious Brain*. New York: Random House, 1976.

Sagan, Carl. *The Dragons of Eden*. New York: Random House, 1977.

Scarf, Maggie. *Body, Mind and Behavior*. New York: Dell Books, 1977.

Selye, Hans. *The Stress of Life*. New York: McGraw-Hill, 1976.

Wilson, John R. *The Mind*. New York: Time-Life Books, 1964.

"What Causes Dreams?" *Newsweek*: Jan. 16, 1978.

REPRODUCING & AGING

Baltes, Paul B. and K. Warner Schaie. "The Myth of the Twilight Years," *Psychology Today*: March, 1974.

Boy Scouts of America. *Handbook for Boys*. Garden City, N.Y.: Doubleday, 1911 (reprinted by the Boy Scouts of America, 1976).

Butler, Robert N. "Age: The Life Review," *Psychology Today*: Dec., 1971.

Clinton, Charles A. *Sex Behavior in Marriage*. 1935.

Edwards, Allan E. and June R. Husted. "Penile Sensitivity, Age, and Sexual Behavior," *Journal of Clinical Psychology*: Vol. 32, no. 3 (July, 1976).

Gemme, Robert and Connie Christine Wheeler, eds. *Progress in Sexology*. New York: Plenum, 1977.

Karacan, Ismet. "Sleep-Related Penile Tumescence as a Function of Age," *American Journal of Psychiatry*: Vol. 132, no. 9 (Sept., 1975).

Kastenbaum, Robert. "Getting There Ahead of Time " *Psychology Today*: Dec., 1971.

Long, H.W. *Sane Sex Life and Sane Sex Living*. New York: Eugenics, 1919.

Masters, William H. and Virginia E. Johnson. *Human Sexual Inadequacy*. Boston: Little, Brown, 1970.

———. *Human Sexual Response*. Boston: Little, Brown, 1966.

Neugarten, Bernice L. "Grow Old Along With Me; The Best is Yet to Come," *Psychology Today*: Dec., 1971.

Nobile, Philip. "The Root of All Evil," *Cosmopolitan*: Nov., 1977.

Pengelley, Eric T. *Sex and Human Life*. Reading, Mass.: Addison-Wesley, 1974.

Pfeiffer, Eric, et al. "Sexual Behavior in Aged Men and Women," *Archives of General Psychiatry*: Vol. 19 (Dec., 1968).

Rosenfeld, Albert. "Are We Programmed to Die?" *Saturday Review*: Oct. 2, 1976.

Rubin, Theodore I. and David C. Berliner. *Understanding Your Man: A Woman's Guide*. New York: Ballantine Books, 1977.

Selkurt, Ewald E., ed. *Physiology*. Boston: Little, Brown, 1975.

Sullivan, Walter. "Very old people in the Andes are found to be merely old," *New York Times*: March 17, 1978.

Tavris, Carol. "Good News About Sex," *New York*: Dec. 6, 1976.

Vance, Ellen B. and Nathaniel N. Wagner. "Written Descriptions of Orgasm: A Study of Sex Differences," *Archives of Sexual Behavior*: Vol. 5, no. 1 (Jan., 1976).

Waister, Elaine and Ellen Berscheid. "Adrenaline Makes the Heart Grow Fonder," *Psychology Today*: June, 1971.

SENSUALITY & SEXUALITY

Arafat, Ibtihaj S. and Wayne L. Cotton. "Masturbation Practices of Males and Females," *Journal of Sex Research*: Vol. 10, no. 4 (Nov., 1974).

Bell, Arthur. "Everybody's *not* doing it," *Village Voice*: Jan. 23, 1978.

Bell, Robert R. "Sexual Satisfaction Among Married Women," *Medical Aspects of Human Sexuality*: Vol. 6, no. 12 (Dec., 1972).

Berg, D.H. "Sexual Subcultures and Contemporary Interaction Patterns Among Adolescents," *Adolescence*: Vol. 10, no. 40 (Winter, 1975).

Berne, Eric. *Sex in Human Loving*. New York: Pocket Books, 1971.

Brown, Howard. *Familiar Faces, Hidden Lives*. New York: Harcourt Brace Jovanovich, 1976.

Brozan, Nadine. "Teen-agers discuss sexuality in the 70's," *New York Times*: April 17, 1978.

Byrne, Donn. "A Pregnant Pause in the Sexual Revolution," *Psychology Today*: July, 1977.

Calderone, Mary, ed. *Sexuality and Human Values*. New York: Association Press, 1975.

Cohen, John, ed. *The Essential Lenny Bruce*. New York: Ballantine Books, 1967.

Comfort, Alex. *The Joy of Sex*. New York: Simon and Schuster, 1972.

———. *More Joy of Sex*. New York: Simon and Schuster, 1975.

Dorfman, Dan. "Upstairs, Downstairs at the Ansonia," *New York*: Nov. 28, 1977.

Dullea, Georgia. "A lack of sexual desire emerges as a contemporary condition," *New York Times*: May 1, 1978.

Ellis, Havelock. *The New Spirit*. Philadelphia: Richard West, 1973.

Fromme, Allan. *Dr. Fromme's Book on Sex and Marriage*. New York: Barnes & Noble, 1950.

Goldberg, Herb, Ph.D. *The Hazards of Being Male*. New York: Signet, 1976.

Gross, Amy. "Beyond Sex: The Joy of Touching," *Mademoiselle*: Dec., 1977.

Grotjahn, Martin. "Don't Laugh: Sexuality and Humor," *Psychology Today*: July, 1972.

Harris, Mark. *The Southpaw.* Indianapolis: Bobbs-Merrill, 1953.

Hessellund, Hans. "Masturbation and Sexual Fantasies in Married Couples," *Archives of Sexual Behavior:* Vol. 5, no. 2 (March, 1976).

Hunt, Morton. *Sexual Behavior in the 1970's.* New York: Dell Books, 1975.

Julty, Sam. "For Men Only," *Bride's:* March; 1976.

——. *Male Sexual Performance.* New York: Grosset and Dunlap, 1975.

Jung, Carl G. *Man and his Symbols.* New York: Dell Books, 1968.

——. *Modern Man in Search of a Soul.* New York: Harcourt Brace Jovanovich, 1955.

Kaplan, Helen Singer. *The New Sex Therapy.* New York: Quadrangle, 1974.

Kinsey, Alfred C. *Sexual Behavior in the Human Female.* New York: Pocket Books, 1953.

——. *Sexual Behavior in the Human Male.* Philadelphia: W.B. Saunders, 1948.

Klein, Fred. *The Bisexual Option.* New York: Arbor House, 1978.

Komarovsky, Mirra. "Cultural Contradictions and Sex Roles," *American Journal of Sociology:* Vol. 78, no. 4 (Jan., 1973).

McCarthy, Barry. *What You (Still) Don't Know About Male Sexuality.* New York: Thomas Y. Crowell, 1977.

McLuhan, Marshall and Quentin Fiore. *The Medium is the Massage.* New York: Bantam Books, 1967.

Nederland, Harold. "Asexuals have problems too," *Village Voice:* Feb. 25, 1971.

"New Morality, the" *Time:* Nov. 21, 1977.

Pietropinto, Anthony and Jacqueline Simenauer. *Beyond the Male Myth.* New York: Signet, 1978.

Pomeroy, Wardell B. "Alfred C. Kinsey: Man and Method," *Psychology Today:* March, 1972.

——. "The New Sexual Myths," *Glamour* Oct., 1977.

Raphael, Bette-Jane. "When He Says, 'I Have a Headache...'," *Ms.:* Sept., 1976.

Rindfuss, Ronald and Charles F. Westoff. "The Initiation of Contraception," *Demography:* Vol. 11, no. 1 (Feb., 1974).

Rogers, Carl R. *Becoming Partners.* New York: Delta Books, 1972.

Rubin, Lillian Breslow. "The Marriage Bed," *Psychology Today:* Aug., 1976.

Rubin, Theodore I. *Compassion and Self-Hate.* New York: Ballantine Books, 1976.

Saghir, Marcel T. and Eli Robins. "Male and Female Homosexuality: Natural History," *Comprehensive Psychiatry:* Vol. 12, no. 6 (Nov., 1971).

Shannon, Thomas W. *Nature's Secrets Revealed.* Marietta, Ohio: Mullikin, 1914.

Silverstein, Charles and Edmund White. *The Joy of Gay Sex.* New York: Crown, 1977.

Spillane, Mickey. *The Last Cop.* New York: Signet, 1973.

Tavris, Carol. "40,000 Men Tell About Their Sexual Behavior, Their Fantasies, Their Ideal Women and Their Wives," *Redbook:* Feb., 1978.

——. "Woman and Man," *Psychology Today:* March, 1972.

Tripp, C.A. *The Homosexual Matrix.* New York: Signet, 1976.

Udry, J. Richard and Naomi M. Morris. "Frequency of Intercourse by Day of the Week," *Journal of Sex Research:* Vol. 6, no. 3 (Aug., 1970).

Westoff, Charles F. "Coital Frequency and Contraception," *Family Planning Perspectives:* Vol. 6, no. 3 (Summer, 1974).

——. "Trends in Contraceptive Practice," *Family Planning Perspectives:* Vol. 8, no. 2 (March–April, 1976).

Wolff, Charlotte. *Bisexuality: A Study.* London: Quartet Press, 1977.

Zilbergeld, Bernie. *Male Sexuality.* Boston: Little, Brown, 1978.

FITNESS & DISORDERS

Benet, Sula. "Why They Live to be 100 or Even Older in Abkhasia," *New York Times Magazine:* Dec. 26, 1971.

Brody, Jane E. "Personal Health," *New York Times:* Nov. 23, 1977.

Burke, Christopher W. *The Adrenal Cortex in Practical Medicine.* Forest Grove, Ore.: Gray-Mills, 1973.

Chandler, G.N. *A Synopsis of Gastroenterology.* Baltimore: Williams & Wilkins, 1963.

Dietary Allowances Committee and Food and Nutrition Board. *Recommended Dietary Allowances.* Washington, D.C.: National Academy of Sciences, 1974.

Eckholm, Erick and Frank Record. "The Affluent Diet," *The Futurist:* Feb., 1977.

Complete Runner, The. Eds. of *Runner's World.* New York: Avon Books, 1978.

Fixx, James F. *The Complete Book of Running.* New York: Random House, 1977.

Jones, Ben Morgan and Oscar A. Parsons. "Alcohol and Consciousness: Getting High and Coming Down," *Psychology Today:* Jan., 1975.

Jones, Kenneth L., et al. *Total Fitness.* San Francisco: Canfield Press, 1972.

Kogan, Benjamin A. *Health.* New York: Harcourt Brace Jovanovich, 1976.

Labuza, T.P. and A. Elizabeth Sloan. *Food for Thought.* Westport, Conn.: Avi Publishing, 1977.

Maness, Bill. "What Do You Really Know About Exercise?" *Today's Health:* Nov., 1975.

Mayer, Jean. "The Bitter Truth About Sugar," *New York Times Magazine:* June 20, 1976.

Nager, Norman R. "Apathetic Hearts," *Human Behavior:* Feb., 1976.

Null, Gary. *Alcohol and Nutrition.* New York: Pyramid, 1977.

Robbins, Stanley L. *Textbook of Pathology.* Philadelphia: W. B. Saunders, 1962.

U.S. Department of Health, Education and Welfare. *What are the Facts About Genetic Disease?* Washington, D.C.: U.S. Government Printing Office, 1976.

White, Abraham, et al. *Principles of Biochemistry.* New York: McGraw-Hill, 1964.

Haber, Deborah. "Exercise," *New York:* Oct., 1977.

Harper, Harold A. *Review of Physiological Chemistry.* Los Altos, Ca.: Lange Medical Publications, 1967.

Harrison's Principles of Internal Medicine. New York: McGraw-Hill, 1974.

WORKING MEN

Battaille, Janet. "Debate on nepotism rules grows with a rise in working couples," *New York Times:* May 9, 1978.

Bender, Marilyn. "When the Boss is a Woman," *Esquire:* March 28, 1978.

Bennetts, Leslie. "Studying the woes of working nights," *New York Times:* April 5, 1978.

Burgen, Michele. "The Problems of Women Bosses," *Ebony:* Nov., 1977.

Burke, Ronald J. "Occupational Stresses and Job Satisfaction," *Journal of Social Psychology:* Vol. 100 (1976).

Chesler, Phyllis and Emily Jane Goodman. *Women, Money and Power.* New York: Bantam Books, 1977.

Clarke, Thomas E. "The Work Environment and Mental Health," *Studies in Critical Psychology:* Vol. 3, no. 2 (Oct., 1971).

Coleman, John R. *Blue Collar Journal.* Philadelphia: J. B. Lippincott, 1974.

Dullea, Georgia. "Vast changes in society traced to the rise of working women," *New York Times:* Nov. 29, 1977.

Feiffer, Jules. "Men Really Don't Like Women," *Look:* Jan. 11, 1966.

Friedman, Morton. "Success Phobia and Retarded Ejaculation," *American Journal of Psychotherapy:* Vol. 27, no. 1 (Jan., 1973).

Garson, Barbara. *All the Livelong Day.* New York: Penguin Books, 1977.

Harragan, Betty Lehan. *Games Mother Never Taught You.* New York: Rawson Associates, 1977.

Heller, Joseph. *Something Happened.* New York: Ballantine Books, 1975.

Hennig, Margaret and Anne Jardim. *The Managerial Woman.* New York: Doubleday, 1977.

——. "Women Executives in the Old-Boy Network," *Psychology Today:* Jan., 1977.

Horn, Jack. "Bored to Sickness," *Psychology Today:* Nov., 1975.

"How Men Adjust to a Female Boss," *Business Week:* Sept. 5, 1977.

"How to Avoid the Director's Disease," *The Director:* May, 1976.

International Business Machines, Inc. *IBM: About Your Company.* Armonk, N.Y.: 1977.

Janeway, Elizabeth. *Man's World, Woman's Place.* New York: William Morrow, 1971.

Kanter, Rosabeth Moss. *Men and Women of the Corporation.* New York: Basic Books, 1977.

——. "Why Bosses Turn Bitchy," *Psychology Today:* May, 1976.

Kent, Malcolm. *On Becoming a Corporate Ace.* New York: Laddin Press, 1972.

Korda, Michael. *Male Chauvinism!* New York: Berkley, 1976.

——. *Power! How to Get It, How to Use It.* New York: Ballantine Books, 1976.

——. *Success!* New York: Random House, 1977.

Lerner, Melvin J. "All the World Loathes a Loser," *Psychology Today:* June, 1971.

Levinson, Daniel J. *The Seasons of a Man's Life.* New York: Alfred A. Knopf, 1978.

Levinson, Harry. *Executive Stress.* New York: Mentor Books, 1975.

Levi-Strauss, Claude. *Triste Tropique.* New York: Pocket Books, 1977.

Lewis, Paul. "Group, not line, builds sewing machines," *New York Times:* March 18, 1978.

McClelland, David C. and David H. Burnham. "Good Guys Make Bum Bosses," *Psychology Today:* Dec., 1975.

Maccoby, Michael. *The Gamesman: The New Corporate Leaders.* New York: Simon & Schuster, 1977.

Mead, Margaret. *Coming of Age in Samoa.* New York: William Morrow, 1971.

Molloy, John T. *Dress for Success.* New York: Warner Books, 1976.

Nichols, Jack. *Men's Liberation: A New Definition of Masculinity.* New York: Penguin Books, 1975.

Ogilvie, Bruce C. and Albert L. Porter. "Business Careers as Treadmill to Oblivion: The Allure of Cardiovascular Death," *Human Resources Management:* Fall, 1974.

Pogrebin, Letty Cottin. "The Intimate Politics of Working With Women," *Ms.:* Oct., 1975.

Press, Robert M. "Men rediscover secretarial jobs for themselves," *Christian Science Monitor:* May 13, 1975.

Quinn, Robert E. "Coping With Cupid: The Formation, Impact and Management of Romantic Relationships in Organizations," *Administrative Science Quarterly:* March, 1977.

Report of the President's Commission on Campus Unrest. New York: Avon Books, 1971.

Ringer, Robert J. *Looking Out For Number One.* New York: Funk and Wagnalls, 1977.

——. *Winning Through Intimidation.* New York: Fawcett World Library, 1976.

Roberts, D.G. "Stolen Kisses," *Gentleman's Quarterly:* Dec., 1976–Jan., 1977.

Sheehy, Gail. *Passages.* New York: Bantam Books, 1977.

Terkel, Studs. *Working.* New York: Avon Books, 1975.

Toffler, Alvin. *Future Shock.* New York: Bantam Books, 1971.

Townsend, Robert. *Up the Organization.* New York: Fawcett World Library, 1975.

U. S. Department of Health, Education and Welfare. *Work in America.* Cambridge, Mass.: MIT Press, 1973.

Weitz, John and Everett Mahlin. *Man in Charge.* New York: Macmillan, 1974.

Whyte, William H., Jr. *The Organization Man.* New York: Simon & Schuster, 1972.

Williams, Dana and Michael King. "Sex Role Attitudes and Fear of Success as Correlates of Sex Role Behavior," *Journal of College Student Personnel:* Vol. 17, no. 1 (1976).

Witchel, Sam. "Dear Personnel Manager,..." *New York Times:* March 29, 1978.

Woodward, Chris. "Tight job market forces men into women's jobs," *Los Angeles Times:* Sept. 15, 1977.

FRIENDS

Bach, Richard. *Jonathan Livingston Seagull.* New York: Avon Books, 1974.

Bock, E. Wilbur. "Aging and Suicide," *The Family Coordinator:* Jan., 1972.

Booth, Alan and Elaine Hess. "Cross-Sex Friendship," *Journal of Marriage and the Family:* Feb., 1974.

"Cardinals name Bud Wilkinson," *New York Post:* March 2, 1978.

Changing Men. Monthly newsletter of the Men's Resource Center: Portland, Ore.

Chesler, Phyllis. *About Men.* New York: Simon & Schuster, 1978.

Christgau, Robert. "Are You Ready for Men's Liberation?" *Ms.:* Feb., 1974.

Fasteau, Marc Feigen. *The Male Machine.* New York: Delta Books, 1975.

Gillies, Jerry. *Friends.* New York: Coward, McCann & Geoghegan, 1976.

Gross, Amy. "Your Friends, My Friends, Our Friends," *Redbook:* May, 1977.

Haller, Scot. "How to Keep Sex From Screwing Up a Friendship," *Mademoiselle:* Dec., 1977.

Harry, Joseph. "Evolving Sources of Happiness Over the Life Cycle," *Journal of Marriage and the Family:* Vol. 38, no. 2 (May, 1976).

Jacobson, David. "Mobility, Continuity, and Urban Social Organization," *Man:* Vol. 6, no. 4 (Dec., 1971).

James, Muriel and Louis M. Savary. *The Heart of Friendship.* New York: Harper & Row, 1976.

Jaynes, Gregory. "As boyish dreams change, miners' sons inherit the dark," *New York Times:* April 1, 1978.

Jesser, Clinton J. "Middle-Aged Married People and Multiple Relationships," paper delivered to the American Sociological Association: 1977.

MacDonald, Mairi St. John. "Informal Helping Relationships Among Adults," Educational Resources Information Center (ERIC): 1969.

Mannarino, Anthony P. "Friendship Patterns and Altruistic Behavior in Preadolescent Males," *Developmental Psychology:* Vol. 12, no. 6 (Nov., 1976).

Mariani, John. "Man Talk," *Viva:* March, 1978.

"Men in McSorley's toast status quo," *New York Times:* Aug. 9, 1970.

Newsletter of the Chicago Men's Gathering (monthly). Chicago.

Pleck, Joseph H. and Jack Sawyer, eds. *Men and Masculinity.* Englewood Cliffs, N.J.: Prentice-Hall, 1974.

Powers, Edward A. and Gordon L. Bultena. "Sex Differences in Friendships of Old Age," *Journal of Marriage and the Family:* Vol. 38, no. 4 (Nov., 1976).

Powers, Tom. "Can Friendship Survive Success?" *Ms.:* Jan., 1975.

Rabe-Cochran, Marsha and Allison Wilson. "Focus on Friendship," *Seventeen:* Nov., 1977.

Rooney, James F. "Friendship and Disaffiliation Among the Skid Row Population," *Journal of Gerontology:* Vol. 31, no. 1 (1976).

Saint Exupery, Antoine de. *The Little Prince.* New York: Harcourt Brace Jovanovich, 1971.

Shulman, Norman. "Life-Cycle Variations in Patterns of Close Relationships," *Journal of Marriage and the Family:* Vol. 37, no. 4 (Nov., 1975).

Tiger, Lionel. *Men in Groups.* New York: Vintage Books, 1970.

Van Horn, Michael. *The Phoenix.* San Francisco: Shields Publishing, 1975.

Vinocur, John. "Pilots who hit Hanoi meet to remember—and forget," *New York Times:* April 14, 1978.

Weiss, Robert S. "The Contributions of an Organization of Single Parents to the Well-Being of its Members," *The Family Coordinator:* July, 1973.

Werner, Laurie. "Can Men and Women be Friends? Answers from Famous Men and Women," *Redbook:* Oct., 1977

COUPLES

Arafat, Ibtihaj S. and Betty Yorburg. "On Living Together Without Marriage," *Journal of Sex Research:* Vol. 9, no. 2 (May, 1963).

Austin, Richard B., Jr. *How To Make It With Another Person.* New York: Pocket Books, 1977.

Bach, George R. and Ronald M. Deutsch. *Pairing.* New York: Avon Books, 1971.

Bengis, Ingrid. *Combat in the Erogenous Zone.* New York: Bantam Books, 1977.

Berne, Eric. *Beyond Games and Scripts.* New York: Grove Press, 1977.

Broadbent, W.W. *How To Be Loved.* New York: Warner Books, 1977.

Cantwell, Mary and Amy Gross. "You and Men," *Mademoiselle:* Jan., 1978.

Cohen, John, ed. *The Essential Lenny Bruce.* New York: Ballantine Books, 1967.

Cuber, John G. and Peggy B. Harroff. *Sex and the Significant Americans.* New York: Penguin Books, 1966.

Dinnerstein, Dorothy. *The Mermaid and the Minotaur.* New York: Harper and Row, 1976.

Friedan, Betty. *The Feminine Mystique.* New York: Dell Books, 1964.

Gelman, David. "How Men Are Changing," *Newsweek:* Jan. 16, 1978.

Harrison, Barbara Grizzuti. "Is Romance Dead?" *Ms.:* July, 1974.

Hennessee, Judith Adler. "What Do Men Really Want?" *Psychology Today:* Feb., 1978.

Hipple, John L. "Perceptual Differences Between Married and Single College Men for Concepts of Ideal Woman," *Adolescence:* Vol. 11, no. 44 (Winter, 1976).

May, Rollo. *Love and Will.* New York: Laurel Editions, 1974.

O'Reilly, Jane. "Never Trust a Handsome Man," *Glamour:* Sept., 1975.

Parker, Dorothy R. *Collected Poetry.* New York: Modern Library, 1944.

Peele, Stanton. *Love and Addiction.* New York: Signet, 1976.

Peplau, Letitia Anne, et al. "The Sexual Balance of Power," *Psychology Today:* Nov., 1976.

Quindlen, Anna. "Relationships: independence vs. intimacy," *New York Times:* Nov. 28, 1977.

Rogers, Carl R. *Becoming Partners.* New York: Delta Books, 1972.

Schwartz, Tony. "Living Together," *Newsweek:* Aug. 1, 1977.

Steinmann, Anne, et al. "Self-Concept of College Women Compared to Their Concept of Ideal Woman and Men's Ideal Woman," *Journal of Marriage and the Family:* Vol. 32, no. 3 (Aug., 1970).

Tavris, Carol. "40,000 Men Tell About Their Sexual Behavior, Their Fantasies, Their Ideal Women and Their Wives," *Redbook:* Feb., 1978.

Vreeland, Rebecca S. "Is It True What They Say About Harvard Boys?" *Psychology Today:* Jan., 1972.

Wagenvoord, James, ed. *The Man's Book.* New York: Avon Books, 1978.

Walster, Elaine, et al. "The Hard-to-Get Woman," *Psychology Today:* Sept., 1973.

MARRIAGE & SEPARATIONS

Beier, Ernst G. "Nonverbal Communication," *Psychology Today:* Oct., 1974.

Bergman, Ingmar. *Scenes From a Marriage.* New York: Bantam Books, 1977.

Bernard, Jessie. *The Future of Marriage.* New York: Bantam Books, 1972.

Billings, Victoria. "Are Break-Ups Harder on Men or Women?" *Glamour:* Dec., 1977.

Bruce, Lenny. *How To Talk Dirty and Influence People.* New York: Playboy Press, 1976.

Burton, Arthur. "Marriage Without Failure," *Psychological Reports:* Vol. 32 (1973).

Campbell, Angus. "The American Way of Mating," *Psychology Today:* May, 1975.

DeCrow, Karen. "40, single again, and absolutely no regrets," *New York Times:* Jan. 11, 1978.

Dienstag, Eleanor. "The Myth of Creative Divorce," *Psychology Today:* April, 1977.

Epstein, Joseph. *Divorced in America.* New York: Penguin Books, 1975.

Glick, Paul C. and Arthur J. Norton. "Marrying, Divorcing and Living Together in the U.S. Today," *Population Bulletin:* Vol. 32, no. 5 (Oct., 1977).

Horn, Jack. "Personality and Divorce," *Psychology Today:* Oct., 1976.

———. "The Life-Giving Properties of Marriage," *Psychology Today:* Jan., 1977.

Hunt, Morton and Bernice Hunt. *The Divorce Experience.* New York: McGraw-Hill, 1977.

Koch, Joanne and Lew Koch. "The Urgent Drive to Make Good Marriages Better," *Psychology Today:* Sept., 1976.

Krantzler, Mel. *Creative Divorce*. New York: Signet, 1975.

Krich, Aron, ed. *Facts of Love and Marriage for Young People*. New York: Laurel Editions, 1962.

Lederer, William J. and Don D. Jackson. *The Mirages of Marriage*. New York: W. W. Norton, 1968.

Lerman, Rhoda. *The Girl That He Marries*. New York: Holt, Rinehart & Winston, 1976.

Martin, J. David. "Note on a Mathematical 'Theory' of Coital Frequency in Marriage," *Journal of Sex Research:* Vol. 6, no. 4 (Nov., 1970).

Meislin, Richard J. "Poll finds more liberal beliefs on marriage and sex roles, especially among the young," *New York Times:* Nov. 27, 1977.

"Men's Lib Movement Trains Its Guns On Divorce Courts," *U. S. News and World Report:* Sept. 12, 1977.

Morris, Loverne. "Working it Out for 56 Years," *Ms.:* Feb., 1978.

Nash, Ogden. *Versus*. Boston: Little, Brown, 1941.

National Association of Record Manufacturers. *NARM Consumer Research Study: The Growing Adult Market*. 1976.

Nordheimer, Jon. "The family in transition: a challenge from within," *New York Times:* Nov. 27, 1977.

Roiphe, Anne. "Keeping and Carrying the House Together," *New York:* Oct. 25, 1976.

Scrocki, Merrill Rogers. "What Divorced Fathers Miss Most," *McCall's:* Nov., 1977.

Seldin-Schwartz, Ethel. "Diary of a Middle-Aged Divorce," *Ms.:* April, 1976.

Shain, Merle. *Some Men Are More Perfect Than Others*. New York: Charterhouse, 1973.

Simon, Werner and Gayle K. Lumry. "Suicide of the Spouse as a Divorce Substitute," *Diseases of the Nervous System:* Sept., 1970.

Stein, Peter J. "Singlehood: An Alternative to Marriage," *The Family Coordinator:* Oct., 1975.

"Study of female killers finds 50% were abused," *New York Times*, Dec. 19, 1977.

Tavris, Carol and Carole Offir. *The Longest War*. New York: Harcourt Brace Jovanovich, 1977.

Thurber, James and E.B. White. *Is Sex Necessary?* New York: Harper & Row, 1975.

U. S. Department of Health, Education, and Welfare, National Center for Health Statistics. "Advance Report: Final Divorce Statistics, 1975," *Monthly Vital Statistics Report:* Vol. 26, no. 2 (May 19, 1977).

———. "Advance Report: Final Marriage Statistics, 1975, "*Monthly Vital Statistics Report:* Vol. 26, no. 2 (May 9, 1977).

———. "Annual Summary for the United States: Births, Deaths, Marriages and Divorces, 1976," *Monthly Vital Statistics Report:* Vol. 25, no. 13 (Dec. 12, 1977).

———. *100 Years of Marriage and Divorce Statistics: United States, 1867–1967*. Washington, D.C.: U.S. Government Printing Office, 1973.

———. "Provisional Statistics: Births, Marriages, Divorces and Deaths for 1977," *Monthly Vital Statistics Report:* Vol. 26, no. 12 (March 13, 1978).

———. *Remarriages: United States*. Washington, D.C.: U.S. Government Printing Office, 1973.

———. *Vital Statistics of the United States, 1974: Volume III—Marriage and Divorce*. Washington, D.C.: U.S. Government Printing Office, 1977.

Williams, Roger. "Alimony," *Psychology Today:* July, 1977.

Wilson, Angela. "Taking the Pulse of a Marriage," *Ms.:* Feb., 1978.

Zemon-Gass, Gertrude and William C. Nichols, Jr. "Take Me Along—A Marital Syndrome," *Journal of Marriage and Family Counseling:* Vol. 1, no. 3 (July, 1975).

FATHERING

Binstock, Jeanne. "Motherhood: An Occupation Facing Decline," *The Futurist:* June, 1972.

Brazleton, T. Berry, M.D. "Helping Husbands to be Better Fathers," *Redbook:* May, 1977.

Brozan, Nadine. "If the decision is abortion, what is the man's attitude?" *New York Times:* June 11, 1975.

———. "Teen-age abortion: Do parents have the right to be informed?" *New York Times:* May 22, 1978.

Buchwald, Art. "Father's Day notebook: memos to celebrate by," *Washington Post:* June 20, 1976.

Cherry, Rona. "We've Won the Right to Legal Abortion, But We're Still Learning the Physical and Emotional Effects," *Glamour:* Jan., 1978.

Clinebell, Howard. "Creative Fathering," in Edward V. Stein, ed., *Fathering: Fact or Fable?* Nashville: Abingdon Press, 1976.

Daley, Elliot A. *Father Feelings*. New York: William Morrow, 1977.

Francke, Linda Bird. *The Ambivalence of Abortion*. New York: Random House, 1978.

Gilman, Richard and David Knox. "Coping With Fatherhood: The First Year," *Child Psychiatry and Human Development:* Vol. 6, no. 3 (Spring, 1976).

Ginsberg, Allen and Louis Ginsberg. "...Violets are blue: on Father's Day, the Ginsbergs 2" (dialogue from a joint poetry reading), *New York Times:* June 16, 1974.

Gurwitt, Alan R. "Aspects of Prospective Fatherhood: A Case Report," *Private Practice:* Vol. 31 (1976).

Hetherington, E. Mavis, et al. "Divorced Fathers," *Psychology Today:* April, 1977.

Jonas, Gerald. "Jonas and Daughters," *Ms.:* May, 1974.

Klemesrud, Judy. "'Sexist' cards are greeted with disdain," *New York Times:* June 13, 1974.

Koubek, Richard F. "A Father's Instincts," *American Home:* June, 1977.

Lacoursiere, Roy. "The Mental Health of the Prospective Father: A New Indication for Therapeutic Abortion," *Bulletin of the Menninger Clinic:* Vol. 36, no. 6 (Nov., 1972).

Lees, Robert Barry. "Men and the Abortion Experience: Anxiety and Social Supports," Ph.D. dissertation, University of Michigan, 1975.

Leonard, John. "The Fathering Instinct," *Ms.:* May, 1974.

Milling, Eileen. "The Men Who Wait," *Woman's Life:* April, 1975.

Morrow, Lance. "An Essay on the Unfairness of Life," *Horizon:* Dec., 1977.

Nathanson, Bernard. "Deeper into Abortion," *New England Journal of Medicine:* Nov. 28, 1974.

Roiphe, Anne. "Can You Have Everything and Still Want Babies?" *Vogue:* Dec., 1975.

Rosen, R.A., et al. "Health Professionals' Attitudes Toward Abortion," *Public Opinion Quarterly:* Vol. 38, no. 2 (Summer, 1974).

Rossman, Michael. "Where Are Our Children? A Requiem for the Unborn," *Mother Jones:* May, 1978.

Steinberg, David. *Fatherjournal*. Albion, Ca.: Times Change Press, 1977.

Sullivan, Ellen, et al. "Legal Abortion in the United States, 1975–1976," *Family Planning Perspectives:* May–June, 1977.

Sutherland, Donald. "Childbirth is Not for Mothers Only," *Ms.:* May, 1977.

U. S. Department of Health, Education and Welfare, Center for Disease Control. *Abortion Surveillance, 1975*. Washington, D.C.: U. S. Government Printing Office, 1977.

Wilde, Oscar. *The Picture of Dorian Gray*. New York: Dell Books, 1956.

"Working Fathers," *Ms.:* May, 1974.

INDEX